REDEFINING THE STATE IN LATIN AMERICA

edited by
Colin I. Bradford, Jr.

ORGANISATION FOR ECONOMIC CO-OPERATION AND DEVELOPMENT

ORGANISATION FOR ECONOMIC CO-OPERATION AND DEVELOPMENT

Pursuant to Article 1 of the Convention signed in Paris on 14th December 1960, and which came into force on 30th September 1961, the Organisation for Economic Co-operation and Development (OECD) shall promote policies designed:

— to achieve the highest sustainable economic growth and employment and a rising standard of living in Member countries, while maintaining financial stability, and thus to contribute to the development of the world economy;

— to contribute to sound economic expansion in Member as well as non-member countries in the process of economic development; and

— to contribute to the expansion of world trade on a multilateral, non-discriminatory basis in accordance with international obligations.

The original Member countries of the OECD are Austria, Belgium, Canada, Denmark, France, Germany, Greece, Iceland, Ireland, Italy, Luxembourg, the Netherlands, Norway, Portugal, Spain, Sweden, Switzerland, Turkey, the United Kingdom and the United States. The following countries became Members subsequently through accession at the dates indicated hereafter: Japan (28th April 1964), Finland (28th January 1969), Australia (7th June 1971) and New Zealand (29th May 1973). The Commission of the European Communities takes part in the work of the OECD (Article 13 of the OECD Convention).

The Development Centre of the Organisation for Economic Co-operation and Development was established by decision of the OECD Council on 23rd October 1962.

The purpose of the Centre is to bring together the knowledge and experience available in Member countries of both economic development and the formulation and execution of general economic policies; to adapt such knowledge and experience to the actual needs of countries or regions in the process of development and to put the results at the disposal of the countries by appropriate means.

The Centre has a special and autonomous position within the OECD which enables it to enjoy scientific independence in the execution of its task. Nevertheless, the Centre can draw upon the experience and knowledge available in the OECD in the development field.

Publié en français sous le titre :
REDÉFINIR L'ÉTAT EN AMÉRIQUE LATINE

* * *

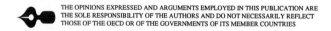

*
* *

Foreword

Organised jointly by the Inter-American Development Bank and the OECD Development Centre in the context of its programme on "International Policy Issues" and as part of its external co-operation activities, the IVth annual meeting of the International Forum on Latin American Perspectives was held in Paris in November 1993. This book is based on the papers and deliberations heard at that meeting.

Table of Contents

Third Part
ECONOMIC POLICY

Fourth Part
CONCLUDING REFLECTIONS

Preface

In 1990, the Inter-American Development Bank and the OECD Development Centre created the International Forum on Latin American Perspectives as an annual mechanism for bringing together the expertise available in OECD Member countries, particularly in Europe, with the experience of Latin American specialists. This volume represents the results of the IVth International Forum on Latin American Perspectives which was convened by the two institutions in Paris in November 1993 and is the fourth publication based on this series of conferences. The Forum is designed to provide an opportunity for an exchange of views among experts, policy makers and opinion leaders, in the expectation that these exchanges themselves may produce new insights on current problems and contribute to policy thinking in the international community.

This book explores new dimensions, new definitions and new perceptions of the state in Latin America. It attempts to move beyond old visions of the state embodied in ideologies and models from the past, to open a discussion reflecting the broader agenda of the 1990s and new ideas about how the state relates to and interacts with both civil society and the private sector.

The current situation in Latin America is at once difficult and promising. The crisis of the state is real in both financial and functional terms. Realism requires an understanding of the limitations inherited from the past which constrain the scope and scale of state activity in the future. On the other hand, major progress in economic policy reform in recent years has not only improved economic prospects in the region but unburdened the state of some of the excesses of the past. At the same time, thanks to their vitality, initiative and drive, the private sector — including the informal sector — and civil society have provided a new context for public policy and state behaviour in Latin America.

A redefinition of the state in Latin America must take account of the new developments in the region. In a world of global competition and new forms of industrial organisation, old patterns of industrialisation and protection are clearly outmoded, but simplistic ideas regarding the possibility that free markets can spring up without institutional development to resolve economic and social ills are also insufficient. In a region which has experienced a continuous decline in real incomes through the 1980s and a steady increase in the numbers of people in poverty, the state cannot deny its share of responsibility for and its impact on society in a context of increasing social tensions and disparities. Neither can the state attempt to solve the social problem on its own. Now that democracy has returned to most of the countries in the region, the issue of the role of the state and its redefinition is in the hands not only of the governing group of the moment, but of society as a whole.

The state and its future in the evolving context in Latin America will continue to excite discussion. This book seeks to bring some fresh concerns and viewpoints to a wide audience and to stimulate further debate and progress, within our respective institutions and beyond them, especially in Latin America itself.

Jean Bonvin   Enrique V. Iglesias
President   President
OECD Development Centre   Inter-American Development Bank
Paris   Washington, D.C.

February 1994

First Part

INTRODUCTION AND OVERVIEW

Some Initial Thoughts

Jean Bonvin

Redefining the role of the state has become a topical question everywhere — in the North, South, East and West — because of the failure of socialist experiments and the continuation of the world economic crisis. Many countries are now carrying out a transition towards a market economy and political democracy at the same time. If the convergence of economic and political freedom marks "the end of history", to use a well-known formulation, then the paths of history are sometimes like seemingly unending tunnels!

That is why Latin America is a valuable focus for our discussions. The Latin American countries provide a large sample, with differing areas, numbers of inhabitants, per capita incomes, political systems, and institutions. Nonetheless, the common cultural heritage of these countries facilitates appropriate comparisons.

The problem of the role of the state in the economy and society remains timely because past attempts at solutions have often been disappointing. In developing countries the emphasis on state intervention since the Second World War closely reflected the dominant theories of the time. Until the 1970s, state involvement was considered a factor that would speed up the processes of accumulation and industrialisation. The need for state intervention was also justified by the low levels of private investment, by discounting the rationality of private economic actors and by great inequality of incomes. The state and its agencies often appeared to be the only structure that could prevent countries from disintegrating, and could ensure a minimum of cohesion and national economic independence. These ideas inevitably led to the control of markets and prices, and to expansion of the public sector as the only way to allocate resources efficiently. It was forgotten that a state-oriented development strategy conforming too closely to the leaders' interests tends to substitute a political rationality for economic rationality, and introduces a system of incentives in which rent seeking — and often corruption — become widespread.

Through various statistical tests[1] it has gradually been shown that the growth of the state can have a negative effect on economic growth rates, and that beyond a certain threshold, it becomes essentially a redistributional state. Such conditions made programmes for reducing state expenditure necessary, and, because of the

11

effects of the debt crisis of the 1980s, led to a reduced state role, accompanied by privatisation, liberalisation of trade and prices, and an opening of markets.

There have been two major refinements in the theory of state intervention since the end of the 1970s. On the one hand, there is the credibility that is essential for efficiency and the success of state policy. Yet the variables affecting this credibility are largely political and institutional; they are those which make a government more or less autonomous and more or less popular. Consequently, some basic decisions, like state policies affecting the market, depend on relations between the government and the people.

The recognition that the East Asian countries owe their rapid development to an active presence of the state does not legitimise public intervention under all circumstances. It is also no longer possible unequivocally to condemn nationalisation because of the failure of public enterprises in Africa and Latin America.

On the other hand, public choice theory shows that state actors, like private actors, try to maximise their own utility functions. The general interest can certainly be a major factor in these functions, but only as mediated by personal or ideological conceptions. Moreover, personal interest can be expressed directly, either by the "rents" that can be appropriated, or simply by holding onto power. In such cases, decisions are significantly different from optimal policies based on maximising a theoretical social welfare function. Thus, it would be rash to define an "optimal state", with a precise and unchanging role, in the absence of insight into how the state is organised.

There are many features of state organisation. The first obviously concerns the type of political system and institutions. In the period from the 1950s to the 1970s, it was widely assumed that an authoritarian regime was essential for carrying out unpopular reforms and providing leadership for an inefficient administration. The risks of political instability associated with Western democratic systems seemed to be too great for the requirements of development. The dominant view held that there had to be a compromise between economic development and political democracy. In fact, pluralism has costs in terms of social tension and conflict, and competition between parties, trade unions and different interest groups gives preference to the people's short-term aspirations and strengthens vested interests. On the other hand, an authoritarian state has a more long-term outlook than an elected government: its leaders generally change less frequently; it is less subject to popular pressure and special interests; it is easier in principle for it to make decisions conforming to economic rationality; and being more hierarchical, it can more easily prevent or repress protests.

These hypotheses have been challenged by studies of Latin American countries in particular. They show that authoritarian governments' economic performance has not been better than that of other goverments at all stages of development. Some econometric studies[2] have even found a significant positive correlation between economic growth and the existence of democratic institutions.

Like all governments, autocratic regimes seek to retain power. This can make them very sensitive to political pressure in the short term, even though they do not face electoral risks. Consequently, they often increase the number of politically advantageous transfers entailing significant price distortions. These distortions, in turn, retard the rate of long-term economic growth. The absence of elections may mean that there are more strikes, demonstrations, riots, and *coups d'état*.

Although there is a temptation to seek a direct causal link between economic liberalisation and the establishment of democratic institutions, an orderly relationship between the state and organised groups is a necessity for economic efficiency. The abundant literature devoted to the balance of power between interest groups and governing coalitions has shown that regimes in the process of transition towards democracy are especially fragile and that re-election constraints influence the continuity of economic policy.

More generally, interest group theory stresses that the aim of fragile governments is to maximise the advantage to be gained from fiscal redistribution, even at the risk of being reduced to the role of intermediary between organised groups. That is why one of the main consequences of the redistributional state is to change social behaviour. Knowing that the government can be susceptible to pressure, individuals and coalitions are stimulated to engage in rent seeking from the public sector and in efforts to obtain measures that modify the operation of markets in their favour. On the other hand, these groups rarely support reforms that might threaten their vested interests, resulting in what can be called the "tyranny of the status quo".

That is why another theme is important, namely a democratic state's ability to undertake reforms and, more generally, its ability to exercise power, to be an initiator or an arbitrator, rather than a simple intermediary between rival forces. No government has complete control over the implementation of its decisions; no decision-making process is ever completely centralised. The final decision is the result of strategic bargaining, first among a government's members, then between government and the civil service. The economic theory of bureaucracy calls into question the purist assumption that the administrative officials in charge are either completely submissive to the political leadership, or are only motivated by serving the public interest.

This theory leaves some important issues still to be resolved. What factors determine the degree of a government's control over its bureaucracy? To what extent can the bureaucracy make coherent decisions in continuity? How can the central civil service be shielded from various public and private pressures? Bureaucratic theory, however, cannot simply be transposed to developing countries: cultural and historical factors, institutional conditions and methods of political control should all play a major role in this analysis.

It is indisputable, however, that investment in human resources (notably in education) is a condition for training a competent and relatively independent civil service. It is also one of the foundations of an open political system: for a given income level, an improvement of the social indicators is related to increased freedom. Modern endogenous growth theorists not only consider the development of human capital to be a motor of growth, but recognise that political instability tends to decline with an increase in educational and income levels[3].

The Latin American experience provides an opportunity for testing these ideas and verifying the relevance of these theories. Characterised as the "middle class continent"[4], as it belongs both to the Third World and to the Western world, Latin America is an ideal terrain for analysis.

It is clear that an in-depth analysis of the state's role cannot avoid dealing with a part of the world where the state is often considered as the supreme regulator, co-ordinator and pacifier of the nation, if not as an autonomous despot that is a source of power and riches. That is undoubtedly why there is such intense and sometimes violent competition for power. Despite national differences, the continent's history reveals a common expansion of state power and a multiplying of state agencies and enterprises. This history has also often been associated with a strong populist tradition in which the state becomes an entrepreneur and actively promotes industrialisation. Consequently, could not this deliberately state-oriented development be considered one of the main obstacles to democracy?

Part of the answer to this question is probably that the 1980s debt crisis and the implementing of successful adjustment programmes have made an impression.

If the last annual report of the World Bank is correct, a consensus is emerging in favour of reforms that would put limits on state intervention, trim oversized civil services, open economies more, and give increased priority to human resources. In this context, will democracy's chances be strengthened by state helplessness in the face of crisis, as well as by the weakening of pressure groups?

Unfortunately, the ability to formulate and carry out projects is also weakened in the sectors which remain the state's responsibility: educational development, environmental protection, and improvement of infrastructure. However, is not the willingness to put intentions into practice a major step towards reform?

This question is all the more decisive since socio-political studies undertaken in different Latin American countries suggest that reforms are not immediately and automatically viewed negatively by the people, and that the reforms can even gain temporary support as long as their negative consequences are not felt by large or leading categories. These studies also show that once discontent reaches a certain level, authoritarian regimes are as vulnerable as democracies. Consequently, the way reforms are introduced, the order in which they are introduced and the time they take to be implemented may be considered as determining factors for their success.

Notes and References

1. LAL, D. (1987), "The Political Economy of Economic Liberalization", *World Bank Economic Review*, 1 (2): 273-299.

    LEFTWICH, A., ed. (1990), *New Developments in Political Science*, Hants., Edward Elgar Publishing Ltd.

    SCULLY, J.W. (1989), "The Size of the State, Economic Growth and the Efficient Utilization of National Resources", *Public Choice*, 63 (2).

    SINGH, R.D. (1985), "State Intervention, Foreign Economic Aid, Savings and Growth in LDC's: Some Recent Evidence", *Kyklos*, 38 (2): 216-232.

2. GRIER, K.B. and G. TULLOCK (1989), "An Empirical Analysis of Cross-National Economic Growth, 1951-80", *Journal of Monetary Economics*, 24 (2): 259-276.

    HAGGARD, S. and R. KAUFMAN (1989), "Economic Adjustment in New Democracies", in Nelson, J., ed. (1989), *Fragile Coalitions: The Politics of Economic Adjustment*, New Brunswick, Transaction Books.

    POURGERAMI, A. (1988), "The Political Economy of Development: A Cross-National Causality Test of the Development-Democracy-Growth Hypothesis", *Public Choice*, 58 (2): 123-42.

3. LUCAS, R. (1988), "On the Mechanics of Economic Development", *Journal of Monetary Economics*, July.

    Revue économique, Vol. 44, No. 2, mars 1993, numéro spécial, « Nouvelles théories de la croissance économique ».

4. TOURAINE, A. (1988), *La Parole et le sang : politique et société en Amérique latine*, Paris, Odile Jacob.

Redefining the Role of the State: Political Processes, State Capacity and the New Agenda in Latin America

Colin I. Bradford, Jr.

Introduction: the primacy of politics

This book focusses on three dimensions of the role of the state in Latin America — political processes, state capacity and new agenda issues — and, perhaps most important, the interaction among these three elements. There appears to be a widespread sense in Latin America that the state is over-extended, over-indebted and ineffective in promoting a viable form of economic and social development which can embody the broad public interest of society. This is at once a failure of politics and a failure of governance, a failure of leadership and of public management, of articulation of values and vision and of execution. As a result, there is a connection between the need for reform of the state and the need for renovation in politics so that **through politics** the purposes of reform are clearly defined, supported, acted upon, and sustained.

There are substantial differences of views about the future **role of the state** in Latin America. The various dimensions of political processes — the dynamics of political party behaviour, the interaction of interest groups in society, public debate, elections, legislative-executive interactions, legal and judicial procedures — all will affect whether and how a society eventually defines a new role for the state, converting it into a form that better reflects contemporary (and perhaps future) needs. The political process itself, in this formulation at least, is democratic in the broadest sense, requiring society-wide debate, consensus, decision(s) and actions.

Redefining the role of the state is not the only public issue of transcendent importance in Latin America today. On the contrary, the decade of the 1990s seems different from previous decades in the wide range of issues which command public and policy priority. The economic debate in the 1980s was extremely narrow, focussing on structural adjustment, trade policy and exchange rate reform as if they constituted the entire economic agenda. Economic issues overwhelmed all other policy priorities in the 1980s. In contrast, the 1990s — with new imperatives for social equity, growth and environmental sustainability, as well as for political and state reform — seems to be a new era in the scope of the policy agenda. The significance of this new agenda for policy making and for the role of the state is clear.

The urgency of social reform and greater economic growth to sustain the return of democracy to the region as well as the economic reforms undertaken in the 1980s would by themselves force the reform of the state onto the public agenda. The effective integration into policy making of environmental issues — which are horizontal in nature and cut across various policy instruments and government agencies — also requires institutional changes. Hence, even if there were no crisis of the state in Latin America, the pressure arising from these new issues would be sufficient to bring to the fore the reform of the state and redefinition of its role.

The new agenda of the 1990s is not alone, however, in creating the imperative to redefine the role of the state. The crisis of the state in Latin America would exist in any case. It has roots in the past as well as a future (Tomassini, 1992, p. 106); it is both economic (Bresser Pereira, 1993) and developmental (Tomassini, 1992, Chapter 5; dos Reis Velloso, 1994*); it is also a crisis of capacity in the narrow sense of the administrative capacity of public sector management to cope with the demands upon it (the World Bank's work on "governance" defines the challenges confronting the state in this narrow sense).

These major dimensions of the subject are highly interactive with one another. The new agenda, which is generated by underlying social and economic conditions, is transmitted into the public domain by the political process. It affects, and is affected by, the capacity of the state to act effectively on a more complicated agenda. The capacity of the state to provide strategic direction for national energies, to implement political, economic and social reform and to affect the polity, the economy and society positively is conditioned by both the political process and the new agenda. The dynamics of the political process is, in fact, the most powerful determinant of the interaction of the three dimensions affecting the role of the state in Latin America. Political processes, in the broadest sense, are channels and vehicles for the flow of forces and energy that connect actors, issues and institutions. It is the politics of reform which are at the centre of the force field which will determine the future of democracy, economic reform and social equity in Latin America.

Tensions, theories and issues: the conceptual framework

The issues raised by a focus on the interaction of the new agenda, state capacity and political processes are revealed by tensions between democracy and economic reform, between models of liberalisation and competitiveness, between civil society and the state itself, and between economic reform and social policy.

An asterik (*) indicates the research carried out in the context of the IDRC/ECLAC/ Development Centre project described on p. 22, collected in Bradford, ed., (1994*) .

Democracy versus economic reform

Throughout the literature and in some chapters of this book there is an underlying concern over the tension between democracy and economic reform. Recent history has revealed a disturbing tendency for high economic performance to be associated with authoritarian political regimes. The success stories of the East Asian newly industrialising economies are the focus of particular attention: the dynamic economic development that was sufficient to transform these economics from developing countries to nearly industrialised economies in 25 years occurred with a noticeable lack of democratic process. Not all authoritarian regimes engender high-performance economies, of course, but the most dramatic examples of "catch-up" industrialisation in East Asia have occurred under authoritarian governments which began to liberalise the political regime only **after** dynamic economic development was well under way.

Nevertheless, the choice of political regime is not often, and certainly not always, determined by economic considerations. Democracy is the prevailing political form in Latin America in the early 1990s. The question then becomes how economic reform can be accelerated and supported within a democratic framework, rather than what political regime will best facilitate dynamic development. The examples of the East Asian economies have raised doubts about whether democratic regimes can be disciplined enough to implement reforms effectively and consistently so as to sustain the changes necessary to achieving high growth. They have also raised issues concerning the degree to which insulation from political pressure may be essential to high economic performance (Haggard, 1990, p. 45).

> In this view, the key to the superior economic performance of the Asian "tigers" is "state autonomy" defined as a combination of the "capacity" of the state to pursue developmentalist policies with its "insulation" from particularistic pressures. (Przeworski and Limongi, 1993, p. 56)

This view is even more strongly expressed by Pranab Bardhan:

> The East Asian success story of development has led to an emerging **consensus** about one of the **necessary** (though far from sufficient) conditions of a development state: a large degree of insulation that the development-minded decision-makers can have against the ravages of short-run pork-barrel politics and their ability to use the discipline of the market (guided possibly by world market signals) against the inevitable lobbies of group predation. (Bardhan, 1993, p. 46; emphasis added)

A question also raised by these cases is whether the existence of a technocratic elite capable of steering the country towards economic goals in the common good is a necessary element in success. Williamson (1994) has developed a political economy theory of the role of the "technopol" (a technocrat-become-politician) who implements a broad reform programme. The technocratic agenda, in this formulation, is based on normative economics in which the objective of economic policy is posited as the promotion of the general good. The central issue for Williamson is how to strengthen the political muscle of those politicians (cum-technocrats) who are most driven by a concern for the general good rather than by particular interests.

We can discern four different theories of the politics of economic reform (Bradford, 1994a). One is the **new political economy**, a kind of neoclassical economic theory of politics in which agents rationally pursue their self-interest within a political framework. This theory goes a long way to explaining rent seeking and what Williamson calls the "favour-granting state". A **pluralist theory** of politics sees policy as driven by competition among interest groups: competition in the political marketplace drives the agenda towards policies that promote the public interest, just as competition in the economic marketplace leads to efficiency.

The third theory is Williamson's own, which one might call the **technopol model**. This theory would say that if there is a crisis, if there is a window of opportunity (a honeymoon), if the opposition is fragmented, if the regime type is favourable (the nature of a favourable regime is rather unclear), if there is a mandate (or an opportunity for surprise), if there is a leader with vision, if there is a consensus within the team, if the reforms are radical and comprehensive, if there is public support, and if external influences are positive, then the conditions are ripe for an economic policy reform directed towards the general good, rather than towards satisfying particular interests. In this model, the state pursues what most economists assume should be the objectives of government policy, and, accordingly, it becomes an umpire rather than a favour-granting mechanism. This means that the state and political actors are detached from the political process, and that technopols are neutral players for the common and general good.

Robert Bates' **partisan theory**, in which the motivation of politicians is to implement policies in the interest of certain sectors of society, is the fourth. This theory implies that market-oriented reforms are not apolitical. It is consistent with Merilee Grindle's chapter in Meier (1991), which offers an alternative model of politics to the neoclassical (NPE) approach that dominates the Meier volume. Her model rests much more on historical and contextual factors and focusses much more on dynamics and interactions within the state (such as relations between the executive branch and the Congress, within the legislature, between parties, or between agencies), between the state and society, and between elements within society, such as interest groups and their constituents or the media. In other words, she focusses on the dynamics of politics — its flux and flow — rather than on a set of static conditions in which interests are being maximised.

Meier himself concludes that the new political economy is limited because it rests too much on instrumental rationality rather than on procedural rationality. Given this limitation, he argues for the need to:

> seek a more eclectic approach that combines the old and new political economy. From the perspective of the older political economy we should give special attention to the influence of historical tradition, social structure, ideologies, and institutions. An explanation of the motivations of policy makers is then too mixed to be understood only by rational choice models of the new political economy. (Meier, 1991, p. 307)

The more inclusive approach of Bates and Grindle avoids seeing technopols as isolated from the political process, and instead **embeds** them in that process as political actors with interests like those of everyone else, including the desire to survive. However much the general welfare may be advanced by a particular set of reforms, there is still going to be a deep-seated power struggle in which the reformers are fully involved in the flux and flow of the historical process (Bradford, 1994a).

No matter how helpful "state autonomy" and "insulation" appear to have been in the East Asian cases, they over-simplify the social forces and political processes that reformers must contend with in Latin America. The technocrat as politician becomes a political actor and is involved in the political process in which he or she must make or influence policy. Politicians, even technocratic ones, can not act on the system from outside but are themselves players in a complex field of conflicting forces composed of many other actors, especially in democratic countries. The question is how political processes can be used to reinforce economic reforms and how the reform process can strengthen democratic process rather than circumvent it.

Haggard and Kaufman (in this volume) reach the same conclusion. They distinguish between initiation and consolidation of reforms:

> The consolidation of both the constitutional system and the economic policies themselves ultimately depends on the development of institutionalised channels of representation which provide political support for a given policy regime. In the absence of the consultation and oversight required to generate such suppport, economic reforms are likely to be unstable and subject to extensive and rapid reversal.

In other words, broad, inclusive political processes are necessary for the sustainability of economic reforms over the longer term. Margaret Keck (in this volume) persuasively demonstrates the likely failures of technocratic solutions to environmental problems, and the need for democratic politics to involve relevant constituencies in environmental policy making as a vital element to the sustainability of policy solutions. In this view, democratic politics — redefining the relationship between economic policy makers and the polity from insulation to engagement — is vital to the success of the economic reform process, rather than a factor in conflict with it. Democracy and development are potentially complementary, in this formulation, rather than the trade-offs they appear to be when one examines the East Asian cases. This conclusion restores political processes to centre stage in the analysis of the role of the state in Latin America.

The question then is how to achieve development discipline while strengthening democratic political processes and participatory development (Jaguaribe, 1991). Another way to perceive this tension is in the juxtaposition of the need for state engagement with the private sector, which inevitably entails discretionary involvement, against the need "to distance contract enforcement, property rights, and bankruptcy proceedings from political decisions [so that the state] can foster investor confidence and increase the likelihood that new competitors will enter domestic markets" (Cafagna, in this volume).

Liberalisation versus competitiveness: the new paradigm of the "civil economy"

Despite the turbulence, disorder and disarray at the macroeconomic level in Latin America in the 1980s, there has been a great deal of transformation, structural change and shifts in *modus operandi* in micro-level industrial and social organisation. These significant changes have taken place at the base of both the economy and society, rather than at the apex. New modes of economic and social organisation have occurred at the level of the firm, including inter-firm relations, and at the level of local community organisations. What has evolved in the last 20 years, underneath all the macro-level disturbances, is a new paradigm for the organisation of production and for the organisation of society. A dramatic development in recent years has been the evolution of "civil society" as a myriad of private initiatives, activities and entities to carry out basic societal functions, some of which were previously carried out by the state. There has also been a parallel evolution in economic activity which could be called the "civil economy".

The new economic paradigm rests on changes in modes of production from large-scale integrated manufacturing facilities to decentralised networks of smaller firms capable of greater adaptability to shifting tastes, technologies or prices. This new form of industrial organisation is responsive to changes in basic trends in global patterns of production: the rapid rate of generation of new knowledge and innovation; the broad applicability of new information-handling technologies across a broad spectrum of economic activities; the reduction of labour costs as a proportion of total production costs; shifts in the nature of produced inputs for production processes through technological change; shorter process and product life cycles; the predominance of the quality of the product over cost competitiveness; the growing importance of responsiveness to customer needs, including quick delivery times; and the need for aggressive marketing and efficient distribution networks (Dahlman, 1994*).

These pressures to move to a more flexible, decentralised form of the organisation of production places greater emphasis on certain features of the national economy which vitally affect firm behaviour. These include: a favourable macroeconomic environment, adequate physical infrastructure — especially in transportation and communications — a literate and skilled workforce, and an adequate institutional infrastructure which includes the legal system, the financial system, export promotion and technology support (Dahlman, 1994*).

These "new elements of competitiveness" coalesce in the redefinition of industrial relations, which are no longer based on efficient firms but on a competitive network of R&D units, suppliers, producers, distributors, wholesalers, retailers and service centres. This production chain is now more important than the production function within the firm. The nature of inter-firm, inter-institutional and intra-firm relations along this chain is what determines effectiveness today. "Competition is now more between systems and networks than between individual firms" (Dahlman, 1994*).

This new paradigm of industrial organisation has significant implications for economic policy. These new elements of competitiveness which transcend the boundaries of the firm translate into a need for a systemic approach to competitiveness. The dimensions and implications of such an approach are being explored in a joint project of the OECD Development Centre, the International Development Research Centre (IDRC) of Canada and the United Nations Economic Commission for Latin America and the Caribbean (ECLAC)*.

It is clear that the increasing importance of information, innovation processes, institutional relations, investment in plant and equipment, infrastructure and human resource development has implications for core economic, financial and trade policies. There is a need for a broad policy approach that attempts to focus on points of interaction among critical policies and variables, such as the tax system and investment; financial institutions and innovation; exchange rates, tariffs, subsidies, public investment and exports; capital markets and human capital; wages and productivity; and monetary policy and fiscal deficits. (See Fanelli and Frenkel, 1994*; Ffrench-Davis, 1994*; and Ramos, 1994*.) To bring together the various elements within these points of interaction and to create coherence among them, integrative strategies are necessary for public policy. The new paradigm of systemic competitiveness also demands broader strategies on the part of firms, private sector institutions and non-profit agencies, not just the state. This, in turn, leads to the need for these strategies to relate to each other and, hence, for the different entities to interact.

The new paradigm leads to two important roles for the Latin American state in the future. First, the fact that the systemic approach leads to the need to integrate policy across various instruments and institutions recasts the state towards a more strategic role — setting a development direction, and shaping policies which are a coherent expression of it. This strategic role of the state is essentially a **political** role requiring political leadership skills in articulating a vision, mobilising support and setting policy priorities. Strategic vision is not economic planning: there is certainly no necessary implication of heavy-handed intervention in the economy, nor for a state role in directly productive activities. Quite the opposite. Rather, what is implied is setting the strategic framework within which civil society and the private sector assume functional responsibility for the preponderance of economic and social activities.

Second, to enhance competitiveness, growth and exports, the state needs to have an interactive relationship with the new "civil economy". For this relationship to be effective, new ways must be created for associating the state with private sector initiatives, for bringing related economic agents together so they can exploit the potential yields latent in their common endeavours and for supporting enterprise and industrial development. This catalytic role is more consistent with the role of the state in the East Asian growth experiences (Birdsall, in this volume; World Bank, 1993; dos Reis Velloso, 1994*; and Bradford, 1994b). It is not the interventionist, inward-looking role identified with import-substitution industrialisation of the post-war era in Latin America. Nor is it the minimalist role identified with the trade and market liberalisation of the neoliberal period in the 1980s. The catalytic state requires flexible and innovative mechanisms for the interaction of state and society; it also undoubtedly requires administrative reform in the management of the public sector and large investments in civil service training and reform. Other types of mechanisms and modalities required for this kind of catalytic state need to be identified and elaborated. One example is Valenzuela's discussion (in this volume) of labour organisations best able to interact with the state, especially those pursuing a development path of skill upgrading and international insertion. Whether or not the discretionary policy behaviour implied by the new strategic and catalytic roles of the state is compatible with the transparency and uniformity needed in antitrust reform is an issue posed by Cafagna in this volume.

Civil society and a redefinition of the state

If the new paradigm of the "civil economy" requires a redefinition of the role of the state, the evolution of civil society demands a redefinition of the state itself. There have been two strands of evolution. One is a normatively positive development of civil society into autonomous or quasi-autonomous social organisations. These carry out vital representational functions and economic transactions, have social responsibilities, and may be legal or illegal, formal or informal, religious or secular entities. Civil society

> obliges us to recognise institutionally that a diversity of interests and social aspirations exist which are not reduceable to either great groups according to class or to political party representation. The strength of civil society is related to the existence of diverse and viable spaces for individual, social and political action. (Garretón and Espinosa, 1992, p. 40)

This strength of civil society created survival mechanisms against both the political and economic pressures of recent years.

The other evolutionary line is a normatively negative evolution of civic culture, which consists of the "cognitive visions, values, attitudes, feelings and information that a society has...and the ways of organising the political system" (Tomassini, 1994, p. 8), and the consequent erosion of the cohesive function of politics in nurturing a stable society. Part of this negative evolution and erosion has occurred because of the economic pressures of the 1980s, and some of it has occurred under the corrosive hand of military regimes. Where these pressures have been acute,

> the primary, basic phenomenon is generalised desolidarisation... The (consequent) atomisation of society mirrors and accentuates the disintegration of the state... The pulverisation of society into myriad rational/opportunistic actors and their anger about a situation that everyone — and, hence, nobody — seems to cause has a major scapegoat: the state and the government. (O'Donnell, 1993, pp. 16-19)

These pressures have obviously been major causes of the crisis of the state in Latin America.

The positive and the negative evolution both generate pressures for a redefinition of the state to correspond to the imperatives for change in the current conjuncture.

> It is a mistake to conflate the state with the state apparatus, or the public sector or the aggregate of public bureacracies. These, unquestionably, are part of the state, but they are not all of it. The state is also, and no less primarily, a set of social relations that establishes a certain order... But it is in an order, in the sense that manifold social relationships are engaged on the basis of stable (if not necessarily approved) norms and expectations... We see that the law is a constitutive element of the state: it is the "part" of the state that provides the regular, underlying texturing of the social order existing over a given territory. (O'Donnell, 1993, p. 3)

This implies a comprehensive definition of the state, including the means by which it relates to the functioning of the economy and society, not just its relations with the polity in terms of formal democratic (or authoritarian) determinations between ruler and ruled. This definition moves the focus to a broader and more complex set of issues that go beyond policy issues to the setting of norms, standards and procedures for social participation in policy making itself. The state "is the agent of the values and interests of the political culture" (Tomassini, 1992, p. 33). This definition involves the state as an autonomous entity that strengthens both civil society and the market economy, which are autonomous entities themselves. It suggests a completely different dynamic between the state, the private sector and civil society than occurs in what Garretón calls the "classic matrix", in which these elements are either merged or subordinated one to the other. Under merger, the state, the private sector and civil society collapse into each other, according to Garretón, so they cannot draw mutual strength through interaction. Under subordination, one element dominates the other two (Garretón and Espinosa, 1992, p. 9).

The severe societal problems are often created by the merger or subordination syndromes of the classic matrix. Even in formal democratic regimes, basic individual rights can be violated so that the regime has no liberal content, even though it may have liberal form. Furthermore, the dynamic gains possible from a context in which civil society can flourish are also diminished in the classic matrix. The solution is not just to remove the dominating element acting through the state, but to create ways to engage the state with civil society and the private sector. This requires a broad reform agenda to make the state a more responsive mechanism capable of greater interaction with civil society (Garretón and Espinosa, 1992, pp. 24-36). Further elaboration of the reform agenda is needed. (See Tomassini's chapter in this volume.)

Economic reform and social policy

The legacy of the 1980s in Latin America is an increase in the number and percentage of people living in poverty, even in some countries experiencing positive economic growth. Structural adjustment has been a burden on the poor, even though some programmes have mitigated the social effects of adjustment. Teresa Albánez (in this volume) concludes that "the structural adjustment programmes do not include any real social development strategy". Trade liberalisation towards more open, market-oriented economies has also increased social tensions: the search for greater international competitiveness creates downward pressure on wages. This has led to a situation in which "nowadays the state can not allow the market to be the only mechanism which determines who should have access to goods on which depends, not only the well-being of its citizens, but in some cases their survival" (Albánez).

As a result, an economic policy without social content lacks legitimacy, sustainability and effectiveness. The crisis of the state is in part a failure to come up with a viable economic strategy to provide social hope. "To this extent, the social question is not a sectoral problem but a national problem: not only the public sector but society as a whole bears responsibility here" (Albánez). Democracy and economic reform without social change are not viable. The question is how to include the social agenda as part of both the economic agenda and the agenda for reform of the state.

Joseph Ramos has pointed out that:

There is no such thing as **an** employment policy, for no single instrument can be applied to promote employment... Employment policy is horizontal... An integrated or systemic approach is required; only thus can one ensure that this "secondary" effect of different policies on employment is systematically taken into account. (Ramos, 1994*)

Integrating employment and social policy concerns into the core economic policy agenda is thus a difficult task, both at the analytical level and at that of economic policy co-ordination. Horizontal issues such as employment and environmental questions require cross-cutting policy making and public sector management. This means that these new horizontal questions need to be woven together with economic, social and state reform. None is sufficient without the other.

The reform of social services — health, education, social security, and social protection — needs to be put on an economically viable basis (Hausmann, in this volume). Spending more public resources is not only unfeasible but, without complementary reforms of social services, undesirable. Qualitative changes in the delivery and content of social services need to accompany the increased priority and resource commitment these sectors require. There may be no area in which building state capacity is more important than in social services reform (IDB/UNDP, 1993, Chapter 4). The links between social reform, state reform, social spending, reduction in military expenditures and tax reform for greater revenue generation and greater equity need to be established as integrated elements in a serious reform agenda. Hausmann points out that social reform may not be a positive-sum game but, rather, may consume more resources than it generates in both political and economic terms.

Massively increasing the scope and scale of human resource development programmes is clearly a critical part of any economic or social reform. The new paradigm of competitiveness rests on the human resource base more than on any other factor. Reductions in military expenditures need to be tied to an increased commitment to human resource development as a means of justifying economically the cuts in defence budgets needed to finance significant increases in investment in human resources. The recent shift in the tax base in many Latin American countries from exports to income transforms tax policy from largely a revenue-raising device to an instrument of social as well as economic policy (Perry, in this volume). This fundamental shift brings an old instrument into a new arena where careful thought is required. Tax policy is an example of a horizontal instrument which affects not just one policy objective but many, including the environment, which complicates policy design and impact. No other policy instrument has a greater effect on social equity than tax policy. As a consequence, tax reform is a highly political matter.

The new social imperatives in Latin America and the varied dimensions of social policy illustrate perhaps more clearly than any other policy area the need for a systemic approach to policy reform and the need for an integrated policy framework for dealing with the multiple challenges of the 1990s.

Conclusions: the politics of participation and of reform processes

The tensions dealt with above between democracy and economic reform, between liberalisation and competitiveness, between civil society and the state, and between economic reform and social policy indicate the centrality of political participation in addressing these tensions. Haggard and Kaufman (in this volume) make it clear that economic reform is not possible without consolidation of democracy. Keck shows that technocratic solutions to environmental problems are not sustainable without political consultation, support and participation. The new paradigm of the "civil economy" embodied in new forms of organising production involves a strategic role for a catalytic state able to engage with the private sector in shaping supportive policies within a market economy framework. The evolution of civil society in recent years and the redefinition of the state to include social relations, the "texturing of the social order" by law as a "constituent element of the state" (O'Donnell) and the enhancement of "viable spaces for individual, social and political action" (Garretón) imply a different state in form and function from the past — a state that is "associative, representative and empowering" (Tomassini). The rise of social policy to a priority in economic reform requires a "new social contract" with social organisations which will act as "intermediaries between the state and those whose resources are few" (Albánez).

These conclusions call attention to the modalities of participation. Within the framework of democracy, political parties stand out. Haggard and Kaufman conclude that "the nature of the party system is a crucial variable in understanding the possibility of reconciling democratic consolidation and economic reform". Valenzuela makes a strong case that the greater penetration of national perspectives into union leadership, as contrasted with over-reliance on base support, is likely to make a critical difference in labour's attitude concerning the challenges of skill upgrading, flexible organisation and innovation processes needed for competitiveness and insertion into the world economy. Both the structure of labour organisations and the mental maps of the leadership of unions directly affect the degree to which labour can become part of the process of change or an obstacle to it.

The National Forum in Brazil is a vehicle for "a partnership with society" based on a modern democratic commitment involving a minimum of solidarity on the part of the major economic actors — the state, businessmen, trade unions — about a modern, social-based form of capitalism (dos Reis Velloso, in this volume). The National Forum is "an independent institution that is a politically pluralist instrument of civil society" and an example of the kind of consultative, consensus-forming and collaborative mechanism that can enhance the dynamics between the public and the private sectors, providing a stabilizing force for modernisation. The question is whether the National Forum model is transferable to other countries in the region and whether such organisations can effectuate change as well as articulate it.

From this overview of the chapters in this book, it appears that the crucial issue in redefining the role of the state in Latin America is the inter-relationship between the state and society, polity and economy. Modalities and mechanisms both in society and in the state define the nature of the interaction between these elements. Enhancing the strength and autonomy of civil society, political parties and the private sector through means which engage the state in supportive, facilitative and innovative relations with them seems to be the crux of the matter. Instead of getting out of the economy, the state is being engaged with it on a new basis. Instead of acting on society, the state is interacting with society. Instead of being responsive to purely clientelist political pressures, the state is opening the channels of policy formation to broad representative political participation. This is a messy process, but it may be the only way to achieve legitimacy, effectiveness and sustainability for governance in Latin America. It may be the only way to make economic, social and political reforms viable by inextricably binding them into a single political process which focuses and forces action on the inter-connectedness of these individual and often separate reform endeavours.

References

ALBERT, M. (1991), *Capitalisme contre capitalisme*, Éditions du Seuil, Paris.

BARDHAN, P. (1993), "Symposium on Democracy and Development", *Journal of Economic Perspectives*, Vol. 7, No. 3 (Summer).

BARROS DE CASTRO, A. (1993), "Renegade Development: Vigor and Demise of State-Led Development in Brazil", in W.C. Smith, C.H. Acuna and E.A. Gamarra, eds, *Democracy, Markets and Structural Reform in Latin America*, North-South Center/Transaction Press.

BRADFORD, C.I., Jr. (1994a), Comment on Papers by José Cordoba and Miguel Urrutia in Williamson, ed. (1994).

BRADFORD, C.I., Jr. (1994b), *From Trade-Driven Growth to Growth-Driven Trade: Reappraising the East Asian Development Experience*, OECD Development Centre, Paris.

BRADFORD, C.I., Jr., ed. (1994*), *The New Paradigm of Systemic Competitiveness: Toward More Integrated Policies in Latin America*, OECD Development Centre, Paris, forthcoming.

BRESSER PEREIRA, L.C. (1993), "Economic Reforms and Economic Growth: Efficiency and Politics in Latin America", in L.C. Bresser Pereira, J.M. Maravall and A. Przeworski, *Economic Reforms in New Democracies: A Social-Democratic Approach*, Cambridge University Press, New York, pp. 15-36.

DAHLMAN, C.J. (1994*), "New Elements of International Competitiveness: Implications for Developing Countries", in Bradford, ed. (1994*).

DOS REIS VELLOSO, J.P. (1994*), "Innovation and Society: The Modern Bases for Development with Equity", in Bradford, ed. (1994*).

FANELLI, J.M. and R. FRENKEL (1994*), "Macro Policies for the Transition from Stabilization to Growth", in Bradford, ed. (1994*).

FFRENCH-DAVIS, R. (1994*), "The Macroeconomic Framework for Investment and Development: The Links between Financial and Trade Reforms", in Bradford, ed. (1994*).

FISHLOW, Albert (1990), "The Latin American State", *Journal of Economic Perspectives*, Vol. 4, No. 3 (Summer), pp. 61-74.

FREY, B.S. and R. EICHENBERGER (1992), *The Political Economy of Stabilization Programmes in Developing Countries*, Technical Paper No. 59, OECD Development Centre, Paris, April.

GARRETÓN, M.A. and M. ESPINOSA (1992), "Reforma del estado o cambio en la matriz socio-politica?", Documento de Trabajo, Serie Estudios Sociales No. 30, FLACSO (Facultad Latinoamericana de Ciencias Sociales), Santiago, August.

GERCHUNOFF, P. and J.C. TORRE (1992), "What Role for the State in Latin America?", in S. Teitel, ed., *Towards a New Development Strategy for Latin America: Pathways from Hirschman's Thought*, Inter-American Development Bank, Washington, D.C., pp. 259-280.

HAGGARD, S. (1990), *Pathways from the Periphery: The Politics of Growth in the Newly Industrializing Countries*, Cornell University Press, Ithaca, New York.

INTER-AMERICAN DEVELOPMENT BANK and UNITED NATIONS DEVELOPMENT PROGRAMME (1993), *Social Reform and Poverty: Towards an Integrated Development Agenda*, Washington, D.C.

JAGUARIBE, H. (1991), "Economic Strategies and Public Rationality in the Promotion of Development", OECD Development Centre, mimeo, Paris, November.

LAFAY, J.-D. and J. LECAILLON (1993), *The Political Dimension of Economic Adjustment*, Development Centre Studies, OECD Development Centre, Paris.

MEIER, G.M. (ed.) (1991), *Politics and Policy Making in Developing Countries: Perspectives on the New Political Economy*, International Center for Economic Growth, San Francisco.

NELSON, J.M. *et al.* (1989), *Fragile Coalitions: The Politics of Economic Adjustment*, Overseas Development Council, Washington, D.C.

O'DONNELL, G. (1993), "On the State, Democratization and Some Conceptual Problems (A Latin American View with Glances at Some Post-Communist Countries)", Working Paper No. 192, April, Helen Kellogg Institute for International Studies, University of Notre Dame, Indiana.

PRZEWORSKI, A., and F. LIMONGI (1993), "Political Regimes and Economic Growth", *Journal of Economic Perspectives*, Vol. 7, No. 3 (Summer).

RAMOS, J.R. (1994*), "Employment, Human Resources and Systemic Competitiveness", in Bradford, ed. (1994*).

TOMASSINI, L. (1992), *Estado, gobernabilidad y desarrollo*, Temas del Foro 90, CINDE (Corporacion de Investigacion para el Desarrollo), Santiago de Chile.

TOMASSINI, L. (1994), "Governance and the Role of the State in an Integrated Policy Framework", OECD Development Centre, Paris (mimeo).

TOURAINE, A. (1988), *La Parole et le sang : politique et société en Amérique latine*, Éditions Odile Jacob, Paris.

WILLIAMSON, J., ed. (1994), *The Political Economy of Policy Reform*, Institute for International Economics, Washington, D.C.

WORLD BANK (1993), *The East Asian Miracle: Economic Growth and Public Policy*, Oxford University Press, New York.

The IDB and the Modernization of the State

Luciano Tomassini

This paper suggests changes in the state to prepare it for the new development strategies that are being adopted in Latin America. Whereas the development models followed by Latin American countries in the past were one-dimensional and/or sectoral, the current strategies are multi-dimensional and systemic.

From the last century until the 1930s, the economic policies of the countries in the region centered on the export of those primary commodities in which their production sectors specialized. Following the Great Depression of the 1930s, economic development in Latin America was implicitly based on state-planned and protected industrialization, an approach which became explicit toward the end of the 1940s, when Raúl Prebisch formulated his first propositions through ECLAC. The objectives were to achieve import substitution and eventually to generate export growth that would allow these countries to overcome the stranglehold on external finances caused by the depression and the war. In the 1960s, after this approach ran its course, the region's economies were hit by the crisis in the world economy and by rising oil prices. They responded to this situation first by borrowing abroad, and later by introducing structural policies intended to service the resulting debt, all of which entailed economic and social setbacks.

The economic strategy of Latin American countries today, in the context of an ever-changing and increasingly complex international integration, can never again be as simple as in the past. Countries and their governments have realized that current strategy depends on (a) technological modernization and transformation of the productive apparatus; (b) increased liberalization of foreign trade and greater international competitiveness; (c) development of a new approach to productivity that accompanies the above processes and, at the same time, stimulates creation of a broader entrepreneurial base; (d) expansion and strengthening of credit institutions and financial markets; (e) rapid incorporation of the poor into modern sectors of the economy; and (f) adaptation of state attitudes and structures to these processes. Becoming aware of such a broad and complex range of challenges is as important as recognizing that these challenges are intricately interdependent and must be addressed as a whole[1].

The state's need for modernization

The success of the new economic policies adopted in Latin America, the creation of a new entrepreneurial culture, and the incorporation of the poor into the productive process, as well as the creation of an essentially innovative society and economy, imply a thorough revision of the structure, attitudes, and role of the state. Even a modernized and vital private sector cannot be relied on to assume increasing responsibility for development or to stimulate its most creative elements, if state institutions are not modernized at the same time.

The state that these countries inherited was formed when requirements for a large state prevailed in the world. This phenomenon is explained by the crises undergone by humanity, from the Great Depression of the 1930s, through the strenuous effort required in World War II, to the outbreak of the Cold War. The world opted for a large, welfare-oriented, interventionist state. Furthermore, developing countries like those in Latin America, which were at a stage of development in which the private sector was very weak or practically non-existent, could not hope to be incorporated into the modern world without the leadership of the state. Many things have changed since then, and the countries of the region are beginning to move in a new direction.

The reforms to the state initiated by the countries in the region are designed to strengthen public administration and the state's capacity to analyze, plan, and implement economic and social policies; to improve tax policies, tax administration, and fiscal management; and to establish regulatory controls as a counterweight to ongoing privatization and deregulation programs. It has become clear, however, that while improvements in the public sector are essential, they are not sufficient. Other recognized areas of need include providing legislatures with support services and a legal framework; modernizing judicial systems; strengthening social security systems and their financial viability; achieving significant advances in administrative, financial, and managerial decentralization; introducing more effective mechanisms for integrating the poor into the productive process; and, above all, forming better and closer associations between the state and the private sector. This, in turn, implies an understanding of the systemic nature of current development strategies.

Social culture today is characterized by a greater reliance on society and the market, and by a search for greater complementarity between these two and the state. Since reflection on the role of the state was frozen between the time the interventionist state was in force and the time it was attacked by neoliberal thinking, the re-emerging concern over the issue is highly fragmented and appears very confused. Today a number of unrelated partial and constricting notions about the state exist side by side. In order to overcome this schizophrenia, it is advisable to distinguish between the *public sector*, made up of that part of the economy which is controlled by the state, and the *government*, which comprises the public authorities — the executive, the legislature, and the judiciary — and the interaction of these authorities with political parties, labor unions, and other citizens' organizations through which the process of government is properly channeled and conducted. It is also necessary to differentiate between, on one hand, the public sector and government, and on the other, the new forms of state and public association designed to manage public interests jointly in the most diverse sectors.

Today many private institutions are devoted to fulfilling tasks of public interest, either directly or in association with the government. The state has given up responsibilities that it has deemed more appropriate for other economic and social actors, and private organizations are now being formed to perform public services.

All of the countries which have undergone fundamental changes in economic policy have been faced with the task of bringing their state apparatus in line with these changes. This adaptation is extremely important in dealing with radical changes such as those experienced in Eastern European and Latin American countries. Following the painful "lost decade" of the 1980s, these countries are now decidedly adopting policies to liberalize, open, and modernize their economies. It is impossible to carry out a sustained productive modernization, an exhaustive social reform, a change in entrepreneurial culture, and a firm effort to enhance international competitiveness without the guidance and support of the state — a state, however, that has been completely reformed.

This new state, which seeks complementarity with its citizens and with the private sector, is more enterprising than bureaucratic. It tends to empower its citizens, its enterprises, and its social organizations, rather than to control or subsidize them. It strives to anticipate problems instead of just attempting to solve them as they arise. It is more concerned with generating resources than with consuming them. It decentralizes authority and adopts more participatory forms of administration. It promotes competition among suppliers and seeks to have its agencies provide good services to its citizens. It fosters results-oriented agencies rather than ones that merely fulfill bureaucratic regulations. It is dedicated not only to providing public services, but to acting mainly as a catalyst, empowering all economic and social sectors so that they can solve community problems on their own.

Modernization cannot be achieved through initiatives focused on individual sectors, but must be integrated and systemic in nature. This implies that while modernization may be introduced gradually in specific sectors, it should be carried out against a backdrop of systemic vision. It would be foolish to think that a dynamic pace of development could be sustained if the actions of economic entities, as effective as these may be, were held back by impediments in the legislative process, the courts, labor relations, city or regional management, or environmental issues, to name just a few examples.

The countries of Latin America are initiating reforms directed at streamlining public administration and making it more efficient; strengthening their ability to analyze, plan, and adopt economic and social policies; improving fiscal and budgetary policies; improving tax systems and tax administration; introducing better regulatory controls to counterbalance ongoing privatization programs; and re-examining social security systems and their financial viability.

Improvements will also be needed in other areas of public authority. Arrangements designed to promote closer co-operation between state entities and the public will need to be strengthened and expanded, so that duties once exclusively fulfilled by the state can be decentralized and better performed closer to the people. These efforts are now viewed by countries in the region as essential for successfully implementing their current development strategies and for managing their political systems.

The IDB's contribution to this task

Most Latin American countries have adopted development strategies designed to modernize their economies, restructure their production processes, absorb technological changes, incorporate less productive workers into the modern sector of their economies, achieve inter-sectoral integration, open sectors to foreign trade, and develop a sustained international competitiveness. The integrated or systemic character of these strategies demands that more attention be paid to the current relationships between the state, the economy, the private sector, the public, and social organizations, and that radical changes be made to many of these relationships.

Governments in the region feel the need for change, and the Bank has been made aware of this need both through its ongoing dialogues with governments and through the specific requests they have begun to make for help in their efforts to introduce structural changes in their state apparatuses.

The *Report on the Eighth General Increase of Bank Resources* points out that those structural changes "have encompassed efforts to achieve a strengthened, but smaller, fiscally disciplined government which complements the private sector". Expanding on this appraisal, the same document points out:

The objective of such reform is to strengthen public administration, including the capacity to analyze, formulate, and implement economic and social policy, to manage public expenditure, to improve the design of tax policy and tax administration, and to introduce an appropriate regulatory framework for complementing ongoing privatization programs...

It also encompasses modernization of judicial systems, provision of basic support services to enhance the efficacy of the legislative process and strengthen the financial viability and efficiency of the social security systems. These efforts, aimed at modernizing, focusing, and strengthening the machinery of the state, are essential to accelerating economic and social development. (Chapter 1, 1.1; Chapter 4, 1.16)

The Bank's management has given great importance to these ideas, even though they are preliminary, and is taking the first steps to implement them. Some ideas, such as those dealing with fiscal, tax, and budgetary systems, have been around for a long time. Others, such as support to the judicial and legislative processes, or improvements in public management of various state sectors, are more recent. This year the IDB organized seminars on Social Reform and Poverty (with a strong emphasis on equipping the state for this task), on Judicial Administration, and on the Stability and Development of the State. The Bank is also considering, or already granting, scholarships for degrees in public administration, public and social policy planning, social evaluation of projects, and macroeconomic policies at the Instituto Torcuato di Tella, the Institute of Advanced Studies in Management (IESA) in Venezuela, the University of Chile, the Latin American Economic Research Corporation (CIEPLAN), ILADES, la Universidad Católica de Chile, and la Universidad de los Andes in Colombia. Through these initiatives, the Bank has begun to develop a systematic and diversified program to build modern management cadres, trained to plan and manage public policies in its member countries.

The main initiatives that the Bank will most likely undertake in the judicial sector were announced at the close of the seminar on Judicial Administration in Latin America and the Caribbean, held in San José, Costa Rica. In general, these actions are also applicable to and useful in other areas of state activity. The first initiative — creating a nucleus within the Bank to organize its ideas on the problem — has already been carried out. Another step is currently under way: organizing a technical co-operation network in the region to diagnose and give voice to concerns of member countries on these topics. A third option involved the possibility, at the country's request, of granting technical assistance at the national level to identify needs and to map out solutions. Fourth, the advisability of incorporating these elements into the Bank's current programs was pointed out. Finally, the Bank is, as a matter of course, preparing to study loan requests for modernization projects in specific sectors of the state. The Bank is also beginning to process and evaluate, in collaboration with the countries, their initial requests for projects for modernizing judicial systems, strengthening the technical support relied on by legislatures, improving public agency and public policy management, as well as other similar issues.

The notion that the Bank should contribute to member countries' efforts to modernize their states is very recent. The President of the Bank, Enrique V. Iglesias, had already suggested in Caracas, in 1989, that there was a need for broader collaboration with the public sector. It was at the 1993 Hamburg meeting, however, that he placed greater emphasis on state modernization and included in this concept not only the public sector, with whose agencies the Bank has historically worked, but all state agencies. The Bank has adopted this focus on the basis of the following appraisal, which is shared by its member countries: the renovation of the state cannot be achieved through isolated efforts of modernization that overlook important aspects of the government, the legislature, or the judiciary. Although in practice these reforms need to be carried out gradually, they must reflect a united vision and a systemic approach.

Once the Bank announced that it would collaborate with member countries in the overall modernization of their state, it was necessary to recognize that the institution had no experience in many aspects of the process, and to accept the need for systematic work to obtain a complete and current perspective on the topic. It was in response to this need that the seminars were held, a number of documents were prepared on the subject, and, more important, a Working Group on Modernization of the State was created. Represented in this group are all Bank departments with assigned responsibilities in this area, whether through studies they write, through technical assistance operations or fiscal planning they periodically carry out in the countries, or through loan projects.

On the basis of its initial months of work, the group suggested that the Bank would most likely become involved in the following sectors: 1) modernization of the public sector and of state fiscal matters — an area, it should be noted, where the IDB has already contributed significant work; 2) the broad spectrum of public authorities, i.e. the executive, the legislature, and the judiciary, on whose competence and interaction the results of state actions and related policies depend; 3) issues related to modernization of the management of public policy and institutions, including issues related to new organizational structures, decentralization, deregulation, and the adoption of new forms of administration and management; 4) the realignment of responsibilities between the state and public sectors, including, in the latter, market mechanisms, the private sector, labor groups, and social and local organizations, which can share with the state responsibility for carrying out public duties, especially in the social domain; 5) the role of responsibility, transparency, and ethics in carrying out public services.

The Bank's experience in the region during these past few decades has shown that economic growth goes hand in hand with greater social integration, with a new productivity culture, and with an in-depth modernization of the state; these elements are also basic conditions for creating democratic and participatory societies. The link between these diverse issues, which in the past were thought of as unrelated, does not lead away from or complicate the view of the basic problems of development. On the contrary, this link leads to a more realistic and mature vision of development. It is a perspective which, perhaps for the first time, reflects not only the perception of the experts, but also that of the citizen and the average Latin American, who feel that these matters taken together affect in equal measure the expectation of a better society and better quality of life.

The Bank's main areas of activity

The five principal sectors identified by the Bank as priority areas are presented in the table below:

Public sector	Government and public authorities	Management of government agencies and policies	Relationship between the state and public sectors	Ethics, responsibility, and transparency

Within these sectors, the following are among the activities identified by the Bank as those that, based on previous experience, offer the least risk and, at the same time, are already the subject of dialogue between the Bank and member countries, or are the subject of specific requests:

1. *Modernization of the legal and judicial systems.* Generally, this area involves Bank assistance to member countries in their efforts to bring judicial codes in line with the new requirements for economic and social development, to strengthen trends that make laws responsive to these requirements, and to redefine the role of the law and jurisprudence in regulating economic and social relations. These efforts are intended to create a climate that stimulates and facilitates development. In particular, the Working Group has developed, thanks to the seminar and several follow-up initiatives, an overview of the countries' ideas regarding the main initiatives the IDB could undertake to support programs (whether they are under way or are being planned) to improve the countries' judicial systems. These programs mainly aim to improve the management of judicial power; enhance the training and careers of judges; streamline

36

judicial procedures; identify alternative ways to solve conflicts; create broader access to the courts; and adapt the law and justice to conform with the new demands arising from the globalization of societies and economies, and, therefore, from the greater international integration of the countries concerned. In this regard, the Working Group has already had the opportunity to carry out studies and advisory work and to receive and evaluate requests from member countries. These activities have allowed the group to acquire the integrated perspective that is the subject of this discussion.

2. *Support for legislative initiatives.* Although parliaments in most Latin American countries are co-legislative bodies that govern together with the executive power, they have a critical responsibility for creating and enacting laws that fit the needs of society and development. As is well known, however, parliaments are not always organized and technically prepared to fulfill this responsibility effectively. The complexity of economic and social life today has made this task highly technical and increasingly specialized. Although the Bank's activities in this area are still to be defined, subject to further consultations and visits to various countries, one could expect main areas of future Bank activity to entail improving the effectiveness of legislative functions; strengthening relations with the executive power (as a co-legislative body) and other non-governmental and state entities; redefining and broadening representation in parliaments by supporting measures that would strengthen their contacts with interest groups and their familiarity with national issues on which they must rule; enhancing the parliaments' abilities to deal with fiscal policy issues, as incorporated in their respective constitutions; and developing a data base that would provide parliaments with the background and reference materials needed to carry out their work effectively, allowing them, for example, to harmonize enacted and proposed legislation to avoid repetitions and contradictions in the countries' governing laws. As each country's predicament is different, the Bank will have to deal directly, on a case-by-case basis, with the parliaments and their staffs, or with the firms that have been created in these countries to provide and receive legislative assistance.

3. *Management of state institutions and public policies.* Substantial changes are required in the way state institutions and public policies are managed, since these are linked to changes in the social culture of Latin American countries, the evolution of their economies, and advances in the field of organization theory concerning both state agencies and, especially, private firms. This involves introducing organizational structures, management styles, and decision-making processes that are not only compatible with a modern organization, but are also in tune with the innovative, enterprising, and decentralized character of the new development strategies currently in force in Latin America. It is a question of supporting modern policy-making processes that are less bureaucratic and less centralized, while encouraging greater co-ordination not only among government agencies, but between the government and private entities as well. It is

also a question of assigning to the state a role that is less interventionist and less dependent on the use of public resources, equipping the state to act as a catalyst for endowing and empowering other economic and social agents. In this area, the Bank will need to pay special attention first of all to the introduction and dissemination of modern forms of management among agencies responsible for public, social, and economic policies that affect the states; second, to the establishment of efficient and customized mechanisms to regulate and supervise the activities of various non-state sectors, especially sectors involving privatized firms or deregulated areas; and, third, to the analysis, dissemination, and customizing of practices for decentralizing administrative, financial, and decision-making processes, at both the municipal and regional levels. The importance of the subject, and the implications it holds for all state institutions, make it useful to expand further on this topic.

Modernization of public management

It is practical to assume that state modernization does not involve only structural changes. It is possible, and even likely, that reorganized state institutions could continue to operate in the old manner even after structural changes have been instituted. Any change in the organizational structure of public agencies must therefore be accompanied by similar changes in management.

The need to modernize management of agencies and public policies does not relate just to specific sectors but represents a new style of management and decision-making that needs to spread gradually across all public management. Furthermore, the new style of management now taking hold worldwide finds application in both public and private sectors, taking into account the differences specific to their functions. The same management style should also be applicable to all types of organizations — ministries, municipalities, hospitals, labor unions, companies — thus closing the gap between private and public sectors. Among the various elements of modern management of public agencies and policies, the following deserve specific mention:

- Establishment of governments beyond partisanship, which have great technical competence and the upper echelons of which are appointed according to merit. The change from a controlling state to one that provides guidance and delegates power to its economic and social sectors presupposes reliance on personnel able to issue appropriate directives and provide guidelines on a daily basis.

- Conversion of hierarchical or pyramidal state structures to more flexible ones that are able to establish networks among agencies and civil servants and to promote interaction between the state, the private sector, and social or local organizations.

- Modernization in the management of the state's human resources. State employees should be granted greater freedom of initiative and, at the same time, assigned greater responsibilities, in order to overcome the state's

38

current bureaucratic culture, which tends to saddle employees with rigid structures and regulations.

– Improvement of the decision-making systems at all levels. The quality of public management and its outcome are highly dependent on the timeliness of the procedures through which decisions are made and plans carried out. Traditionally, decisions have been slow and not very creative since they were the outcome of bureaucratic, hierarchical organizations. Procedures and attitudes are needed that endow decision makers with greater flexibility and initiative. It is necessary, therefore, to reform the structure, path, impediments, timing, and results of decision processes, to identify their shortcomings, and to propose measures for making them more efficient.

– Strengthening transparency and honesty in the discharge of public duties has received increased worldwide attention from the public. Such efforts should be intensified in Latin America.

– Modernization of budgetary techniques for the purpose of expanding budget-structuring practices, assigning goals to various budget allocations, emphasizing evaluation of results, and proposing multi-year programs for projects that exceed ordinary fiscal periods. These are indispensable tools of modern public management.

– Control of the activities of state-controlled and decentralized organizations, privatized sectors, and certain important markets that are vital to the success of economic and social policies. Such control is another important element of a modern management system. The General Comptrollers of the Republic have traditionally been very proficient in controlling the legality and integrity of administrative proceedings, in protecting the public patrimony, and in carrying out certain auditing roles by maintaining their line of authority and independence before the courts. There is disagreement, however, concerning the advisability of easing *ex ante* control on the legality and redress of administrative proceedings, and of creating greater *ex post* control on state activities and other areas where efficient operation is a matter of public interest. The reason for this is to avoid problems when undertaking initiatives and assuming risks.

Congress, particularly the House of Representatives, plays an important supervisory and investigative role. This is inherent in a democratic system. However, the resources on which legislators rely to fulfill their duties and, especially, to carry out this role are limited.

Finally, there is a need to establish procedures for allowing the community to exert control on public policies and measures that affect its interest by creating mechanisms similar to those embodied in the public defender's office of some countries.

The relationship between the state and the private sector

The economic reforms currently undertaken by Latin American countries are assigning a greater importance and a broader role to the private sector. Since old debates have been overcome, there is no longer any doubt among governments that the private sector has been called upon to provide, first of all, an important contribution towards modernization of production, technical innovation, and the export capability of countries in the region. It has also been called upon to make possible a social reform that, by incorporating the population's poorest sectors into the productive process, will be effective in helping to relieve poverty in the short and long terms, and to enhance economic competitiveness. Since neither the international financial organizations, nor the state, nor public enterprises can provide sufficient financing on their own to modernize the economy and incorporate the poorer sectors into it, the Bank considers modernization of the state to be closely linked to strengthening the private sector. Therefore, the Bank wishes to intensify its efforts through policies and programs to offer the efficient and timely help needed for private sector development in the region.

It is important to keep in mind that success of the economic reforms and access by the poorer social sectors to the resulting benefits, not to mention the strengthening of democracy itself, make it necessary to offer opportunities for participation in the modern economy to the largest possible number of people, whether they are entrepreneurs, investors, or workers. Doing so not only empowers the poor to escape from poverty by offering them jobs and raising their income levels, but it also strengthens their commitment to the region's economic, social, and political systems.

Financing private sector investments has been part of the Bank's activities since the beginning of its operations, as its Articles of Agreement mandate. While there is no legal requirement for public guarantees for these loans, the Bank's policy has wisely required these guarantees. During the 1960s and 1970s, the Bank carried out these operations through global loans, an arrangement that was consistent with the economic strategies in vogue at that time. The strategies emphasized the importance of government support for encouraging economic growth, strengthening the private sector, and channeling credit earmarked for that sector, especially public sector credits. Those who ultimately benefited from these operations were private companies, particularly those in the industrial and agricultural sectors, whose credits were channeled through public agencies and public policies. These loans were granted at subsidized interest rates, and were focused on those sectors that needed stimulation. Several evaluations have demonstrated that while that approach was consistent with the economic policies of the time and did, in fact, fill a void, it had several drawbacks: the sub-loans were concentrated on a small number of middle- and high-income producers; and many of the national development banks that brokered those loans became insolvent because of their reliance on high service commissions, subsidized interest rates, and high administrative costs, at a time when concessionary funds lent at subsidized interest rates were becoming scarce.

Recognition of these limitations, along with the fact that these activities made extension of short-term credit the only viable course in a highly unstable financial market, led to the conclusion that this approach did not provide a reliable basis for developing the private sector, and that the national development banks were not the only, or the best, vehicles for handling this process. This belief coincided with a dramatic change in the economic policies of the borrowing countries. The Bank's new focus on private sector financing underlines the need to put trust in the sector's initiative, to help create a competitive environment, and to expect the utmost efficiency from financial institutions and private sector producers that participate in these credit arrangements. For this purpose, the Bank has emphasized opening lines of credit to different sectors involved in private activities, thereby enhancing equal opportunity and competitiveness in gaining access to credit. This contrasts with public programs that focus their financing on particular sectors. At the same time, the Bank has encouraged the role of private financial institutions in disbursing these credit lines, and has also encouraged government development banks to act as second-tier banks in such operations. Of course, in qualifying private financial institutions to broker its lines of credit, the Bank applies its own evaluation criteria, taking into account factors such as the banks' capitalization, profitability, and portfolio quality. The Bank has also tried to broaden the range of eligible private financial institutions, to include banks linked to financial companies, leasing companies, and other companies that operate at market interest rates. One goal of this effort — a point which has not been emphasized sufficiently — is to integrate into the credit network a larger number of private sector entities, including medium, small, and very small companies.

In summary, the Bank is pursuing three main objectives through these policies: to increase the efficiency and solvency of private financial institutions, to make small producers eligible for credit, and to stimulate deposit-taking for savings and investments. The Bank is also aware that the fulfillment of these objectives is a necessary condition both for incorporating the disadvantaged social sectors into the productive process and for consolidating democracy. According to this vision, achieving greater social integration through broader financing, building a wider entrepreneurial base, and strengthening democratic institutions go hand in hand.

It is almost impossible to ignore the fact that these objectives still clash with Latin America's current entrepreneurial culture. In this region of the world the private sector was for the most part born under the protection of the state. This has advantages but also disadvantages. Initial protection was necessary, but often it implied granting monopolies, tariff protection, or subsidies to the private sector, thereby creating a profit-oriented and conservative entrepreneurial culture that was averse to risk-taking, innovative ideas, and engagement in medium- and long-term productive projects. Fortunately, this culture is changing. The countries in the region will have to stimulate this process if they want to incorporate technological changes and attract the foreign investments and partnerships needed to accelerate restructuring of their production sectors, rates of growth, and access to international markets. The state has a very important role in this process. In the past, the state protected its production sectors; today, its role lies in its ability to provide guidance, to create a capacity at the national level for anticipating future trends, to provide the necessary signals to the various social and economic sectors, and to fulfill an enabling and endowing role for these sectors by providing them with information, advisory services, and other necessary forms of support.

The state has always played a crucial role in establishing the legal framework of labor relations and in preserving good labor relations within companies. Achievement of constructive and consensus-building labor relations is an essential element in Latin America's current development strategies. On one hand, this presupposes maintaining the traditional reliance on strong and independent organized unions. On the other, improvement of labor relations implies a growing understanding by workers of the importance of preserving the economic balances and productivity of companies, and that employers become increasingly accustomed to linking the workers' productivity to salaries. All of these issues depend on the legal framework, economic balances, relations between unions and the private sector, and the preservation of an appropriate development and investment climate — tasks in which the state will have an irreplaceable role.

Concluding ideas

At the closing of the seminar in San José on Judicial Administration in Latin America and the Caribbean, the IDB President announced the main initiatives that the Bank was likely to undertake in this area, initiatives which, generally speaking, would also seem viable and appropriate for other areas of state activity.

The need to bring the state closer in line with society is an imperative of the times. Only a few of the approaches needed to face this challenge have been mentioned here. The need presupposes that significant changes be gradually implemented within state agencies and institutions. Again, it is a question not of bringing about a total change, but of achieving gradual changes on both the institutional and personal levels, and of endowing a traditional institutional system, which is becoming increasingly modernized, with new mechanisms and tools. Global winds are blowing in favor of the development of individual freedom, social organizations, and the private sector, but they do not detract from the guiding and regulatory role that will always belong to the state as a guarantor of public well-being.

Modernization of the state does not mean improvements only to its administrative institutions, though these are important, but a significant realignment of functions between the state and public society. These issues need to be stressed. Included in this context are the operations of the market, the private sector, labor organizations, grassroots social organizations, and regional and local entities, which have a great desire to participate and a growing capacity to help solve public problems that directly affect them. In this regard, many things need to be accomplished or devised. First, there is a need to strengthen government agencies that can provide assistance to the weakest links in the productive system, to promote training for this sector, and to encourage the dissemination of technological innovations throughout the economy (including small, medium-sized, and even very small businesses, as well as other private sector entities whose access to the market and to the incentive programs still provided by the state is extremely limited). Second, it is necessary for a portion of the investments and credit extended to be channelled to viable and profitable opportunities that involve creative and small business activities. Such activities offer the greatest chances for generating employment and often can help considerably in restructuring a country's productive and export base. Third, agencies and policies responsible for carrying out the government's social programs must be made less bureaucratic. This can be done by getting agencies accustomed to working more closely with grassroots organizations and more in tune with the way these organizations work, since a great degree of solidarity, experience, and motivation can be found in these organizations. Fourth, the state should directly promote co-operation with the private sector or grassroots organizations and promote training programs for social managers. Today these programs are mainly vocational in nature and self-taught, compared with the state's ability to train company managers or managers for public entities. Finally, largely dependent on community co-operation are sensitive issues such as the protection of underprivileged groups, improvements in citizen safety, or awareness of epidemic diseases, to mention just a few examples. In fact, the community is taking many of these problems into its own hands. This is a critical area insofar as it calls into play the state's ability to bring decisions closer to the people.

Most Latin American countries have relatively small and open economies that depend strictly on investments, technology, and international trade, and that must operate within a framework of international relations characterized by significant changes and a great deal of uncertainty. This calls for enhanced ability and professionalism in foreign policy, as well as greater proficiency and integration among the different entities that handle foreign affairs, an area where much progress is still needed. It is a question not only of improving the foreign services of these countries, but of emphasizing the need to have an international policy based on a medium- and long-term strategic vision. Reforming the ministries of foreign affairs would not be sufficient. It would also be necessary to create a true institutional system of foreign policy, since management of the countries' foreign interests is shared by various agencies. The structures and functions of the ministries of foreign affairs should be improved and somewhat decentralized, whereby the traditional roles of management and foreign representation would prevail, providing better, more analytical, and flexible forecasting results. Professionalism of the ministry staff, with selection and promotions based on efficiency and merit, is an essential condition for making foreign policy that has the clarity, support, and stability required of a state policy. As an increasing portion of the countries' foreign trade is conducted by the private sector, the relations between institutional foreign policy and this sector should become smoother and more systematic.

Note

1. This paper focuses on the Inter-American Development Bank's activities and views related to the modernization of the state. Therefore, this document does not contain an academic bibliography. The main conceptual sources for the Bank's treatment of this subject are found in a book by IDB President Enrique V. Iglesias, *Reflexiones sobre el desarrollo económico; hacia un nuevo consenso latinoamericano* (IDB, Washington, D.C., 1992), pp. 159 ff. Other sources are: Iglesias' opening address at the Seminar on Judicial Administration in Latin America and the Caribbean, San José, Costa Rica, 4-6 February 1993; his opening address before the Bank's Board of Governors, Hamburg, Germany, 1993; Tomassini, *Estado, gobernabilidad y desarrollo*, written in November 1992 and published in 1993 in a collection of IDB monographs; various sections of the *Report on the Eighth General Increase of Bank Resources*; and documentation being developed by the IDB's Working Group on Modernization of the State.

From the Mobilising State to Democratic Politics

Alain Touraine

It is generally agreed that after a phase of structural adjustment — *ajuste* — which in Latin America as in other parts of the world has had positive economic consequences but severe social ones, priorities must now be shifted from economic objectives to broader political and social action. This recognition can have at least two very different implications, however.

The first, which is closest to previous economic analyses, is that for current structural reform to succeed, the state must improve its ability to regulate the economy. It must be able to conduct privatisations, revamp the tax system — which in Latin American countries is usually quite inappropriate — and negotiate with international institutions. It must above all free itself from the clientelism and corporatism that ruled its action in the preceding period. This calls for the state to be made both leaner and stronger.

The other implication is that the state must be made capable of restoring a constantly deteriorating social situation. The urban crisis has become so acute in some countries that public security is requiring more and more resources and, in the case of Peru, state reinforcement is growing out of the army's struggle against the *Sendero Luminoso* insurgency. Above all, increasing exclusion and inequities have been jeopardising national social unity and integration, and could lead to violent uprisings, even military coups, as in Venezuela and in Argentina, where Presidents Alfonsín and Menem were threatened. This second perspective is quite different from the first in that it breaks with the idea that economic reform can in itself solve a country's main social problems. It is the better point of departure, for within the very broad framework it defines there is room for analyses of the first type, whereas the opposite is not true.

We must therefore keep clearly in mind that after a phase of structural adjustment and direct anti-inflationary action, Latin American countries are again considering the matter of their form of development and of how they are to work as societies; this has brought them to be just as concerned about the fight against social inequity and exclusion as about the growth of investments and production.

To see things from this perspective, it is essential to define the economic situation in Latin American countries from the point of view of their political institutions, while in the first perspective it might be enough to define the best methods for achieving economic reforms.

The mobilising state

The situation can no longer be completely defined in strictly Latin American terms. The globalisation of economic and cultural exchange and the triumph of world markets have been more or less directly associated in all parts of the world with a crisis in the socio-political model of the mobilising state, which has prevailed throughout the 20th century.

Since 1970, there has been a striking simultaneity in the decline and fall of the communist regimes, of nationalisms in the formerly colonised countries, of national-popular regimes in Latin America and, more recently, of the European social democracies and their equivalents in Australia, New Zealand and Canada. This dissolution culminated in 1989 with the fall of the Berlin Wall and the emancipation from Soviet domination of countries such as the Baltic states, Poland, Czechoslovakia and Bulgaria, while Romania and some of the countries that were part of the Soviet Union went only half-way. Hungary differed in that it had already been engaged in a deep transformation process since 1968. In western Europe, social democracy was elected out of government — as in Sweden, Austria and France — or had to adopt free-market policies to remain in power, as in Spain and Australia. In China, and possibly in Vietnam and Cuba, communist governments are calling upon foreign investments, which in certain regions are changing society into something quite different from that which remains under close political control at the central level.

The current situation is governed by the fall of the mobilising state as a general political model. To understand the situation, we must define the model.

The mobilising state embodied, though less radically in Latin America and in western Europe than in other parts of the world, three types of objectives: political (national integration), economic (growth) and social (redistribution of income). It did not separate economic policy and social policy, modernisation, and the strengthening of national unity; in fact it tried to combine them all in a single model that was designed by the state, not negotiated at a parliamentary level by the social partners themselves.

In many parts of the world, the mobilising state replaced a state that had been guided by strictly political or national policies, was extremely cut off from civil society, and wherein the most active collective social actors were often defined in cultural or regional terms. The mobilising state arrived as an instrument of integration of the socio-political scene. In addition, throughout the 19th century, before the mobilising state, while central Europe was occupied with the question of nationalities, national states in western Europe entered into struggles and rivalries. At the same time, a practically unmanaged capitalism developed, while the important political and social debates were devoted to constitutional issues, secularity or the nature of taxes. Political, economic and social problems thus appeared to be founded on totally separate logics.

46

The United States was experiencing an analogous situation: the problems involved in the conquest of the West and in immigration were for a long time considered as having nothing to do with those involved in the slavery-based society of the South, in the formation of large-scale capitalism centred on New York and Chicago, and in the judicial and constitutionalist spirit that had been present since independence. Before the New Deal, social, economic and political problems in the United States had, as in Europe, mostly been dealt with separately, which made parliamentary activity and state intervention a very complex matter. Similarly, in Latin America, before the mobilising state, the state concentrated mainly on building national unity after the era of *caudillos*, while economic activity generally remained focussed on international trade. Ethnic issues, especially in the Andean countries and in Central America, were treated in a very autonomous framework.

The mobilising state marked the integration of politics, economic activity and the social actors. This interpretation of the mobilising state as a historical model is important because it will serve to explain that state's current decline and disintegration. Some people consider the mobilising state as a temporary deviation that should be dismantled so as to return to a situation where political, economic and social problems are strongly differentiated. It is also conceivable, to the contrary, that after the fall of the mobilising state and a transition period dominated by the unleashing of a market economy, a new model of national society will necessarily arise having a higher and more efficient level of integration of political, economic and social problems than had the mobilising state. This essay should be governed by this question.

The contrast between the political life of the 19th century and that of the 20th can be seen everywhere. Triumphant capitalism presided over the 19th century, and at the end of the century, anticapitalist, anti-imperialist and anticolonialist movements of a social, cultural and political nature began to develop. The end of the 20th century offers the opposite picture: after nearly a century of triumph, starting with the Mexican and the Soviet revolutions, the model of political determinism has run its course and the first thing happening after that is a return to the liberal idea of a purely economic management of economic activity. The mobilising state had adopted a position that was completely opposed to the differentiation of social subsystems, except in one case: mobilising states generally accepted or reinforced the separation of religion and politics, at least in the communist countries, in national-popular governments of the Mexican type and in Nasserian nationalism. The mobilising state had asserted the need for an increasingly all-encompassing mobilisation of social and cultural forces. The 20th century has been profoundly antiliberal all over the world, from the Third World to Japan, from France and Italy with their post-war nationalisations to the economic nationalisms of the member states of the Bandung group. First, national awareness was mobilised, but more recently mobilisation efforts have been directed at least as much to ethnic and ultimately even to religious affiliation.

Like other parts of the world, Latin America had 50 years of what Gino Germani (1962) was the first to call "national-popular" regimes. Seen from the angle we are working with, their main feature was the intermingling of social, economic and political actors. Apart from the Monterrey group in Mexico, few entrepreneurs on the continent did not have their own fates linked to that of the state. Most entrepreneurs enjoyed rents that were protected by the state, and in many countries industrialisation was driven by public enterprises following a pattern of action that was as much political as it was economic. Brazil, in particular, from the time of Getulio Vargas onwards, developed a nationalist industrialisation policy. Unions that were not controlled by government were just as rare, as were unions that were not incorporated into the state apparatus in a neocorporatist fashion. Neither the Peronist nor the Mexican unions — the latter were established by the state in the same way as Brazilian unions were — followed the British-type trade-union tradition, and Bolivian unions were for a long time more the instrument of Juan Lechin's political career than organisations for negotiating labour demands. At the same time, the national-popular state, because of its mobilising nature, set out for itself social and economic tasks, as much as strictly political ones. It sought to reinforce national integration by redistributing outside resources and by speeding up import substitution.

This socio-political matrix, as Manuel Antonio Garretón calls it, is based on dependence on outside resources and models and on the preservation of social dualism and exclusion, but also and sometimes even more so, on the growth of the domestic market, *hacia adentro*, and the extension of social and political participation to vast sectors of the urban population. This multiplicity of forms and objectives accounts for the instability of the model. In Argentina, Venezuela and Panama, the matrix tended towards populism; in Mexico and especially in Brazil, it was of a nationalistic nature; and in Chile it combined a conception of European-style representative democracy with elements of national populism, which were present as much in Ibañism and the socialist party as in Christian democracy.

The fragility and instability of this model explain the deep crisis that shook the continent in the 1980s. The crisis had both internal and external causes, the former being, as most often they are, the most important. Inflation was largely induced by the pressure of social demands, especially those coming from the groups closest to the state; the weakness of industrialisation and of the entrepreneurial sector is best explained by the economic behaviour of the oligarchy, its speculative investments and capital flight; indulgence in *plata dulce* explains an indebtedness suddenly made heavier by deterioration of the terms of trade and the rise in interest rates leading to the dramatic 1982 crisis.

At that time in the Soviet Union, growth had been slowing down since the 1970s, new nuclear and electronic technologies were not being mastered, and there had been military defeat in Afghanistan. All of this led to Gorbachev's adoption of *perestroika* and *glasnost* to surrender totalitarian control over Soviet society and over the Comecon (CMEA) countries. Elsewhere in the world there were many instances of the mobilising state's collapsing — as in Egypt after Nasser's military defeat — and of its progressive stifling, as in Algeria.

The fall

The most striking aspect of all this is that almost none of these mobilising states was toppled by a popular uprising. Poland had been upset by the Solidarity movement in 1980-81, but as from 1989, the disintegration of the communist regime was gradually and shrewdly managed by the Round Table negotiators. Czechoslovakia's velvet revolution was altogether quite pacific compared to the Hungarian revolution of 1956, and in Russia an attempted putsch by conservative forces, not a popular uprising, is what sped up the disappearance of the political power. In Latin America, neither in Brazil nor in Argentina, neither in Uruguay nor in Chile were the military regimes swept away by popular uprisings such as the one which dealt a death blow to Ceaucescu in Romania, but which did not completely liquidate the communist power élite.

In earlier times, capitalist domination had been opposed by the mobilisation of social and political forces; for the mobilising state, the main agent of its downfall was of a strictly economic nature: the need and the determination to free the economy from the political control to which it had been subjected. The silence that took hold of grass-roots groups and intellectuals is so widespread that nobody even notices it anymore. Yet, when referring to the *decada perdida* in Latin America, when income per capita was seen to be sharply regressing in most countries, and poverty spreading, would not one have been tempted to describe this as a revolutionary situation? Would not one have expected to see a new state mobilising the claims, the fears and the hopes? What happened instead was the opposite. During the period of rapid growth in Latin America, voices were raised to denounce domestic imperialism and colonialism; today those voices have practically disappeared and the dominant political ideology gets by with speaking of democracy in terms so vague and so formal that they can certainly not satisfy those who are threatened with poverty or underemployment.

There are reasons for this virtually universal silence. The first is that the mobilising state absorbed the social actors and took away their ability for autonomous action and even for autonomous thinking. The mobilising state was opposed by critical intellectuals and, when it was repressive, by dissidents and exiled critics; in the wake of its disintegration, however, it has left silence. Poland, a country of speech and challenge, rose up in 1980 on the wave of a social, national and democratic movement. Ten years later, it is voiceless: Solidarity has weakened; and the intellectuals, whose academic salaries have become meagre, are seeking substitute sources of income at home or abroad while the most prominent amongst them have become directly involved in political action and are struggling with a difficult situation.

The same is true for Latin America, even in countries where military regimes had eliminated a populism that had become revolutionary. In Chile, as of 1983, political demonstrations and union actions shook General Pinochet's regime but stopped after a fairly short period, mainly as a consequence of the economic recovery conducted by Minister H. Buchi. When a campaign demanding a referendum was launched, leading to the fall of the dictator, the predominant theme of the campaign was one of reconciliation, not of liberation. The fall of the mobilising state does not free social actors who have previously been prisoners of state repression or seduction, it leaves the social scene bare and silent. Only in countries where the former type of state has not completely disappeared, as in Romania, do social and intellectual opposition movements preserve a certain vigour.

The 19th century had ended on the din of revolutionary movements and declarations in Berlin, Paris, St Petersburg and Chicago. The 20th century ends, instead, in the silence of battles unwaged, not lost: the social actors have disappeared. Mobilising states are being opposed not by ideas, but by structural adjustment, that is, by freeing the economy from the political control to which it had been subjected. Western countries, accustomed to both the power of liberal capitalism and the force of social and political opposition movements, are finding this situation hard to understand.

The liberal shock

Many observers have been tempted to think that the mobilising-state model, and especially the national-popular state in Latin America, has been replaced by another model, that of a liberal society, which should ultimately take hold of the whole world. Market economy, political democracy, cultural tolerance and secularisation would be interdependent aspects of this universally triumphant model. In Latin America, democracy is being re-established despite a situation of severe economic crisis, while at the same time structural adjustment policies are being developed. In addition, one could conceivably agree with those for whom the new Chilean democracy is the natural complement to the economic reforms undertaken by an authoritarian regime, but which are now calling on economic and social actors to be independent rather than to submit to an absolute power. One could similarly heed those who trust Mexico to evolve, and finally to abandon the political monopoly of the PRI and respect election results.

This analysis is fallacious and unacceptable in its simplification of the whole of observable evolutions. Furthermore, this simplified view contradicts the central tradition of liberal political thought, which from Rousseau to de Tocqueville and John Stewart Mill has always clearly separated political liberalism and economic liberalism; today the two tend to be confused. Comparison with the early 19th century is edifying. At that time, political liberalism prevailed, owing to the need to oppose absolute monarchies and the dictatorial power generated by the French Revolution. Today, economic liberalism is taking over under the pressure of international financial agencies and to counter unbridled inflation. It is therefore tempting to limit political solutions to the elimination of authoritarian regimes, to limit democracy to the organisation of free elections capable of easing political tensions and confrontations, even where the representativeness of competing candidates is often hazy.

The main error in defining the current situation as the triumph of the liberal solution is to confuse two operations that history, on the contrary, differentiates: the destruction of the old system and the building of the new. In political change, continuity is rare when the object is to eliminate a regime that exercises vast control over many aspects of social life. It is possible to progress in stages and continuously from a policy of economic protectionism to a free-trade policy — this is what has happened in the past half-century in western Europe — but a continuous, controlled progression from a communist regime to a democracy, for instance, is not possible. The former has to be destroyed first, along with all of the forms of its hold on society. Today, the only known means of doing this efficiently is to implement the market economy, for it is much less a positive principle of economic and social organisation than a weapon against political, ideological or bureaucratic control of the economy.

Let us therefore stop seeing in the triumph of the market economy the foundation of a new type of society. A market economy is the absolute weapon against the mobilising state and especially against the totalitarian state, and this gives it today a fundamental historical role, but it does not in itself bring forth any form of political or economic organisation. The market economy does not *per se* lead to the development of entrepreneurs and a large domestic market; similarly, it can be combined equally well with an authoritarian regime, a democracy limited to formally pluralistic elections or a democracy producing a deep change in the distribution of rights, income and power.

The destruction of the mobilising state is a long and difficult process. In Latin America, its most important aspect is the reform of the public sector. This involves the state's surrendering of public enterprises, which were less economic agents than they were sources of income and *clientèle* for the parties and the unions associated with the government. An important part of state reform is therefore just one aspect of economic reform: enterprises must submit to an economic logic that they had previously failed to apply, a failure that produced a tax deficit, which in turn triggered or exacerbated inflation. Another imperative, especially in post-communist countries, is to strip the communist power élite of all the functions it had taken over, whether in economic activity or in academic and cultural life. Party spirit or the spirit of clientelism cannot be driven away without some breaks, which are sometimes as sharp as those that produced the shift from a capitalist to a centralised regime. Russia provides a brilliant illustration: Gorbachev's refusal to break with the communist power structure led, especially as of the end of 1990, to a forceful comeback of the communist apparatus, which was visible as much in the Lithuanian crisis as in Moscow. This ultimately led to what could be called by a Latin American term, the *autogolpe* of August 1991, since it was principally Gorbachev's own ministry that took the initiative in what the communist dignitaries considered to be the continuation of the previous months' policies and the defence of what was essential to the regime, rather than a true *coup d'état*.

Once the break is accomplished, it is final. In eastern Europe, even in countries where former communists have returned to power or have kept it, chances that the communists will once again have political control over society are very slim. In Poland, for example, the peasants' party, allied to the former communist party, has announced its intention to further a liberal economic policy. This is even more true in Hungary, where at the end of the communist regime the socialists had already practised a very active open economic policy.

Nowhere was the break with the past as dramatic as in Argentina and, as of 1985, in Bolivia. The Argentine case is the most impressive, for President Alfonsín had re-established democracy, tried and condemned the leaders of the military regime, resisted coup attempts and won the favour of international opinion. It is therefore understandable that after the economic collapse of the country, the president's resignation, the hunger riots, and the rise of Carlos Menem and his small team to control of the *Justicialista* party and subsequently of national power, violent protest from both intellectual and political circles should have denounced the practices, ideas and mores of the new government. Much of this criticism is justified, but it does not touch upon the essential: Argentina's need to break with an economy of guaranteed income, a protectionism that destroys all competitiveness and an extreme neocorporatism, associated with a crushing public sector deficit and the deterioration of many public services. Nothing ensures that in Argentina the shock of the Cavallo plan will produce an economically efficient and politically democratic society, but even if it fails to accomplish this transformation, the need for the break it has just effected would be no less evident. Argentine public opinion made no mistake about it: despite the difficulties encountered, it voted decisively for the president's candidates who had cut the Gordian knot.

The case of Bolivia is even more astonishing. There, the main leader of the national-popular revolution of 1952, Victor Paz Estenssoro, was the one to break in 1985 with hyperinflation and the political and social disintegration of a country that his old rival, Hernán Siles Suazo, could no longer control and to impose a complete change resulting in an economic policy that has been maintained by all his successive leaders, from Paz Zamora to Banzer.

It does not necessarily follow that the break with the mobilising state must be violent. The example of Chile, or better yet that of Brazil, shows that even a military dictatorship can be ousted without violence or an open break. The necessary upshot of all this is that appealing to market economics and to the verdict of the international economy is much less a foundation for the building of a new type of society than the weapon for overthrowing the previous state. In just a few years, a large part of the world has abandoned the mobilising-state model, and wherever this model still survives, it is on the defensive. Intellectuals, whose criticism was merely directed at getting the mobilising state to intervene more decisively, were proved so wrong by events that they were reduced to silence, as were the European intellectuals who sang the glories of the Chinese cultural revolution.

The national and populist reaction

Before examining the conditions for the reconstruction of a societal system and the forms it will take, we must take another moment to consider the break with the old system. We could be tempted once again to compare the current situation to that of Europe at the beginning of the 19th century, when the development of civil society — that is, of economic society — induced extreme violence in capitalist domination. The social impact generated by economic adjustment has been, and still is, very fierce. Brazil, which has not yet completely accepted the transition to a new form of economic management, is experiencing an inflation that in no way hinders its economic activity but which increases social inequalities distressingly: the poorer sectors need to keep their income available to cover their daily subsistence, and they are not able to invest it in such a way as to make it offset the sliding scale. Increasing poverty, violence and crime have brought about a law-and-order backlash, even in the rich countries of the North, which have been hit much less hard.

This situation is a large factor in the breakdown of political life and the weakening of collective action: social conflicts, political struggles and debate over a society's choice of orientation are pushed into the background by the opposition between the victims of exclusion and those who are "inside": the general tendency of the latter to protect themselves against the real or imagined threats represented by the former, and of the former to consider that political debates about issues related to the "inside" world are meaningless and do not deserve their participation.

When the lower classes express themselves, they do so to demand protection against the effects of the economic reforms. The clearest case is that of Poland, where economic reform was introduced early in 1990 by the government of T. Mazowiecki, an heir to Solidarity. The violence of the consequences — which had been accepted by this "left-wing" government as the *sine qua non* for the destruction of the party's and the power élite's control over society — soon reinforced a conservative Catholic right wing intent on re-establishing the church's hold on social life in an opposite spirit to that of Solidarity. Representatives of this neonationalist and populist right wing were subsequently brought into the government until Mrs Suchoka returned to a more balanced policy combining economic reforms and social measures. The change of policy did not prevent the outburst of mass discontent, this time with support from the former communists.

In Latin America, these tendencies have generally been weak, even though they had important political consequences in Ecuador and were an important factor in Fujimori's victory over the political parties in Peru. The same populism of protest was also used in Argentina and Venezuela to support military uprisings. The most important and tragic illustration occurred in Guatemala where the development of large-scale export farming first led to the destruction of community equilibrium in the native Indian world as well as to an urban crisis, then brought about both an Indian movement, mostly in Quiché country, and an urban guerrilla movement, which religious groups tried to unite. This caused an extremely violent reaction from the army and ended in genuine ethnocide with lasting terror.

On the whole, however, it is surprising to note the deficiency of grass-roots reactions, whether Bonapartist, populist or revolutionary. This is a reminder that, contrary to common belief, Latin America is a continent where there has always been a shortage of social actors, a continent full of revolutionary situations but where in the past 50 years actual revolutionary movements have rarely occurred, save for the mass revolutionary actions conducted in Bolivia and, much later, in Nicaragua. Similarly, despite some strong economic growth, the continent has produced few entrepreneurs or great industrial leaders, and we have already mentioned the weakness and the lack of autonomy of the unions, with the sole, important exception of the mining unions (more in Chile and Peru, than in Bolivia). The general weakness of social actors was formerly explained by the mobilising state's hold; today, it is due more to the prevailing and practically exclusive role played by economic reform in the destruction of the old system. As much in the liberal transition period as in the former mobilising state, social actors play a less important and less independent role in Latin American countries than in countries that have known endogenous development.

The general conditions of reconstruction

The inevitable discontinuity between the destruction of the mobilising state and the construction of a new social and political system forces us into a certain discontinuity in this analysis. In considering this new situation, the elements arising from the observation of facts are not entirely sufficient to understand the trends of Latin America's social and political life. We need to step back a little and examine the general conditions of economic and social development; this is all the more necessary in that we have ruled out the idea that the market economy *per se* leads to the improvement of living conditions and political freedom. We must examine the elements that are necessary in theory and in practise for the building of a society with endogenous development, where the establishment of a market economy is only the first stage.

We would like to think that economic growth, political democracy and cultural tolerance are mutually stimulating and that, all in all, democracy is more favourable to growth than is an authoritarian regime. In an analogous line of thinking, many observers have come to the conclusion that democracy can be achieved only above a certain level of well-being without which political rights are void of content, for what can freedom mean to a human being who is starving? There is a large part of truth in these two assertions: development does have to be defined in terms that are at once economic, social and political, and it is certainly not acceptable to assert that the economy is the driving force of change and that political and social organisation are merely a consequence of the economic situation. Classical thinkers expressed deeper ideas when they contended that progress is ordained by the triumph of reason, and therefore that of science, technology and freedom of thought and of conscience. Still, such trust in reason is not nearly enough to account for historical processes. It is preferable to set out the general hypothesis that development is a result of the combination of three main interdependent factors: a high level of savings and of well-chosen investments; mechanisms for redistributing the products of growth as extensively as possible; and an integrated political whole, bearing laws and regulations that ensure safety and justice for inhabitants who feel they are citizens of their country.

This central proposition needs to be completed in two ways. First, the market economy is not directly an element of development, but it is, as we have been emphasizing, an important and often necessary condition for development, insofar as it opposes domination over the whole of society by a state that imposes its own objectives, whether they be political, ideological, social or cultural. This leads to the second complementary hypothesis, which is more precise. For development to take place in the absence of any unifying actor, there must be as much autonomy as possible amongst the three factors mentioned above — more specifically, amongst the agents of investment, of redistribution and of national integration, and therefore amongst economic activity, socio-political debate and judicial and administrative institutions. Each of these categories of actors operates in terms of distinctive values and norms. An entrepreneur can be motivated by the pursuit of profit but also by personal ethics, as Weber thought, or by the idea of national interest. Redistributive agents defend interest groups, but also a concept of justice or of development itself. Judicial and political integration is founded on a concept of nationality, on an idea of justice and also on educational doctrines. Contrary to what we would be tempted to think spontaneously, development comes more easily when the different grounds for it to occur are all present at the same time and, consequently, when society has no unity of values, norms and command.

By definition, the mobilising state did not transform economic actors that were already in motion; rather, it transformed social reproduction systems, local powers, tightly controlled economic networks and accumulated privileges. The more immobile or exclusionary the previous forms of organisation, the more drastic was the mobilising state's intervention — by way of a revolution, or in the form of enlightened despotism or of an authoritarian modernisation. Soon, however, the need arose to upset the mobilising state's action and liberate the aforementioned development factors. Some countries have achieved spectacular success; two examples are Germany and Japan, which have applied what has been called the Bismarckian model, that is, an authoritarian modernisation leading to the formation of a civil society, to the emergence of entrepreneurs, unions, and a rule of law reinforced by a vivid national awareness. The model has been applied by other countries, specifically in Latin America by Brazil, as was shown by Luciano Martins (1976) in a classic book that covers the decisive period starting with Getulio Vargas and going from the Estado Novo to Juscelino Kubitschek.

In many other countries, however, the mobilising state concentrated resources under its control and used them to strengthen its own power, sometimes so much as to change itself into a totalitarian state. In other cases, the mobilising state became more concerned about clientelism, distribution and managed participation than about achieving its will through repressive means. This was the case in many national-popular regimes, especially in Argentina, Bolivia and Venezuela, and at certain moments in Peru.

Today, the setting in motion — or modernisation — of societies everywhere in Latin America has progressed enough that the most pressing problem now is strengthening the *movement towards autonomy* of the development factors over the ruins of the mobilising state, whether of the distributist type, or of the type still tempted by authoritarian solutions. We might add that the strengthening of the actors and the agencies of development, precisely because each of them has its own logic, should lead to the strengthening of institutions in charge of *combining* the different modes of action, that is, to the strengthening of a system of political and judicial representation for social demands. The "open" model of development, which is founded on the autonomy of actors, gives a central importance to parliament, considered above all as a clearing-house for social demands. We could say that the most important change that Latin America must bring about is to transfer the central role from the state to a political system in charge of negotiations amongst social actors and of combining the different modes of action.

This problem goes far beyond the often obscure debate on presidentialism versus parliamentarism: the United States, for instance, is a typical example of a presidential democracy, and yet it is one of the countries where parliament, or Congress, plays the most important role. This shows the need to define, more precisely than is usually done in Latin America, the difference between a government centred on the state and one centred on a political-representation system. No Latin American country has, at the time of writing, all three of the following elements: strongly constituted social and economic actors, strong juridical rules and national awareness, and a political system of negotiations for social demands. Chile, Uruguay and Costa Rica have taken decisive steps in that direction, however, and the world was able to admire the solidity of Brazil's political institutions in the recent crisis, as well as the strength of the country's entrepreneurs and unions. Mexico remains more dominated by the mobilising-state model, while Argentina and Colombia are struggling with a difficult mutation, and Venezuela and Peru are still experiencing the crisis of a mobilising state that has lost control over a fractured society that is undergoing an upheaval referred to by J. Matos Mar (1984) as the *desborde popular*. Most countries, however, have accepted opening to the international market; this is incompatible with the central role of a mobilising state and constitutes the prerequisite to the strengthening of autonomous actors of development.

State reform

It is not enough to say that development requires investment, redistribution and national integration. The problem of development must also be considered from a historical perspective in order to establish priorities amongst these three factors. In the case of Latin America, this question takes on dramatic proportions. The continent's most distinctive feature, in the developing world as a whole, is the extent of its social inequalities, which in Brazil reach an exceptional level when the wealthiest 20 per cent of the population is compared with the poorest 20 per cent. Attention has often been drawn to the contrast between the extreme social inequalities in Latin America and the much more limited inequality in Japan and Korea during those countries' periods of great development. Attention has also been drawn to the deficiency of savings and investment in Latin America, which in the past has run countries such as Argentina, Chile and Uruguay into stagnation, an extended *estancamiento*. Attention should furthermore be drawn to the weakness of the state's decision-making capacity, which for a long time was the trademark of countries such as Argentina, Colombia and Ecuador, not to mention extreme cases such as present-day Nicaragua and Panama.

What, strategically speaking, is the most important development factor in Latin America? Should priority be given to redistribution of income, to increasing productive investment or to strengthening the state as an agent of national unity and integration? In order to avoid any misunderstanding, let it be clear that the question is one of which strategy to follow, and that whatever the answer, it cannot lead in any way to dismissing any other development factor as secondary, or dispose of the ultimate need to develop a strong, open political system that is capable of managing the relations between independent modes of action.

Strategic priority should be given in Latin America to strengthening the state, and more precisely, to the development of the *national state*, as a factor of integration. This hypothesis seems to flow directly from the analysis of the previous development model. If the dominant model in Latin America was the national-popular state — that is, a variation of the neocorporatist state, which absorbed a large part of the social actors, entrepreneurs or unions, and which identified the rule of law with paternalism — then nothing is possible unless the state has been reformed, that is, refocussed on its proper functions. This would allow social actors to be autonomous and the political system to develop.

Reform of the state cannot be limited to reducing its size and to privatising unprofitable or badly managed public enterprises, even though such measures are important to separate the logic of political action from the logic of economic actors. The point is to strengthen the rule of law, as well as to raise the quality of public administration, and above all to improve both national integration and the country's ability to build a national project. All of these functions define a state that is more "state-centred" and "national", but less social and especially less corporatist. These changes would be void of content if they were not associated with a sweeping tax reform. Progress in tax collection has been spectacular in Argentina, significant in Chile and even — recently — in Brazil, but in most countries, the state has inadequate resources and the ostentatious consumption of the rich remains shocking, especially in comparison with the growing poverty of large numbers of people. The importance of tax reform derives from the fact that it acts directly both on state reinforcement and on social redistribution, and that in a less direct way, it strengthens investment by taxing luxury spending.

The independence and the quality of public administration are often still inadequate, despite important progress in countries such as Colombia and the attempts at reform made in Argentina. Mexico is the country that first comes to mind when speaking of state reinforcement. President de la Madrid, with technocratic methods, then President Salinas, with a more populist approach, to a large degree accomplished the huge task of releasing the state from the PRI's hold and of checking the importance of the corporatist, labour, farmers' and urban sectors in the state/party, to the benefit of action programmes linked directly to the presidency. This sharp turn into presidentialism involves some risks and weakens the political system, but it is a radical departure from the mobilising-state model.

Other countries have followed the opposite path. In Brazil, where the administration included some well organised sectors — even beyond the widely known example of *Itamarati* — the quality of information and of decision-making deteriorated so much that the country's current crisis could be considered more political than economic. The state has become extremely weak in Haiti, where the country is being ruled by paralegal forces of repression. Conversely, Chile has long had a high-quality public administration that has resisted political contingencies. The state's weakness remains the main obstacle to Argentina's recovery after the successful results of the Cavallo plan, for Argentine capitalists are still more tempted to seek state privileges than to take market risks, especially to face the problems inherent to enterprises involved in production, which require long-term planning and a rationalisation effort in every aspect of production. The role of the state is of paramount importance because in a post-populist situation (or an antipopulist situation of military rule) everything depends on the state, and especially because the social actors act independently of one another, since they are both subjected to economic regulations and engaged in direct negotiations with other social actors.

Two sequences

Once we accept that state reform is the top priority, two complementary sequences are possible: the next priority is either to train entrepreneurs, or to achieve social redistribution through the action of political and trade-union forces. If it is true that all Latin American countries should make state reform their top priority, the decision on which of these two sequences should be followed depends on the type of country.

The clearest case is provided by the countries that have strongly committed themselves to the new *hacia afuera* policy and have adjusted their states to the new situation. For these countries, the idea is mainly to change economic opening into a policy favouring exports, the conquest of new markets and domestic industrial development. The case of Chile is the easiest to describe because it has been the most successful. The rapid development of new exports, especially farming exports, has brought considerable resources into the country, but these resources have mainly benefited a substantially state-subsidised capitalism that has generated few qualified jobs in a context of harsh social policy. The accumulated funds are therefore directed to financial investments, especially abroad; Chilean investments in Argentina are already significant. As yet, there are few high-technology enterprises in Chile capable of exporting industrial goods and services. First steps have been taken, but the true development of the country will depend on the development of these new sectors: although farm exports play a very important role, they cannot carry the modernisation project on their own, especially if the resources generated by copper are not as abundant as they have been in the recent past. The coming of democracy in Chile has led to an increase in state resources and a revival of social policy, especially in the housing area — health care is still extremely dualistic. We must therefore conclude that the time has come for Chile to give priority to training a class of entrepreneurs; an excellent study of this process has been provided by Cecilia Montero and other CIEPLAN scholars (Montero Casassus, 1992).

The situation is much less favourable in most of the other countries that have followed the same economic policy: Argentina, Bolivia and even Colombia. In Mexico, for a long time there was a strong hostility between the Monterrey group — and private entrepreneurs in general — and the Mexico City group, representing enterprises under direct or indirect state control. Recently, the *maquiladoras* strongly boosted activity in the northern border regions, but the Mexican economy appears to be more dependent on NAFTA results and on the increase in investment that NAFTA is expected to generate, than on a direct industrialising effort. In countries where entrepreneurs do not become stronger, there is a high risk that economic opening will merely lead to the country's incorporation into the North American zone as a marginal entity, as is the case for the Dominican Republic, or even into the European zone, as is the case for the French West Indies, or else to increasingly violent social confrontation, as in Haiti.

In countries where the state has maintained more direct control over the economy or where violent domestic conflicts have given the state and domestic security problems pre-eminence over economic problems, social integration must be given priority over economic initiative. The problem here is one of neopopulist situations wherein a strongly dualised society led to a more direct state intervention, both economic and social, as was the case for Peru, marked by the APRA and by Velasco Alvarado's neo-Peronism. This is especially true in Brazil, where despite some regression in recent years the economic actors — enterprises and unions — are more autonomous than elsewhere and where the main issue is to reduce inequalities, which have become unbearable, and to put an end to the violence to which a large part of society is subjected. Similarly, in Venezuela, the state, made wealthy by oil resources, allowed the development of extreme social inequalities, which ultimately triggered the urban riots that military groups recently tried to co-opt. In Peru, the armed struggle conducted by *Sendero Luminoso* is not the expression of a social movement of urban or rural underprivileged classes but the result of a deep crisis in important sectors of society. Colombia's case is quite different, in that it has always suffered from the marginalisation of some sectors of the national society, but its fight is directed less against guerrillas, some of which have joined institutional politics, than against the troubling effects of narcotics trafficking.

The liberal path taken by Bolivia, Chile, Mexico and Argentina, in particular, seems difficult for these countries (even Brazil) to follow. A social policy aimed at reducing inequalities, rather than an economic policy directed at strengthening enterprises, appears to be the only solution to protect these countries from chaos or from a dualisation so extreme that it will endanger national unity. Brazil is the only country where a "left-wing" movement has taken shape, especially around the PT, forming an alliance between working-class groups of the modern Brazil and grass-roots groups of underdeveloped Brazil. Whatever the results of the next presidential election, the dominant issue already appears to be the need to reconstruct the state, which has been weakened by an irresponsible distributist policy, by the fragility of a political life in which "physiological" tendencies are very strong, by the scandal that ended in President Collor's impeachment and by the strong mobilisation resulting from grass-roots demands. In Peru, the support received by President Fujimori from the population against the parties has grown weaker, and the pressure in favour of bold social reforms has grown stronger, while in Venezuela, there is no reason to believe that the principle of alternation between the two traditional parties will be enough to check the risk of social violence.

The political system

The two sequences — *state reform* to *strengthening of enterprises* to *social redistribution*, and *state reform* to *social movements* to *strengthening of enterprises* — lead to a greater autonomy for the state, the enterprises and the socio-political forces of redistribution; consequently, they lead all countries away from the national-popular model, as well as from the antipopulist military dictatorships of the 1970s. How can these three elements of a "developed" society be combined if they are no longer placed under the supreme authority of a president and within a state party, as was the case with the Mexican PRI, the Argentine *justicialismo*, the Bolivian MNR and the Peruvian APRA? The current evolution will be neither complete nor consolidated until a political-representation system has been organised and until these parties — of which Albert Hirschman (1979) rightly said that they had a single-party vocation — have been replaced by a pluralistic political system where the parties uphold different policies and represent, at least to some degree, different social interests. The political systems will probably evolve more towards the American type than the British type, but they could also be inspired by the French semi-presidential model.

The mobilising state can be replaced only by a representative democracy, in any of its forms. Wherever this does not happen — either because the development sequences we have just described have not been observed or because dualisation has progressed and economic growth has come to a stop — authoritarian solutions will arise. This break with the process of democratisation is all the more likely in that it will be able to take its inspiration, not so much from the old national-popular model, but from the economic achievements of current authoritarian regimes such as those of the Republic of Korea, Taiwan, Singapore and Indonesia. The decline of the national-popular model seems irreversible, and simultaneous with that of the revolutionary trends spurred by the Cuban example — which has run its course — or by the Sandinista revolution, which has lost all its appeal since Nicaragua collapsed. This means that Latin America will have to choose mostly between the modernising authoritarian model of certain Asian countries and a representative democracy increasingly open to pressing social demands.

It is difficult to predict what choices will be made, but the Asian model, especially the Korean one, was founded on strong national integration where distances separating social groups were not very significant, and on a strong alliance between the state and the enterprises facing opposition from the unions and students, often united in the grass-roots *minjung* movement. None of these features exists in Latin America, where the national-popular state was economically weak but capable of some social integration emphasized by the populist programmes. This is why we can surmise that Latin America, which Alain Rouquié (1987) called "the Far West" (*l'extrême Occident*), is more likely to resemble the open, scarcely radicalised societies of Europe than the closed societies that are in the grip — at least in the beginning — of revolutionary conflicts that are aroused or enfeebled by the changing international situation.

The representative democracy that has been established in several countries will soon have to confront social pressures; the current weakness of these pressures can only be momentary and is likely to last only in countries that have not yet reformed the state or developed their national enterprises. The stronger civil society grows, the more the current level of social inequalities will become intolerable and bring about uprisings of an intensity similar to those which occurred in western and northern Europe at the beginning of the 20th century, and in Japan in the wake of the first great achievements of industrialisation and modernisation after the Russo-Japanese war and World War I. The political models that have dominated Latin American life for the past 30 years are in the process of disappearing. The future of Cuba has ceased to be the object of passionate interest in Latin America, populism has stopped paying, and the liberal transition is coming to an end, as in eastern Europe, where a great variety of demands are again being formulated by a population that has experienced the violent but probably indispensable aftershock of the destruction of communist management by rapid economic liberalisation.

Latin America is definitely in need of new political models, not just of greater concern for social reforms on the part of the current type of state. One could even suggest that time is short for building new political systems that are capable of managing the growing social tensions between economic and social actors who are increasingly informed and organised. If this fails, the continent will experience explosions that did not occur during the lost decade, even though that was when in most countries the lower and middle classes' standard of living collapsed. The accomplishments of a new economic policy, progressively clearing a surplus that can be distributed, will trigger the development of new, increasingly radical demands.

This is why a close watch must be kept on the Chilean example. With a strong capacity for state action, the reinforcement of enterprises, a recent recovery in the rate of union membership, an active social policy that has reduced the proportion of poor people from 40 to 32 per cent of the total population — perhaps even less — Chile today meets all the conditions of development and will soon become a truly developing country if it strengthens its entrepreneurial capacity and if it speeds up its policy of social and economic reintegration of the underprivileged sectors. At the other extreme of the continent, Haiti is sinking into violence after the failure of a belated national-popular movement.

Hacia afuera or desde adentro

The central importance of the political system as an instrument of integration for both the state and for the problems related to territorial unity with the economic forces and the social actors clearly shows that the mobilising state is not being replaced by a new form of liberalism going back to the English, American or French traditions of the early 19th century, when economic problems (the formation of industrial capitalism) and political ones (the extension of civil rights after the overthrow of absolute monarchies) were more separate than they were connected. In viewing contemporary reality, it would be a mistake to say that a market economy and a form of democracy limited to the organisation of an open political market are what has triumphed over the ruins of the national-popular state and after a period of military dictatorship in a number of countries. It may be true that market regulation has replaced the previous confusion of political and economic aims, but the new social system taking shape mainly features a higher level of integration between political action and economic and social interests. Latin American economies are once again directed outwards — hacia afuera — and are driven by exports of goods or labour and by capital imports, but it is also true that politics has ceased to be dominated by comprehensive social projects: instead, anti-inflationary and more general structural adjustment measures have acquired a primary importance on the one hand, and on the other, the struggle against social and regional inequalities has been increasing significantly and will continue to do so as representative democracy grows stronger.

There is no basis for asserting that this growing interdependence amongst political, economic and social actors will develop in a regular way and lead to highly integrated national policies. The process can break down. Extreme dualisation constantly tends to provoke states to resort to an authoritarian power in the name of national safety or of the struggle against violence and chaos. Another possibility is for the state and capitalism to form an exclusive alliance and impose a very high investment rate on society as a whole while keeping salaries low for an extended period of time in order to make quick profits. Even in such cases, however, the idea is spreading that economic results depend on how all the social resources are used.

One example will be enough to make this clear: Latin America has long given great importance to education, and usually the education issue has been associated with secularity. Today, as in Europe, the emphasis is on the link between schooling and both economic growth and social integration. Although funding has so far been directed towards secondary schooling and especially university studies, there is more and more talk of the struggle against decreasing school attendance of a part of society in the first years and of the need to develop technical and trade schools. Education is less a political and strictly cultural issue than it used to be, and more an issue related to the process of social and economic change.

The most spectacular change has occurred in Mexico, a country where modernity was long identified with the revolution, and therefore with a conception of social change that rested on deliberate political action. In the middle of 1993, Mexican policy seems to be guided above all by preparation for and defence of NAFTA, that is, by a project for economic modernisation.

The mobilising state must therefore be considered retrospectively not as a dangerous but temporary confusion of politics, the economy and social life, but as a first association of these three elements of national life; the deterioration of this association usually led to the confusion of the elements, each of which paralysed the other two. This in turn led not to their separation but to the building of stronger interactions amongst them, founded on recognition of the autonomy of the various orders of action, which cannot be co-ordinated unless each operates according to its own logic instead of their all being instruments serving a political and economic power élite.

Latin American societies are more outwards-oriented than during the triumphant ECLA era, but what ECLA began to build under the inspiration of economists such as Raúl Prebisch, Celso Furtado and Aníbal Pinto, is developing today, after a decade that was lost for social and political modernisation and was almost solely devoted to structural adjustment. We are witnessing the emergence of economic and social policies that are much more integrated than before, wherever the state has been able to re-establish some degree of central control over the functioning of the economy, beyond the dangerous facilities of *plata dulce* and inflation. Latin American societies, at least those that do not succumb to disintegration, are oriented more *hacia afuera*, but are managed more from the inside, *desde adentro*, thanks to the reconstruction of political systems capable of negotiating and arbitrating between various categories of national objectives and social interests.

Possible or real democracy?

It takes the freely managed complementarity of national integration, economic growth and social redistribution to constitute a democracy. In addition, the analysis of political systems is so similar to that which applies to development, that democracy can arguably be considered as the political form of endogenous development (or self-sustaining growth), for democracy, too, contains three principles: respect for fundamental rights and therefore limits to the power of the state, the representativeness of political leaders, and citizenship. Throughout history, these principles have found different combinations in the British, US and French models of democracy, but in all cases the three principles have remained.

The limitation of the power of the state is the principle commanding the autonomy of civil society, as was declared by the British in the Glorious Revolution of 1688, while the social representativeness of leaders implies the government by and for the people to which Lincoln referred, reflecting an egalitarian principle. As for the idea of citizenship, it is both social and political. There is therefore no democracy unless these three components are present and are brought together by governments that are freely elected at regular intervals by the people.

Can Latin America today be said to be democratic because it has generally ceased to be ruled by authoritarian regimes — with the exceptions of Cuba and Haiti, and, partly, of Peru and perhaps Mexico, where the most recent elections were still distinguished by fraud? Although democracy certainly cannot exist without free elections, an open political system and freedom of the press are not sufficient proof of its existence. Countries that produced the deepest changes in their economy and that consequently made the cleanest break with the previous mobilising-state model are the ones where democracy progressed most clearly. This is especially true for Chile, Uruguay and Costa Rica, but also for Colombia and Ecuador. It would also be risky to assert that the danger of military dictatorships has vanished on the continent: in many countries the groups most exposed to violence are tempted to call on the military to restore public order, which is threatened by the consequences of poverty and inequality.

In the realm of political order as well as of social and economic order, Latin America is experiencing not so much the building of a new system as the destruction of the old one. It would be more correct to speak not of democratisation but of political instrumentalism after the fall of the great political and ideological mobilisations. This is a situation quite similar to the one observed in many European countries. It is not a negative conclusion — in fact, it would be too optimistic to think that, as of now, a democratic policy can and should be organised in such a way as to be concerned equally with greater justice and with economic efficiency. This is obviously an essential objective, but the process that can lead to it is so complex that all but a very few countries are far from achieving it.

Democracy is a new idea in Latin America: on the ruins of revolutionary or counter-revolutionary ideologies, it is more common to observe the action of a modernising power as in Mexico, in Argentina or perhaps in Peru, than the organisation of a political debate, which is made doubly difficult by the weight of the marginalised population and by the interests of the leading economic groups, which are focussed more on exports than on developing the domestic market.

Latin America is engaged in a transformation process that is generally directed towards the preparation of democratic development, and this is enough to cast an overall favourable judgement on the current evolution. All the same, a strong dualisation and the significant inequalities are the basis for two real dangers: an authoritarian modernising state linked to the dominant economic interests on one hand, and on the other, a neopopulist or nationalistic state comparable to those which are prevailing or gaining ground in many post-communist countries, from Poland to Slovakia and Lithuania, not to mention the countries of former Yugoslavia. This leads us to complete the previous analyses: state reform logically precedes the training of entrepreneurs, which in turn must often take place before a redistribution policy; for democracy to be established in such a way as to enable continuous endogenous development, however, the grass-roots categories' capacity for expression and for the formulation of claims is inadequate, and this is what is lacking most.

Latin America suffers from the weakness of its parties and unions, which were closely connected to the mobilising-state model. Democratisation can take place on the sole condition that social and political pressures are sufficiently reorganised to defend the interests of the majority. In addition, Latin America suffers, as do other regions, from a lack of ideas and political analysis. Intellectuals, who have been associated more with a nationalist or revolutionary model than with a democratic idea, must contribute more actively to the development of a national project and of social debate, so that the opening of the political system will not entail a growing divergence between the political society and the majority of the population.

Thus, the mutation that began with the deep change in economic policies and in the role of the state will generate a more endogenous model of development only when the political system is able to play its role as mediator between a state giving priority to the building of an integrated national society and social actors capable of negotiating amongst themselves the distribution of the results of economic growth.

Bibliography

BRESSER PEREIRA, L., J. M. MARAVALL and A. PRZEWORSKI, ed. (1993), *Economic Reforms in New Democracies: a Social-democratic Approach*, Cambridge University Press, Cambridge.

CALDER, F. and M. DOS SANTOS, ed. (1983), *Latinoamérica. Lo político y lo social en la crisis*, CLACSO, Buenos Aires.

CARDOSO, F. H. and E. FALETTO (1969), *Dependencia y Desarrollo en América Latina*, Siglo XXI, Mexico.

CAVAROZZI, M. (1983), *Autoritarismo y democracia, 1955-1983*, Centro editora de América Latina, Buenos Aires.

COUFFIGNAL, G. (1992), *Réinventer la démocratie. Le défi latinoaméricain.* Fondation Nationale des Sciences Politiques, Paris.

FAJNZYLBER, F. (1983), *La industrialización trunca de América Latina*, Nueva Imagen, Mexico.

FURTADO, C. (1969), *Teoria e política do desenvolvimento economico*, 3rd edn., Editora nacional, Sâo Paulo.

GARRETON, M. A. (1983), *El proceso político chileno*, FLACSO, Santiago.

GARRETON, M. A. and M. ESPINOSA (1992), *Reforma del Estado o cambio en la matriz socio-política*, Documentos FLACSO, Santiago.

GERMANI, G. (1962), *Política y sociedad en una época de transición*, Eudeba, Buenos Aires.

HIRSCHMANN, A. *in* D. COLLIER, ed. (1979), *The New Authoritarianism in Latin America*, Princeton University Press, Princeton.

JAGUARIBE, H. (1962), *Desenvolvimento económico a desenvolvimento político*, Fundo de Cultura, Rio de Janeiro.

MARTINS, L. (1976), *Pouvoir et développement économique du Brésil, 1930-64*, Anthropos, Paris.

MATOS MAR, J. (1984), *El desborde popular y la crisis del Estado*, IEP, Lima.

MAYORGA, R., ed. (1992), *Democracia y governabilidad. América Latina*, Ediciones Nueva Sociedad, La Paz.

MONTERO CASASSUS, C. (1992), *Los empresarios y el Estado en la transición democrática chilena (1990-92)*, CIEPLAN, Santiago.

O'DONNELL, G. (1985), *Acerca del corporativismo y la cuestión del Estado*, CEDES doc. n° 2, Buenos Aires.

PINTO, A. (1959), *Chile, un caso de desarrollo frustrado*, Editora Universitaria, Santiago.

ROUQUIÉ, A. (1987), *Amérique latine. Introduction a l'extrême-Occident*, Seuil, Paris.

RAMA, G. ed. (1987), *Escenarios políticos y sociales del desarrollo lationamericano*, Seuil, Paris.

TOURAINE, A. (1988), *La parole et le sang*, Odile Jacob, Paris.

Second Part

POLITICAL DEMOCRACY

Democratic Institutions, Economic Policy and Performance in Latin America

Stephan Haggard and Robert Kaufman

During the 1980s, severe fiscal crises combined with substantial international pressure to force widespread transformations in the policies and economic structure of many Latin American societies. By the early 1990s, all of the large countries except Brazil had imposed very tough macroeconomic stabilization measures, and most had instituted wide-ranging "liberal" reforms: trade barriers fell almost everywhere; there were widespread sales of banks, airlines, and utilities formerly in the public sector; financial markets were liberalized; and the role of the state as an investor and regulator was scaled back significantly.

The wisdom of these policies has been hotly debated, but for good or ill, a "first round" of reform appears to be nearing completion. During the next decade and beyond, the principal issues on the economic agenda will concern the consolidation of these reforms and their consequences for growth and equity. From the perspective of the early 1990s, these consequences remain ambiguous. Among the positive achievements have been a halt in hyperinflations, an easing of the fiscal crisis, and a renewed influx of external capital into the region. On the negative side, with the exception of Chile, recoveries have been halting and uncertain. Large balance-of-trade deficits and overvalued currencies evoke disconcerting memories of the late 1970s, and the lag in export-oriented investment has rekindled debate over industrial policy and other forms of state activism. Regardless of whether current market-oriented adjustments lead to recovery, concerns over poverty and struggles over distribution will be highly salient political issues.

One way to understand the types of political challenges posed by these "second round" issues is to distinguish between the conditions associated with the initial design and implementation of reforms, and those linked to longer-term consolidation of economic practices and expectations. Owing to the free-rider problem facing potential beneficiaries of reform and the uncertainties surrounding the prospective benefits, reforms have generally been initiated by executives holding concentrated authority and exercising substantial discretionary power *vis-à-vis* economic interest groups and political institutions[1]. This was the case, for example, in Argentina, Bolivia, and Peru, where incoming presidents were able to claim emergency powers and to exploit opportunities opened by electoral honeymoons and weak, disorganized oppositions.

Consolidation of reforms, however, rests on a quite different, even contradictory, set of political and institutional conditions. Where there have been visibly positive achievements, such as the implementation of more stable macroeconomic policy, one challenge will be to lock in reforms by restricting the discretion of elected executives over key monetary institutions such as central banks. To remain sustainable in a democratic context, moreover, reforms will also require the construction of broad bases of support, drawing on the beneficiaries of the policies in question. Finally, and somewhat paradoxically, the long-term viability of both economic reforms and democratic institutions will depend on patterns of political competition that augment the capacity of governments to correct course as economic conditions change and to respond to the distributive claims of citizens and voters.

No attempt is made in this paper to review the increasingly nuanced debates over the "appropriate" role of the government in addressing these issues. Rather, the purpose is to raise questions about the democratic institutions that frame political contestation over development and welfare policies. A central premise is that the conception of "the state" that prevails in current discussions has been overly narrow, particularly given the transition to democracy that has occurred throughout Latin America. Any discussion of the state must pay attention not only to the government as an actor, but to the matrix of constitutional rules and institutions within which it operates. This institutional matrix is not limited to the bureaucracy; it also encompasses the organizations and channels of representation that govern conflicts among political groups.

In the advanced industrial countries, two key features of the long-term reconciliation between democratic regimes and market institutions have been the gradual incorporation of the working and lower classes into the political system and the development of some forms of social compensation and protection. This process of political and economic incorporation occurred through a variety of mechanisms: the expansion of the franchise and of public education, the creation of institutions for regulating industrial relations, networks of social security, and policies for alleviating absolute poverty. At the same time, as Ruggie has argued, it also rested on a broadly liberal, but by no means *laissez-faire* posture toward integration with the world economy, a stance Ruggie labeled "embedded liberalism"[2].

If they are to survive as institutionalized systems, democratic regimes of Latin America will also have to find ways to provide the economic security demanded by voters, while sustaining the market mechanisms required to allocate resources efficiently and productively. Such compromises will not be easy to achieve. From the perspective of individual governmental leaders, this challenge is captured neatly by Geddes' conceptualization of the "politicians' dilemma"[3]. To maintain office in the face of electoral challenges, politicians and their agents in the bureaucracy use the instruments of public policy to build bases of political support. Although such a strategy may be rational for any individual politician, politically motivated economic policy can weaken the economy, and thus prove counterproductive for the class of political incumbents as a whole.

It is impossible, of course, to predict how the new democratic systems emerging within the region will manage these tensions as they move beyond the initial phases of political transition and economic reform. Sustained empirical analysis is impeded not only by uncertainties over the outcome of economic reforms, but also by the fact that current institutional arrangments are still evolving: shifts in the economic situation and the relative balance of power among contending interests may very well bring about further constitutional changes. After a decade of democratic transition in Latin America and other parts of the developing world, however, it is possible to offer some tentative hypotheses about the way specific political and institutional arrangements affect prospects for economic and political consolidation.

At the theoretical level, speculation in this paper is informed by a growing body of "new institutionalist" literature dealing with the effects on political behavior of various forms of representation, party systems, and executive-legislative relations[4]. For empirical reference, the paper draws heavily on the authors' comparative case studies of six Latin American countries that have both experienced democratic transitions in the last decade and begun wide-ranging economic reforms: Argentina, Bolivia, Brazil, Chile, Peru, and Uruguay. Where relevant, the experiences of other developing countries, both inside the region and elsewhere, are also considered. These include Korea, Turkey, and Thailand, which the authors have also examined elsewhere in some depth[5].

The next section examines the role played by executive authority in the initiation of reforms and the ongoing management of the economy. Subsequent sections then address three contemporary "institutionalist" debates about how interests should be represented: the direct representation of interest groups in economic decision-making, either through social pacts or corporatism; the relative merits of parliamentary and presidential systems; and alternative ways of structuring party competition.

The dilemma of executive accountability

Three types of executive authority are relevant to understanding economic policy-making in Latin American democracies. First, as in most democracies, either the constitution or informal understandings provide executives with some emergency powers to respond to national crises. Second, elected presidents have also typically enjoyed some constitutionally mandated legislative powers, or what Shugart and Carey have labeled "entrenched presidential power"[6]. These include vetoes, the power to introduce legislation, and decree powers. Emergency and entrenched constitutional powers must be distinguished, finally, from the question of explicit or implicit delegation of authority either to the executive or to independent decision-making agencies within the executive branch.

The dilemma — and it is a central one to democratic theory — is how to retain the advantages of strong executive authority with respect to efficiency of action, while providing the institutional checks that guarantee accountability and oversight. The problem is faced by all democracies, but it is likely to be particularly acute in new ones. The arbitrary and repressive excesses of deposed authoritarian regimes may encourage efforts to circumscribe centralized authority and guarantee popular control, yet difficult issues of economic management tend to pull new democratic governments away from these commitments toward more centralized and autocratic styles of decision-making[7].

To evaluate the implications of a strong executive for democratic governance, it is important to maintain a clear distinction between the three types of authority outlined above. Each has different implications for economic management and the consolidation of democracy.

Delegated authority is a common feature of decision-making in a number of issue areas in established democracies. It takes the form both of powers ceded by the legislature to the executive, and of delegation from either the legislature or the executive to insulated bureaucratic bodies, such as central banks, commissions, or quasi-judicial policy-making bodies. These agencies have played a particularly important role in economic policy-making in the advanced industrial states as well as in successful cases of reform in the developing world.

Unlike other forms of executive power to be discussed below, such delegation is associated less with the initiation of reforms, which typically involves a high level of discretionary authority for presidents (or prime ministers), than with a consolidation of rules and policy principles that can survive changes of political leadership. Delegation can be interpreted as a rational response by politicians to the presence of collective-action problems, or as a device for institutionalizing policy changes that favor a particular group[8]. It should be underlined, however, that this form of delegation does not necessarily reflect a decline in democratic oversight or an abdication of legislative responsibility. As McCubbins and Kiewit have argued most forcefully, legislatures maintain a variety of mechanisms through which they can delegate while maintaining effective monitoring of executive behavior[9].

Emergency powers are usually written into constitutions to manage severe external and internal security challenges, rather than economic policy-making *per se*, and they have had their most widespread effect on judicial processes and individual political rights. Nevertheless, emergency powers have at times been granted to the president by legislative majorities to deal with economic as well as political crises; this was the case in Argentina after 1983, in Bolivia during the Paz Estensorro administration (1985-89), and at various times in Peru.

Even where legislated by congresses, such grants of emergency powers have been highly controversial; by definition, emergency powers supersede the "normal" channels of representation and decision-making that new democracies seek to institutionalize. The costs of granting such powers to executives, however, must be weighed against the costs of prolonged political immobilism and rapid economic deterioration that confronted a number of new democratic governments in Latin America. To counter the hyperinflation facing Bolivia in 1985, for example, the incoming administration of Victor Paz Estensorro deployed emergency powers against union leaders in ways that probably exceeded its formal constitutional authority. Yet the tough economic and political measures arguably saved democracy by breaking the impasse over economic policy and by pre-empting military intervention.

In countries seeking to undertake extensive economic reforms, there is also a case to be made for "entrenched executive power" — constitutional provisions that endow executives with legislative authority. In presidential systems, the primary executive check on congressional authority is the veto, which thus constitutes an important weapon in limiting the legislative-executive stalemates that can arise in such systems. Decree powers, the power to introduce legislation, and the ability to introduce legislation that cannot be amended are all powers that can help overcome the collective-action and aggregation problems associated with politically difficult economic policies such as budgeting or trade policy.

Where presidents lack organized congressional backing — as was the case in Brazil under Collor — attempts to rely on decree powers may only increase the political isolation of the executive. Where congressional support is relatively strong, however, presidential use of legislative authority has at times contributed to successful economic management. For example, this was arguably the case during the 1980s and 1990s in Chile and Korea, where executives maintained the right to set spending caps that limited legislative authority over budgets. The authors' case studies also suggest that the power of Uruguayan President Sanguinetti to limit fiscal expenditures and to set public wages helped avert extreme macroeconomic instability during the initial years of the political transition in the mid-1980s.

Regardless of their advantages in dealing with specific problems of reform, however, broad grants of executive authority — whether through the open-ended delegation of emergency powers by the legislature or by constitutional design — can imply far more serious threats to democratic consolidation than does the more routine delegation of authority over specific policies to independent technical agencies. Most directly, of course, claims to emergency authority can provide openings for the long-term assumption of dictatorial power. Yet it is just as important to emphasize that strong executive authority can have indirect effects on the effectiveness and legitimacy of representative institutions.

First, granting extensive legislative authority to the executive, particularly in presidential systems, can undermine the incentives of party leaders to reach compromises on economic issues. This is particularly dangerous where the party system is characterized by sharp ideological cleavages. Valenzuela has argued persuasively that during the 1950s and 1960s in Chile, constitutional reforms that increased presidential powers over the budget contributed directly to increasing party-system polarization, both by reducing legislators' opportunities to secure constituent benefits through congressional logrolling and by increasing the stakes attached to winning the presidency[10]. As Shugart and Carey argue, "an assembly represents the diversity of a polity far better than an executive dependent on the president's whim is likely to do. Because of the diverse forces represented in an assembly, such a body has the potential for encompassing divergent viewpoints and striking compromises on them."[11]

Strong executive powers also increase the likelihood that executives will seek broad popular mandates through media appeals and personalist movements, rather than relying on institutionalized consultation with legislators and interest groups. O'Donnell has coined the expression "delegative democracy" to describe such situations; Przeworski refers to "decretism". Both concepts are closely akin to Weber's notion of "plebiscitarianism"[12]. Such systems may continue to rest on electoral legitimation, but the style of decision-making serves to undermine representative institutions. Delegation may be matched with adequate legislative oversight in established democracies, but the possibility that delegation will degenerate into abdication is greater in the developing world where legal and judicial systems remain underdeveloped, governments confront major adjustment difficulties, and non-elected officials in the military or bureaucracy often continue to control independent resources. In a number of democracies, the commitment of elected politicians to democracy may even be uncertain. Under these conditions, legislative majorities may be willing to grant relatively open-ended powers that open the door to executive abuse and that cannot be effectively controlled by judicial or legislative oversight.

Bresser Pereira, Maravall and Przeworski have argued, finally, that the unchecked exercise of executive authority not only corrodes democracy, but may be economically inefficient as well. Arguments for expanding executive autonomy, they observe, rest on a highly technocratic view of the economic reform process. The economic model is assumed to be correct; enhanced executive power is required to overcome self-interested objections. In fact, reforms occur under conditions of a high degree of uncertainty about whether the model is correct, and feedback is thus crucial for correcting mistakes. If structured correctly, consultation can thus improve the *technical* quality of the program by providing needed information to the government. The authors conclude that "when decisions are hidden from public scrutiny, many important ones are made in haphazard way"[13].

To sort out this debate on the effects of executive authority, we must return to the distinction between the initiation and consolidation of economic reform. Some degree of executive discretion may be functional from the perspective of initiation, and the coherence of certain policies can be enhanced through delegation that insulates decision-making from the everyday pull of politics. But the consolidation of both the constitutional system and the economic policies themselves ultimately depends on the development of institutionalized channels of representation which provide bases of political support for a given policy regime. In the absence of the consultation and oversight required to generate such support, economic reforms are likely to be unstable and subject to extensive and rapid reversal.

In a typical sequence, an unaccountable leader — whether orthodox or populist in policy orientation — fails to deliver on promises concerning economic policy and performance. Credibility and authority deflate rapidly, and support disintegrates. Opposition movements mobilize on the basis of a complete rejection of the government's approach, regardless of its merits. Counter-elites win office, but employ a style of governance that is little different from that they replace. The abrupt shifts from Belaunde, to Alan Garcia, to Fujimori in Peru provide a striking illustration of such a sequence.

As the Peruvian case indicates, one should not assume that democracies characterized by such erratic swings in policy will persist. If reform initiatives fail or generate populist backlashes, then a cycle of political decay leading to the collapse of democracy is altogether possible. Yet even where the reform initiatives of plebiscitarian presidents yield positive economic results, there is substantial risk of a slide into a "soft authoritarianism" in which the ruler uses economic success to chip away at constitutional limits on his power. Menem in Argentina, as well as Fujimori in Peru, indicate the possibilities in this regard.

Functional representation: the prospects for social pacts and corporatism

Representation has long been conceived as a way of checking the dangers inherent in concentrated executive power, but representation may be organized through different institutional means. Throughout the 1980s, the possibility of negotiating agreements among state officials and the leaders of economic peak associations was widely discussed as one possibility[14]. Particularly in countries with high and accelerating inflation, there were grounds for hoping that pacts and/or corporatist institutions might serve to mitigate collective-action dilemmas by increasing transparency and information and by developing the iterated interactions among the principal economic actors that are required to build trust.

In Mexico's dominant-party system, such corporatist mechanisms did play an important role in the implementation of a successful income policy initiated in late 1987 (the Economic Solidarity Pact)[15]. Historically, moreover, many Latin American countries have provided for representation of business and labor groups in regulatory bodies and other administrative agencies, but such corporatist practices rarely included encompassing peak associations and have often involved substantial elements of state control[16].

It is far from clear, however, to what extent such mechanisms can be usefully deployed in more open democratic contexts. During the current period of democratic transition, two different historical experiences have spurred interest in direct representation of peak interest groups in the political process. One model derived from the agreements on key political and economic issues worked out in Colombia and Venezuela during the late 1950s, and during the Spanish transition of the mid-1970s. The mutual guarantees forged during these transitions contributed to the stability of each democratic system; in Spain, they also contributed to the extensive structural adjustments that country undertook concurrently with its political transformation.

A second, more institutionalized model was provided by the "societal corporatist" channels of functional representation that first emerged in a number of small European states during the 1930s and 1940s. Schmitter's influential definition of a corporatist model of politics initially referred to patterns of interest intermediation, and particularly the tendency toward monopolistically organized, hierarchical, state-sanctioned interest associations[17]. As the literature on corporatism evolved, the term also came to comprehend the policy-making processes that accompanied such structures, particularly tripartite "concertation" between peak business and labor groups and the government over the central issues of industrial relations and macroeconomic management[18].

In reality, both sets of comparisons are somewhat misleading as possible models for dealing with the situation of contemporary democratic regimes in Latin America. To begin with, there is substantial conceptual confusion over the nature of social pacts. As Karl has observed, the mutual guarantees and power-sharing arrangements reached in Spain, Colombia, and Venezuela were "foundational pacts" rather than "managerial agreements" on economic policy[19]. Assurances were provided concerning the core interests of key power groups, but specific macroecomic policy issues remained the subject of considerable dispute[20].

The societal corporatist arrangements of the small European countries have undoubtedly contributed to successful economic management, but these arrangements emerged in conditions that differed sharply from those in most of the developing world, including low levels of income inequality, functioning market economies with relatively stable macroeconomic policies and strong export orientations, relatively unified peak associations, and strong social democratic parties.

A review of the efforts at forging social pacts suggests that, with the exception of the still-authoritarian Mexican system and some very limited forms of wage-contract bargaining in Uruguay and Chile, there have been few successes in Latin America. Shortly after Sarney's inauguration in Brazil in 1985, for example, talks were initiated between business, government, and representatives of one of the major labor federations, but these quickly broke down in the face of opposition from the more radical labor confederation, the CUT. In 1986, the government launched the Cruzado plan by decree, attempted a new round of pact negotiations when this collapsed in early 1987, then decreed a new program under Bresser Pereira a few months later[21].

Similar stories can be told for most of the other Latin American countries. In Argentina, Alfonsin moved toward a policy of *concertacion* with the CGT in May 1984, after earlier conflicts over reform of the labor law, promulgated the Austral plan by decree in 1985, then again attempted to build an alliance with labor by appointing a prominent union official to the cabinet in 1987. Throughout this period, however, both business and labor representatives adopted neo-Keynesian stances resisted by officials in the finance ministry and, as in Brazil, the fragmentation within the union movement meant that "there would always be some section of organized labor which would refuse to be bound by any agreement"[22]. In Peru, a more limited form of *concertacion* with the major business association disintegrated when Alan Garcia unilaterally decided to nationalize the private banking system.

After more than a decade of discussion, and of repeated attempts in different countries and under different administrations, it is reasonable to conclude that the failures of social pacts are attributable to something more than the absence of statecraft or insufficient opportunities to learn from earlier mistakes. There are more enduring, structural impediments to both social pacts and corporatism in the cases under consideration here[23]. These fall into two categories: features of the institutional and organizational setting which constrain the possibility of reaching credible agreements; and characteristics of the economic setting.

The first and most compelling difficulty is the relative weaknesses of the relevant players, including both interest groups and parties. The essence of both the social pact and *concertacion* alternatives is that the most important economic actors are capable either of directly negotiating binding agreements on major policy variables (such as wages, investment, and prices) or of providing credible support for bargains struck on key government initiatives (such as macroeconomic and industrial policies). In the European context, these negotiations have typically included labor and the private sector, with the government playing the double role of forum and conciliator.

The negotiation of such binding agreements implies, first, that all of the actors must be internally cohesive. For the government, this implies the ability to manage relations between the executive and the legislature and with coalition partners where they exist. For interest associations, it means the capacity to speak authoritatively for their memberships and to guarantee some minimum level of compliance. Second, the parties to the agreement cannot be of widely differing power capabilities. Where future ruling parties have little interest in adhering to agreements, where large imbalances of power exist among the social parties to the negotiation, or where the participants are severely divided by fundamental social inequalities, there is little incentive to make concessions.

In Venezuela and Colombia, the party elites that framed foundational pacts were relatively evenly balanced in terms of strength, and thus had an incentive to compromise. Parties also had deep roots in society; in Venezuela, these included strong ties with key interest organizations such as labor. In Spain, parties also represented broad and deep ideological affiliations that had persisted for decades. Thus the incentives and capabilities for self-enforcing agreements were already present.

Elsewhere, however, conditions have been far less propitious for reaching pacts of any sort, whether foundational or managerial. In the initial stages of transition in Bolivia and Peru, party systems were characterized by high levels of organizational instability, fragmentation, and political polarization, particularly among the leftist parties. Labor organizations were also divided. In Brazil, the leading party of the mid-1980s, the PMDB, was an amalgam of political bosses, intellectuals, and personalist leaders. As the dominant force on the political scene, it had little incentive to reach ageement with other political groups; as a heterogeneous and undisciplined organization with little centralized authority, it had relatively limited capability of doing so.

In Argentina, a relatively even balance between two deeply rooted parties, the Radicals and the Peronists, might have created an opportunity for reaching a social pact, but the changing balance of power and ideological divisions reduced incentives to move in that direction. Radicals for the first time in their history had defeated the Peronists, and aspired to dominant-party status[24].

The second broad barrier to pact-making is economic. In Europe, corporatist politics initially evolved when capital was less mobile internationally and even small economies were somewhat less open to trade, particularly from lower-wage areas. This made it possible for governments to use the tools of Keynesian demand management, to sustain agreements on wages and social compensation, and to maintain international competitiveness through labor market and industrial policies. With the increasing internationalization of capital markets, the growing import penetration from the Third World, and new waves of immigration, such arrangements have necessarily come under strain within Europe itself.

During the 1980s and 1990s, moreover, Latin American countries contended with even more unfavorable economic circumstances, both structural and conjunctural. Their economies are typically characterized by high levels of under- and unemployment and large informal sectors that are intrinsically difficult to organize. Moreover, the strongest segments of the union movement represent workers in import-substituting industries and the public sector who stand to lose heavily from the current agenda of structural reform.

These structural problems are compounded in situations of high and accelerating inflation. Dramatic stabilization initiatives have proved popular with the public, but the very conditions of high inflation impede negotiated interest-group agreements: time horizons shorten dramatically, the risk of making concessions increases, and the severe constraints on fiscal resources make it extremely difficult for the government to organize the compensatory arrangements that typically cement such pacts and corporatist agreements.

The incentives for cooperation increase where prior reforms have already contributed to a deceleration of inflation and a resumption of growth; in Chile and Mexico, recoveries during the 1980s and 1990s provided actors with a stake in maintaining successful policies. In those countries and others, moreover, successful fiscal consolidation could conceivably provide the basis for both short-term compensation and the more extensive welfare systems that are integral to European corporatism. If such arrangements materialize, however, they would be a *consequence* rather than a *cause* of effective economic reform, which had been achieved under quite different institutional auspices.

Legislative representation: the presidential-parliamentary debate

If not all new democracies have the institutional wherewithal to organize pacts or corporatist forms of intermediation, all of them do have systems of territorial representation. Recent discussions of the optimal way of organizing such systems have centered primarily on the relative merits of parliamentary and presidential constitutions[25]. The debate has been extensive and heated, and has hinged as much on conflicting values, such as the merits of majoritarianism, as on the empirical evidence. Surprisingly, there has been little direct reference to the crucial and profound economic issues that dominate the political agenda of many new democracies. A brief review of several major points of contention, however, suggests that the debate is relevant to the question of reconciling democratic rule with coherent and stable economic policy.

The first criticism of presidentialism focuses on the deleterious effects of fixed executive terms. A parliamentary system makes it easier to replace governments that have exhausted their political support and leadership potential. This may be crucial during periods of extreme crisis or pressing need for policy reform. In Bolivia and Argentina, the combination of economic crisis and lame duck status forced presidents Siles and Alfonsin to resign before the scheduled end of their terms, but these *ad hoc* solutions to the problem of an exhausted presidency increased the economic and political uncertainty surrounding the transition between governments; the transition would arguably have come earlier and more smoothly under parliamentary rule. In Brazil and Peru, where presidents Sarney, Collor, and Garcia outstayed their effectiveness, presidentialism also served to prolong crises.

The most important criticisms of presidentialism, however, stem from the problem of dual democratic legitimacy. The fact that the president and the legislature have separate electoral mandates, and that the tenure of members of each branch is not formally affected by cooperation with the other, is arguably good for providing mutual checks and balances. However, it can result in perverse incentives from the perspective of effective economic policy.

Advocates of parliamentarism for Latin America have argued that it would help overcome the legislative stalemates that not only have contributed to economic difficulties, but have been a motivating factor behind the unsettling concentration of executive power and tendency toward "decretism" discussed above. Under presidential rule, the incentives for legislators to cooperate with the executive are limited. This holds true when the president's own party holds a majority, and is even more marked when executives are limited to a single term or when the president's agenda includes difficult adjustment measures. Belaunde, Alfonsin, Menem, and Siles all faced serious difficulties in containing dissent within their own legislative parties.

Under conditions of divided government, the possibility for stalemate is greater still, as the recent history of the United States has demonstrated clearly. Having few incentives to seek enduring coalitions, presidents tend to resort to particularistic incentives to gain support. For their part, opposition legislators are unlikely to cooperate for the purpose of making the president look good; recent US history again provides numerous examples[26]. Under parliamentary rule, by contrast, legislators arguably have a greater incentive to maintain party discipline and to cooperate with the executive, if for no simpler reason than that the fall of the government can lead to new parliamentary elections.

The separate electoral mandate for executives in a presidential system can complicate relations with the legislature in other ways as well. In a parliamentary system, where cabinets depend directly on legislative support, executives normally ascend to office through party machines and legislative coalitions. In presidential systems, direct elections open a clearer route for the selection of "outsiders", or for leaders appealing to the extreme end of the political spectrum. Horowitz and others have suggested that it is possible to reduce these risks by geographical distribution or runoff requirements that encourage the formation of broad electoral coalitions[27]. Nevertheless, if countries such as Brazil and Peru had had parliamentary systems during the 1980s, it is unlikely that a Collor or a Fujimori would have come to power, or that leaders like Lula or Brizola would have been serious contenders for the Brazilian presidency.

"Outsiders" or "extremists" can come to power without the backing of broadly based party organizations, and they are therefore poorly positioned to develop the legislative support required to sustain their programs. When this weakness leads to prolonged executive-legislative stalemate, the temptation increases to bypass the legislature through decree, or even to use extra-constitutional means. Parliamentary leaders, whose tenure depends on their capacity to maintain legislative majorities, must consult with supporters to retain their majorities, whether within their own parties or among coalition partners. For these reasons, they are also more likely to be able to forge coalitions in support of their programs.

The defense of parliamentarism has not gone unchallenged, and many of the counterarguments are pertinent to the prospects for coherent economic management. First, the statistical evidence is mixed as to whether parliamentary systems are any less vulnerable than presidential ones to usurpation of power, the suspension of constitutional norms, or the assumption of executive powers by the military. Shugart and Carey survey all 20th-century regimes that have held at least two consecutive elections, and find the rate of breakdown among developing countries to be about 52 per cent for presidential systems and just over 59 per cent for parliamentary ones[28]. Not included in this tally, moreover, are the wave of parliamentary breakdowns that occurred during the 1920s and 1930s in Eastern and Southern Europe, or in Japan.

Stepan and Skach, by contrast, find that parliamentary systems are more durable. In one test among several, they examine the set of all countries that became independent between 1945 and 1979. Grouping these countries on the basis of their constitutional form at the time of independence, Stepan and Skach find that the only countries still having continuous democratic rule between 1980 and 1989 were to be found among the parliamentary regimes (36 per cent of those which were parliamentary "at birth"). Of the 52 countries in the non-parliamentary category — presidential, semi-presidential and monarchic governments — none managed to achieve or sustain continuous democratic rule into the 1980s. The vast majority of the "survivors" were island states or former British colonies that had adopted the Westminster model of majoritarian rule, and thus approximated two-party systems; only Israel and Papua New Guinea had more than 2.5 effective parties[29]. This raises the crucial question of whether the real source of stability is parliamentarism or majoritarianism, and whether the small former British colonies are relevant for understanding development in more industrialized and socially heterogeneous middle-income countries such as Mexico, Brazil, or the Southern Cone countries.

The Latin American and Asian cases we have examined in depth also provide no strong evidence that parliamentary systems are more effective than presidential ones in terms of economic management. In a number of cases, some of the central difficulties of economic management centered less on the executive's relationship with the legislature than on the difficulty of controlling the rest of the state apparatus (relations between central and state governments, for example, posed vexing policy problems in the federal systems of Brazil and Argentina, particularly in the area of fiscal adjustment) or securing the cooperation of organized business and labor interests.

Parliamentary systems offer no guarantees that these relationships would be handled more effectively. Indeed, if consultation is seen as an important component of reaching bargains over major adjustment issues, it is not clear that a parliamentary form is necessarily desirable. Where parties rule by absolute majority in a parliamentary system, or where majority coalitions are cohesive, prime ministers can acquire greater discretionary latitude than presidents.

Executive-legislative stalemates are possible in parliamentary as well as presidential systems, though they naturally take a different form. Under parliamentary systems with proportional representation (PR), fragmentation of the party system and patronage demands from party leaders can create dangerous stalemates not only in policy making but in the formation of governments. At least one study of European systems shows that stabilization initiatives become more difficult as the number of parties in the governing coalition increases, because of the larger number of side payments required[30]. Our own work on inflation suggests similar relationships in developing countries[31].

The most striking differences among the cases we have examined appear to turn less on the distinction between parliamentary and presidential systems *per se* than on the number of parties. Whether presidential or parliamentary, the countries characterized by high growth and relatively low inflation generally tended to approximate two-party or dominant-party systems. These included presidential systems such as Chile, Korea, Colombia, and Costa Rica, and parliamentary systems such as Malaysia. Societies with highly fragmented party systems, conversely, had the greatest difficulty combining democratization with macroeconomic stability and growth. Among the presidential regimes, Brazil continued a pattern of policy immobilism and economic decline, and Peru encountered major difficulties on both the economic and political fronts. Among parliamentary systems, economic management in Thailand became less coherent as constraints on multiparty competition were relaxed in the late 1980s; Thailand and Peru were also the only countries in the sample to revert to authoritarian rule since their recent democratization. Similarly, Turkey in the late 1970s shows that parliamentary-PR systems are not immune to either economic crisis or political breakdown.

A constitutional change toward parliamentarism might provide incentives for politicians to strengthen their organizations and broaden the range of legislative alliances. In many fragmented and polarized systems, however, the institution of parliamentarism would carry serious risks if it were not accompanied by the reform of rules that currently generate centrifugal forces in the party system, including electoral rules and district magnitudes. As will be argued in the following section, however, the determinants of fragmentation and polarization go far beyond the electoral rules, and hinge in part on the historical ideological orientations and social bases of the competing actors within the broader political and social system.

Economic reform, democratic consolidation, and the organization of party systems

Social changes associated with the current wave of economic reform have significantly altered the context in which party arrangements will evolve in the future. In many countries, the social base of party development has been altered by the weakening of labor unions, the growing politicization of business elites, and the emergence of new grass-roots groups organized around neighborhoods, the provision of services, and environmental questions, as well as gender and ethnic identities. Similarly, the scaling back of the size and responsibilities of the state has placed greater limits on opportunities for patronage and welfare.

Although these changes have important implications for the political landscape over the long run, the distributional issues surrounding the economic adjustment process are unlikely to disappear from the political agenda, and will continue to structure political cleavages to a substantial extent. There are, however, a number of party-system arrangements that would avoid problems of political polarization and fragmentation, providing stable support for the functioning of capitalist democracy. Three seem broadly relevant to the situation of most Latin American countries: systems in which two "catch-all" parties alternate in office, and multiparty systems dominated by either the center-left or the center-right. The analysis of each case considers some of the socio-economic and political conditions under which these alternative party systems are likely to arise, their likely orientation concerning management of the economy, and the characteristic political conflicts that might affect their stability.

Two-party systems

A two-party system in which broadly based catch-all parties alternate in office is likely to emerge where there is a relatively high degree of elite consensus on the appropriate economic model and a weakly mobilized or controlled left. Interestingly, most new democracies have not opted for institutional designs that would support such a party system[32]. These include an electoral system based on plurality voting with single-member districts, whether presidential or parliamentary, though it may also emerge under "moderate" PR systems which discourage the emergence of small parties[33]. Yet the evolution of such systems might be facilitated by the weakening of popular sector forces during the long period of economic crisis and reform, particularly where ethnic or class conflicts were not highly politicized in the past.

Among established developing country democracies, this system is characteristic of the patronage-based and clientelistic parties of Colombia, Venezuela, and Costa Rica, and former British colonies that inherited the Westminster system. It is also approximated by current patterns of competition between the Peronists and Radicals in Argentina, and to a lesser extent, in Uruguay, where the Colorados and Blancos continue to dominate the presidency despite the presence of an important third force within the party system.

Such a system would provide some role for labor, leftist, and other minority interests, but as distinctly "junior partners" to elite-dominated centrist parties that compete for overlapping cross-class constituencies. Despite the reduction in patronage opportunities, moreover, party competition might provide the basis for a kind of mild reformism and social compensation, perhaps similar to that envisioned in the Alliance for Progress. These two-party systems appear to have a good record in maintaining stable macroeconomic policies, a record that is not irrelevant to the maintenance of electoral democracy as well[34].

These systems nonetheless face characteristic problems. First, parties in such systems may become little more than elite-dominated machines, with the risk of both undermining coherent economic policy and taking on exclusionary features that can undermine support for the political system as a whole. The exclusionary side of such parties accounts in part for the widespread alienation evident in the Venezuelan riots of 1990, and even more fundamentally, for the ongoing guerilla warfare that has characterized Colombia.

The challenge in such systems is to find ways to broaden participation and extend social compensation without recourse to the large and inflationary state sectors that were characteristic of developmentalism in the 1960s and 1970s. Colombia probably comes closest to achieving this objective. Projects of this sort demand an extremely delicate balancing act, however, as is illustrated by Jamaica's experience under Manley in the 1970s. Manley's goal was precisely to broaden the political and economic base of an elite-dominated two-party system, but the expansion of the role of the state coincided with the collapse of the bauxite market and the first oil crisis. Manley's inability to reverse his political commitments contributed to the deterioration in economic performance, which in turn fueled a dramatic increase in political polarization. During the 1980s, both electoral pressures and economic constraints pushed the political system, and Manley personally, back toward the center. Efforts to re-establish elite consensus, however, have once again substantially reduced the scope for participation available to the Jamaican left.

Multiparty systems: center-right dominant

Democratic consolidation might also be achieved in an electoral system in which governing parties or coalitions on either the center-right or the social-democratic left have a strong presence, or are even capable of establishing dominance over the electoral system. From a sociological point of view, these two multiparty alternatives are most likely to emerge in societies such as Chile, Brazil, or perhaps Korea, where ideological divisions have been sharpened by historical partisan loyalties, working-class political subcultures, or the recent mobilization of working-class movements.

In such circumstances, the shape of the party system would turn heavily on the political allegiances of the middle classes and rural sector. Rural and/or middle-class alignment with the right would create the basis for the dominance of conservative coalitions, as in Japan. Long-term alliances of these groups with working-class movements — such as the Swedish "red-green" alliance — would contribute to the formation of relatively stable, European-style social democratic coalitions. Either model could conceivably form a viable basis for the electoral legitimation of democratic capitalist systems, though the styles of capitalism would be very different. Like the other alternatives, however, both face characteristic problems.

The increasing political activism of business elites in many new democracies, along with the weakening of traditional labor movements, provides opportunities for the emergence of a "Japanese model" political system, dominated by a strong center-right party or coalition. This is likely to be predicated on an economic model that emphasizes business prerogatives, investment over consumption and transfers, and an instrumental, legitimating formula based on the promise of rapid growth and, in the case of Japan, a highly institutionalized system of pork-barrel politics and corruption[35]. Organized labor and the left would be relegated to a position of long-term opposition, perhaps even with legal and political "guarantees" that provide various checks on their freedom of maneuver. Examples might include electoral rules that limit the entry of small leftist parties or systems of industrial relations that restrict the political activities of unions.

Whatever the advantages of this model in providing support for growth-oriented policies, its exclusionary features pose greater problems for democratic consolidation than do those of the two-party option discussed above. These systems would require governments to produce high rates of economic growth, substantial opportunities for upward mobility, and at least a modicum of welfare concessions to the opposition. All of these might be undermined by economic forces beyond the government's control.

A second dilemma of the center-right model is more explicitly political. The likely conditions for this outcome include a labor movement weakened by some combination of market conditions and state controls; an ideologically coherent and politically strong rightist bloc, both inside and outside the state apparatus; and middle-class groups that are disinclined to form alliances with the left. Current circumstances in Mexico's dominant-party system approximate these conditions, as do those in countries such as Korea, Thailand, and Turkey. If efforts to establish a dominant center-right coalition are accompanied by the political alienation and marginalization of "radicals" on the left, they could lead to political polarization, the pursuit of anti-system politics on the left, and the emergence of quasi-authoritarian "solutions" in response.

Multiparty systems: center-left dominant

The social-democratic model is in many respects the mirror image of the "Japanese" alternative[36]. The principal elements in this model would be strong, if not dominant, center-left parties. These were based historically on alliances which working-class movements forged first with agriculture and then with the middle class, and they generally evolved toward corporatist systems which integrated peak labor and business associations directly into the policy-making process[37]. More contemporary versions would clearly have to find ways to incorporate the new social movements alluded to above.

Whatever its precise institutional form, the core bargain is that capitalists gain predictability in the overall business and macroeconomic environment and consensual decision-making in exchange for the dominance of center-left governments, welfare state policies, and the involvement of labor and possibly other popular groups in the formulation of macroeconomic, social, and industrial policies. As Katzenstein has argued most clearly for the small European states, this alternative is not necessarily antithetical to the maintenance of open markets; to the contrary, such political systems are likely to invest in labor mobility and training, which facilitates openness[38]. Precisely for this reason, this variant of market-oriented social democracy has been held out as a desirable one for countries seeking to make a transition to a more open, export-oriented development strategy.

Compared to center-right systems and possibly even to the two-party model, inclusionary features of the social-democratic outcome would provide it with a relatively broad base of legitimacy and support. Precisely because of their identification with the left, moreover, social-democratic governments might be in a better position to moderate wage and welfare demands emanating from their core constituency; this point has been made widely in the literature on Western European social democracies[39].

While this model is normatively appealing, it is far from clear that the social and political conditions for its emergence are widespread in the middle-income Latin American countries. As noted above in the discussion of corporatism, the organization of the working class has suffered substantially over the last two decades, first as a result of authoritarian rule, then owing to the recession of the 1980s. As a result, in most countries labor does not yet possess the coherent structure needed to make it a unified and forceful political player or to provide the basis for strong leftist parties. In less developed countries of the region, the problem is structural: the working class is simply not large enough to play a determining political role.

Some countries in the developing world do, of course, retain greater possibilities of forming a strong center-left coalition. Some, such as Chile, can draw on a long-standing alliance between parties of the left and the labor movement; others, such as Korea, have been characterized in recent years by the increasing political consciousness and mobilization of the industrial working class. Even where organized labor remains politically strong, however, its potential as a base for a new center-left model remains unclear. One major issue would be how organized labor would relate to newly emerging popular movements, whose aspirations with respect to gender, employment opportunities, environment, or small enterprise often conflict with the traditional claims of the union movement. A second would be the role to be played by organized labor in the context of more open, export-oriented economies which face substantial pressures to contain wage costs. Such issues are not unmanageable, but with the partial exception of Chile, they remain unresolved. Until they are, center-left coalitions will be unable to provide private sector groups with the guarantees that might form the core of a social-democratic bargain.

A third and even more daunting problem with the social-democratic model, finally, is that it implies a reconciliation of the left with military and business elites, which in many countries remain relatively strong and hostile to the compromises on which such a system must rest. The sources of rightist strength might include the continuing presence of external threats, a memory of "disorder" associated with political openings to the left, or middle classes disinclined to play the role of a swing force because of the factors just cited. Where landed interests remain a significant social and political force, as in Brazil, they are also likely to constitute a barrier to this solution.

Conclusion

As this brief survey of alternative party systems makes clear, none escapes the central political tension between democracy and the market with which this discussion began. Yet this finding may also be read in a hopeful way. Although the options for managing this tension creatively — of striking a compromise of embedded liberalism — are not completely open-ended, they are multiple. To the extent that the analysis of these different party systems implies alternative ways of organizing a market economy, it buttresses other recent work that has emphasized the continuing variety of national economic systems and indicates that there may be multiple pathways to the successful consolidation of democratic capitalism.

Notes and References

1. Haggard and Kaufman (1992a).

2. Ruggie (1983).

3. Geddes (1993).

4. A seminal article is March and Olsen (1984).

5. Extended discussions of these cases appear in Haggard and Kaufman (forthcoming).

6. Shugart and Carey (1992).

7. This theme is developed at greater length in Haggard and Kaufman (1993 and 1992a).

8. Bates and Krueger (1993).

9. Kiewit and McCubbins (1991).

10. Valenzuela (1978). In some instances, however, as Shugart and Carey (1992, p. 187) point out, this may actually facilitate system stability: where parties are organized primarily around regional interests, extensive presidential authority over economic policy can free individual legislators to service local constituencies, while also providing a check against particularism that might undermine the system as a whole.

11. Shugart and Carey (1992), p. 165.

12. Bresser Pereira, Maravall and Przeworski (1993), p. 208; O'Donnell (1992); Weber (1978), pp. 268-271. The last contains several brilliant insights on the relationship between plebiscitarianism and economic management.

13. Bresser Pereira, Maravall and Przeworski (1993), p. 209.

14. In the recent literature on democratization, see for example O'Donnell and Schmitter (1986). The literature on corporatism bears a relationship to the study of "consociational" forms of rule that characterize a number of ethnically plural societies. In these cases, representation is based on ethnic identification rather than functional position in the division of labor. See Lijphard (1968).

15. Kaufman, Bazdresch and Heredia (forthcoming).

16. For the classic statement on this, see Schmitter (1974) and Collier and Collier (1979). See also the discussion in Malloy (1977).

17. Schmitter (1974).

18. See for example Lehmbruch and Schmitter, eds (1982).

19. Karl (1990).

20. This was the case in Uruguay during the mid-1980s, for example. The negotiation of broad agreements of "mutual security" in 1984-85 has sometimes been cited as an

example of the way pact-making can contribute to smooth democratic transitions. While these pacts may well have contributed to a general climate of moderation, they did not preclude bitter contestation over macroecomic policies during the Sanguinetti period.

21. Roborough (1989).

22. Roborough (1989), p. 200.

23. For a parallel critique, see Przeworski (1991), p. 185.

24. See discussion by Torre (1991).

25. A number of the more important pieces have been collected in Diamond and Plattner, eds. (1993); these include Linz (1993a and 1993b), Horowitz (1993), and Lijphard (1993). See also Mainwaring (1989); Shugart and Carey (1992), pp. 28-54.

26. Shugart and Carey (1992), p. 33.

27. Horowitz (1993).

28. Shugart and Carey (1992), pp. 38-43. The criterion of two consecutive elections is aimed at eliminating "ambiguous cases in which one election was held under the watchful eye of a departing colonial power or as a mere 'demonstration' for foreign consumption" (p. 39).

29. Stepan and Skatch (forthcoming). The survivors were Bahamas, Barbados, Botswana, Dominica, India, Israel, Jamaica, Kiribati, Nauru, Papua New Guinea, St. Lucia, St. Vincent, Solomon Islands, Trinidad and Tobago, and Tuvalu.

30. Roubini and Sachs (1988).

31. Haggard and Kaufman (1992b).

32. For reflections on why this might be the case, see Geddes (1990).

33. The authors are grateful to Matthew Shugart for this point.

34. For a more detailed argument of this point, see Haggard and Kaufman (1992b).

35. For different expositions of the "Japanese model", see Curtis (1988), particularly pp. 45-79, and Calder (1988).

36. For an exposition centered on the small, open European economies that might have relevance for some developing countries, see Katzenstein (1985), particularly pp. 80-135. See also Luebbert (1991).

37. See Luebbert (1991).

38. Katzenstein (1985).

39. The theoretical foundation for this argument is spelled out in Lange (1984).

Bibliography

BATES, Robert and Anne O. KRUEGER (1993), "Generalizations Arising from the Country Studies", in Robert Bates and Anne O. Krueger, eds, *Political and Economic Interactions in Economic Policy Reform*, Blackwell, Cambridge, pp. 463-467.

BRESSER PEREIRA, Luiz Carlos, José María MARAVALL and Adam PRZEWORSKI (1993), *Economic Reforms in New Democracies*, Cambridge University Press, New York.

CALDER, Kent E. (1988), *Crisis and Compensation: Public Policy and Political Stability in Japan: 1949-1986*, Princeton University Press, Princeton.

COLLIER, Ruth Berins and David COLLIER (1979), "Inducements versus Constraints: Disaggregating Corporatism", *American Political Science Review*, 73 (4): 967-986.

CURTIS, Gerald (1988), *The Japanese Way of Politics*, Columbia University Press, New York.

DIAMOND, Larry and Marc F. PLATTNER, eds (1993), *The Global Resurgence of Democracy*, Johns Hopkins University Press, Baltimore.

GEDDES, Barbara (1990), "Democratic Institutions as a Bargain among Self-Interested Politicians", paper prepared for the American Political Science Association meeting, San Francisco.

GEDDES, Barbara (1993), *The Politicians' Dilemma: Reforming the State in Latin America*, University of California Press, Berkeley.

HAGGARD, Stephan and Robert R. KAUFMAN (1992a), "Introduction: Institutions and Economic Policy", in Stephan Haggard and Robert R. Kaufman, eds, *The Politics of Economic Adjustment*, Princeton University Press, Princeton.

HAGGARD, Stephan and Robert R. KAUFMAN (1992b), "The Political Economy of Inflation and Stabilization in Middle-Income Countries", in Stephan Haggard and Robert R. Kaufman, eds, *The Politics of Economic Adjustment*, Princeton University Press, Princeton.

HAGGARD, Stephan and Robert R. KAUFMAN (1993), "The State in the Initiation and Consolidation of Market-Oriented Reform", in Dietrich Rueschemeyer and Louis Putterman, eds, *State and Market in Development: Synergy or Rivalry?*, Lynne Reiner, Boulder.

HAGGARD, Stephan and Robert R. KAUFMAN (forthcoming), *The Political Economy of Democratic Transitions*.

HOROWITZ, Donald L. (1993), "Comparing Democratic Systems", in Diamond and Plattner, eds (1993), pp. 127-134.

KARL, Terry Lynn (1990), "Dilemmas of Democratization", *Comparative Politics*, 23 (1): 1-23.

KATZENSTEIN, Peter J. (1985), *Small States in World Markets: Industrial Policy in Europe*, Cornell University Press, Ithaca.

KAUFMAN, Robert R., Carlos BAZDRESCH and Blanca HEREDIA (forthcoming), "The Political Economy of the Pact for Economic Solidarity in Mexico: December 1987 to December 1988", in Stephan Haggard and Steven Webb, eds, *Voting for Reform*, World Bank, Washington, D.C.

KIEWIT, Roderick and Mathew McCUBBINS (1991), *The Logic of Delegation*, University of Chicago Press, Chicago.

LANGE, Peter (1984), "Unions, Workers, and Wage Regulation: The Rational Bases of Consent", in John H. Goldthorpe, ed., *Order and Conflict in Contemporary Capitalism*, Oxford University Press, Oxford, pp. 98-123.

LEHMBRUCH, Gerhard and Philippe C. SCHMITTER, eds (1982), *Patterns of Corporatist Policy-Making*, Sage Publications, Beverly Hills.

LIJPHARD, Arend (1968), *The Politics of Accommodation*, University of California Press, Berkeley.

LIJPHARD, Arend (1993), "Constitutional Choices for New Democracies", in Diamond and Plattner, eds (1993).

LINZ, Juan (1993a), "The Perils of Presidentialism", in Diamond and Plattner, eds (1993).

LINZ, Juan (1993b), "The Virtues of Parliamentarism", in Diamond and Plattner, eds (1993).

LUEBBERT, Gregory M. (1991), *Liberalism, Fascism or Social Democracy*, Oxford University Press, New York.

MAINWARING, Scott (1989), "Presidentialism in Latin America", *Latin American Research Review*, 25: 157-79.

MALLOY, James M. (1977), *Authoritarianism and Corporatism in Latin America*, University of Pittsburgh Press, Pittsburgh.

MARCH, James G. and Johan P. OLSEN (1984), "New Institutionalism: Organizational Factors in Political Life", *American Political Science Review*, 78 (3): 734-750.

O'DONNELL, Guillermo (1992), "Delegative Democracy?", Working Paper No. 172, Kellogg Institute, Notre Dame, IN.

O'DONNELL, Guillermo and Philippe C. SCHMITTER (1986), "Tentative Conclusions about Uncertain Democracies", in Guillermo O'Donnell, Philippe C. Schmitter and Laurence Whitehead, eds, *Transitions from Authoritarian Rule: Prospects for Democracy*, Johns Hopkins University Press, Baltimore.

PRZEWORSKI, Adam (1991), *Democracy and the Market*, Cambridge University Press, Cambridge, New York, Port Chester, Melbourne and Sydney.

ROBOROUGH, Ian (1989), "Organized Labor: A Major Victim of the Crisis", in Barbara Stallings and Robert R. Kaufman, eds, *Debt and Democracy in Latin America*, Westview Press, Boulder, San Francisco and London.

ROUBINI, Nouriel and Jeffrey D. SACHS (1988), "Political and Economic Determinants of Budget Deficits in Industrial Democracies", NBER Working Paper No. 2682.

RUGGIE, John Gerard (1983), "International Regimes, Transactions, and Change: Embedded Liberalism in the Postwar Economic Order", in Stephen D. Krasner, ed., *International Regimes*, Cornell University Press, Ithaca, pp. 195-232.

SCHMITTER, Philippe C. (1974), "Still the Century of Corporatism", *Review of Politics*, 36 (1): 85-131.

SHUGART, Matthew Soberg and John M. CAREY (1992), *Presidents and Assemblies: Constitutional Design and Electoral Dynamics*, Cambridge University Press, Cambridge.

STEPAN, Alfred and Cindy SKATCH (forthcoming), "Constitutional Frameworks and Democratic Consolidation: Parliamentarism vs. Presidentialism", *World Politics*.

TORRE, Juan Carlos (1991), "America Latina: Governing Democracy in Hard Times", paper delivered at the 15th Congress of the International Political Science Association, Buenos Aires.

VALENZUELA, Arturo (1978), *The Breakdown of Democracy: Chile*, Johns Hopkins University Press, Baltimore and London.

WEBER, Max (1978), *Economy and Society*, University of California Press, Berkeley, Vol. 1.

Sustainable Development and Environmental Politics in Latin America[1]

Margaret E. Keck

Sustainable development, defined in the Brundtland Commission report simply as "...development that meets the needs of the present without compromising the ability of future generations to meet their own needs"[2], is a concept whose political dimensions are ambiguous at best. Much economic analysis of what "sustainable development" requires either begs the political questions altogether or makes a number of unwarranted assumptions about commitments to equity. Indeed, the issues of equity between nations (North-South conflict) and equity within them (social justice, poverty, inequality) are often blurred.

Environmental concerns are politically contentious because they entail a redefinition of the boundaries between private and public. This could be a claim to a public interest in the conduct of what previously were seen as private activities, or on the contrary a dispute over private appropriation of what had been seen as public goods. Further contention can arise over the extent of the public concerned — whether for example it stops at the boundaries of a particular nation or includes humankind more generally — or even over what kinds of rights should be accorded to non-human species. Political conflict thus occurs over how environmental issues are defined, over who has authority over and/or the right to be heard on them (which is influenced by how they are defined), and of course, over how they are to be resolved. A wide variety of national and international political actors — governmental, multilateral, and societal — may claim some kind of standing. Such conflicts may raise issues that go well beyond a narrow vision of environmental problems, in questioning states' abilities to know and preside over the public good. Yet few of those claiming to speak for society on these issues are "representative" in the usual sense of the word. Evaluating the *political* conditions for sustainable development, then, requires careful mapping of institutional capacities, the power resources of relevant actors, and political dynamics at each level of analysis.

Several Latin American countries are particularly good examples of the difficulties posed by the political dimensions of sustainable development thinking. Persistent social inequity not only exacerbates environmental degradation but makes it harder to reverse, and long traditions of clientelistic distribution of resources undermine the assumptions of rationality present in most projects designed to address these problems. This essay will focus primarily on Brazil, which provides apt illustrations for these points and which has been a main target of international environmental attention.

Discussion of sustainable development in the 1980s emerged at a time when most Latin American countries were experiencing major economic and political changes. The economic crises of the 1980s, widespread questioning of the developmentalist role of states, and transitions from military to civilian governments created a cauldron of political and social ferment that would affect the (diverse, even contradictory) political meanings that environmental issues would come to have in the region.

Sustainable development

The notion of sustainable development was an important break for the international conservationist community. It stemmed from an attempt to come to terms conceptually with the accusations by developing country leaders that environmentalists cared more about the survival of wildlife than about that of people — a North-South divide over environment and development that crystallized during the preparations for the United Nations Conference on the Human Environment, held in Stockholm in 1972. The concept was publicized in *World Conservation Strategy*, published in 1980 by the International Union for the Conservation of Nature and Natural Resources (IUCN) and prepared with the help of its sister organization the World Wildlife Fund (WWF) and the fledgling United Nations Environmental Program (UNEP)[3]. In 1987, it reached a wider audience as the centerpiece of *Our Common Future*, the report of the World Commission on Environment and Development headed by Norwegian prime minister Gro Harlem Brundtland. By June 1992, when the United Nations Conference on Environment and Development was held in Rio de Janeiro, every major governmental, inter-governmental, and multilateral development agency had espoused sustainable development.

The need for such a concept became evident to the world community in the preparations for the 1972 Stockholm conference when North-South relations became one of the most important dimensions of the conflicts there. Brazil, a leader of the Southern bloc at Stockholm, was one of the promoters of the prior meeting of experts at Founex, Switzerland, called to produce a document on environment and development to enrich the Stockholm debates[4]. The Founex report highlighted the need for a focus on poverty and a view of development as cure rather than cause of environmental problems; it sought solutions in "ecodevelopment" of the kind that theorists like Paris-based economist Ignacy Sachs of the *Centre de recherches sur le Brésil contemporain* were attempting to develop[5].

Latin Americans played an important role in the organizations that shaped these definitions. Like their colleagues elsewhere, the individuals involved were for the most part scientists who had themselves been shaped by decades of uphill battles to protect natural areas. Brazilian biologist Paulo Nogeira Neto, elected to the IUCN

Executive Board in 1970, became Brazil's first secretary of the environment, a post he would hold for 12 years. The Venezuelan Geraldo Budowski was IUCN director-general in the early 1970s, and went on to influence Costa Rica's conservation policy; the Peruvian Marc Dourojeanni has also played a major role in shaping the organization.

By the time the Brundtland Commission issued its report in 1987, the call for development as growth in the initial formulation of *World Conservation Strategy* had been joined by greater attention to equity. The commission's secretary-general equated *sustainable development* with "...growth with equity and growth with caution", and wrote further:

> The concept of "sustainable development" [...] connotes a process of change in which economic and fiscal policies, trade and foreign policies, energy, agriculture, industrial and other sectoral policies, and the political decision processes underlying them all aim to induce development that is both economically and ecologically practical.
>
> "Sustainable development" should be a goal for all nations, industrialized ones as well as Third World states. The changes required in policies and institutions, national and international, are significant, but well within the possible[6].

Twenty years after Stockholm the UN Conference on Environment and Development had progressed to the point of having both terms in the title, but although the rhetoric was more sophisticated, much of the content was similar. If the meaning of "development" is still contested at the end of the 20th century, how much more might the addition of sustainability — an idea intended to reshape development thinking at its core — add to the controversy? Who sustains what, how, and for whom — essentially political questions — have not been seriously addressed by most of the voluminous literature on sustainable development. Indeed, unlike economists, geographers, anthropologists, and of course ecologists, political scientists have come rather late to the analysis of these questions. As a result, literature on sustainable development is replete with passive verbs and "musts", but rather short on active verbs with identifiable subjects.

The political problem stems in part from the fact that from Founex on, the issues of equity among and equity within nations have been blurred, and frequently the first has served as proxy for both. Both have at different times been presented as the essential condition of the kind of inter-generational equity contained in the definition of sustainable development. The espousal by governments of a Third Worldist position calling for global equity in international relations by no means signifies a strong commitment to equity at home. The Brazilian case is an excellent example: the military governments that in the 1970s steered a remarkably independent course in foreign relations, attempting to lead the South in North-South relations, presided over a radical upward redistribution of income in their own country. (Not all dictatorships have done the same; most of the East Asian NIEs pursued rapid development policies while paying greater attention to social equity, though still at a high cost in political repression.)

The confusion among these different references to equity is wonderfully illustrated in an article written by Brazilian ambassador to the United States João

Augusto de Araujo Castro for a special pre-Stockholm issue of the journal *International Organization*[7]. It was the only article in the issue to stake out a developing-world position on environmental questions, and provided a sophisticated introduction to arguments presented at Stockholm as well as others that remain unaddressed to this day. Some of the points made by Araujo Castro have become familiar: he objected to the ecological argument that developing countries cannot hope to attain consumption patterns of developed ones, and to the neo-Malthusian tone of Northern environmental discourse. He argued compellingly that disarmament and peace would help to resolve environmental problems, and prefigured what later became accepted wisdom by espousing the "polluter pays" principle: "By this time it should be clear that most of the existing pollution problems are simply noncomputed social costs of private activities. [...] Were the polluters liable for the damages they cause, incentives would be created to solve environmental problems." He claimed, however, that developing countries were still at a prepollution stage — something that was already highly dubious in his own country. In a clear formulation of what became catchwords at Stockholm (the pollution of affluence and the pollution of poverty), he argued:

> There is a pollution of affluence and a pollution of poverty. It is imperative to distinguish between the two lest some pollution be prevented at the cost of much economic development. Were it not for the dangers arising from the confusion between the two kinds of pollution, there would be no need for calling attention to the precarious housing conditions, poor health, and low sanitary standards not to mention starvation in developing countries. The linear transposition of ecological problems of the developed countries to the context of the developing ones disregards the existence of such distressing social conditions. Wherever these conditions prevail, the assertion that less income means less pollution is nonsense. It is obvious, or should be, that the so-called pollution of poverty can only be corrected through higher incomes, or more precisely, through economic development.

Outlining what ought to be the position of developing countries regarding environmental problems, he made two major points. The one that received the most attention was his defense of national sovereignty, which is what the Brazilian position became known for at Stockholm. He claimed that "...any ecological policy, globally applied, must not be an instrument to suppress wholly or in part the legitimate right of any country to decide about its own affairs". Before his discussion of sovereignty, however, Araujo Castro took great care to stress that the first step in an internationally acceptable approach to environmental policy had to be the "rejection of the principle that the ecology issue, taken on a global basis, can be dealt with exclusively through a technical approach, as suggested by the developed countries". He made this point essentially to reinforce his sovereignty argument and particularly to object to the IBRD's adoption of environmental standards for projects.

Much of Araujo Castro's argument prefigured elements of the sustainable development debate. Nonetheless, the point that no approach to saving the environment would work unless it were "imbued with a solid and well-informed political approach" was lost somewhere along the way, as international institutions and environmental organizations sought incentives to induce individuals and governments to change their environmental behavior, as it were, in spite of themselves. In part, this is due precisely to the political dilemmas posed by many (most) governments' lack of initiative in doing anything about *either* environmental concerns *or* the "desperately low levels of socioeconomic welfare" that Araujo Castro noted in his essay.

In part, the reversion to an essentially technical approach to international environmental policy reflects the disciplinary roots of those most engaged in the environmental debate during the 1970s and 1980s. Biologists, chemists, ecologists, and economists all believed that as much as possible environmental policy should be insulated from politics; politics (viewed as partisanship or self-interested scrambling for a piece of the pie) impeded sound policymaking. Even analysts as sophisticated as Ascher and Healy, for whom attention to equity is central to their model of "virtuous circles" in natural resource policymaking, see political objectives and organization more often as a problem to be overcome than as a central component of the process. Although they see it this way often because of what they perceive as built-in inequities in the political and social structure, they do not see the *existing* political and social structure as the necessary starting point for the process they espouse. The following passage provides a good example:

> The striking lesson to policymakers [of problems with the Sri Lankan Accelerated Mahaweli Development Program] is the importance of addressing flaws in political and social organization. Certainly there is much technical analysis to be done in order for huge, complex ventures like multipurpose dams to be well designed and implemented. Yet in these cases the problem is not so much that the technical burdens are overwhelming, but rather that restrictive policymaking routines, lack of participation, and premature closure of problem definitions render good technical analysis either impossible or irrelevant. The obstacles amounting to the "implementation gap" [...] — regional rivalries, political maneuvering, and bureaucratic inefficiency — are clearly operative in these cases[8].

Ascher and Healy see "flawed" political and social organization as a crucial element rendering the policy process irrational. Other analysts during the 1980s focused more on the incapacity of states, beleaguered by rising socio-political demands and declining resources, to address new issues like the environment while trying to face up to the accumulated grievances that departing military rulers left for their civilian successors to resolve. Still others doubted state capacities for different reasons, seeing statist developmental apparatuses as ineffective and inefficient policy machines.

The next section elaborates on these points, but first the importance of the context in which these arguments developed should be stressed. Once again, the Brazilian example is useful. At the time of the Stockholm conference, Brazil was at the height of the heady confidence from the high-growth years of the "economic miracle", when annual GNP growth rates exceeded 10 per cent and anything seemed possible. The Stockholm conference coincided with the inauguration of the first leg of the Transamazon highway, designed to open up the Amazon to settlement, providing a safety valve for unrest in the impoverished northeast and serving at the same time to foster the kind of national integration dear to geopolitical strategists. In contrast, the 1980s, during which many of the instruments and incentives intended to lure Third World governments into environmental good citizenship were formulated, was known as the "lost decade" for much of the continent. Although the depth of economic crisis increased resentment of environmental conditions in foreign and multilateral development lending, borrowers had very little choice: domestic investment was down to a trickle and the debt crisis made foreign money hard to get. The position taken by multilateral lending institutions was thus extremely important[9].

At the same time, most of the countries in the region underwent a transition from authoritarian to democratic regimes. The result was not only a ferment of political organization, but also a considerable increase in social demands of all kinds. Political parties emerged from clandestinity and new ones were organized; trade unions reorganized or changed their strategies to fit new political opportunities; social movements demanded urban services and, in rural areas, access to land. Environmental organizing also increased significantly in the 1980s, taking a variety of forms: local groups were founded to protect natural areas or protest environmental damage; environmental think tanks were formed, and other think tanks added cnvironmental issues to their agendas; and by the end of the decade, some grass-roots organizations and non-governmental organizations that function as grass-roots support organizations had begun to reframe social demands in environmental terms. The latter process was to a considerable extent a response to donor interest[10].

Environmental issues have rarely made it into the mainstream of representative political deliberations. The key actors have generally not been representative organizations, and congresses have rarely been the site of major decisions. (The passage by Brazil's Constituent Assembly of a chapter on environmental protection is a tribute to the organizing abilities of Deputy Fabio Feldmann, but it also reflects the fact that for most deputies who voted for the chapter — and very few did not — it seemed at the time an essentially costless act.) Instead, decision making normally occurs in bureaucratic organs and occasionally in councils attached to them; deliberations — insofar as they occur — tend to take place far from the public eye. Three issues raised earlier are relevant here. What kinds of "flaws" in political and social organization, to use Ascher and Healy's terms, make a policy process less rational than it might be? Would not an effective policy process try to build upon the existing political and social organization? What constitutes state capacity in the environmental area, and how much is there or should there be? Finally, can or should participation in the policy process be increased, who should participate, and who should decide?

All of this points up another key problem in sustainable development debates: the tendency to define problems at a macro level, propose solutions at a micro level, and fail to bridge the two. Although couched as a macro-level social concept, sustainable development is inconceivable without meticulous attention to the micro level of the social, political, and economic contexts it proposes to transform. In international discussions of sustainable development states are treated as unitary actors; in the implementation of sustainable development policies, however, this unitary image quickly disintegrates. For example, when Brazilian government officials announce in international fora the intent to use ecological economic zoning plans as instruments for rational planning of sustainable use of rain-forest areas[11], it is not *Brazil* that will design and try to implement such plans. Rather, specific constellations of regional government officials, planners, and domestic and foreign consultants and bankers will draw up the plans, and other configurations of political and social actors (local and national) will react to them. In doing so they will call upon allies in both national and international arenas, and each will claim to speak with authority for the public interest. As the notion of sustainable development is by definition attentive to local specificity, it requires recognition that environmental politics is multivocal[12].

Environmental politics

Environmental politics is about access to and use of resources, about the quality of life, and ultimately about the relationship between humankind (and its forms of social organization) and everything else. Our perceptions of each of these three areas are historical constructions. Many of the environmental issues affecting developing countries have been around for a long time under other names. What are now called environmental struggles in the Amazon, for example, were previously called land struggles, or simply local social conflicts. In urban areas people living in poor neighborhoods or shantytowns have been demanding sewers, clean water, and trash collection for generations. Struggles around such issues produced social movement organizations, appeals to local governments and to politicians to act as brokers, and the like, long before "the environment" became a matter of public concern. The reconfiguration of social struggles as environmental issues opens up new political resources and new allies for their protagonists. Labeling struggles as "environmental" can change the grid of political and social relations in which they are embedded.

At the level of governments, environmental politics is rarely limited to those organs specifically established to oversee environmental policy. Agricultural and infrastructural agencies play an especially prominent role. In federal systems, the bulk of environmental responsibility may fall on the states. Understanding the politics of the environment requires investigation of where environmental issues and policies fit into the overall grid of intra-bureaucratic and state-society relations at a particular time. Given jurisdictional confusion and rather fuzzy mandates, the individuals who occupy positions of power within institutions are enormously important, and the ability of environmentalists to affect policy depends largely on their ability to influence sympathetic individuals in parts of the state apparatus.

However much technical planners may want to insulate environmental policy from other areas, the nature of environmental issues makes this unlikely. Establishing parks always involves controversy over land use both within park areas and in the surrounding regions; ensuring a supply of clean water involves regulation of industrial effluents and disposal of domestic waste. Money spent on the environment sometimes benefits powerful social actors (as in water and sanitation projects) and sometimes does not (as in restrictions on beachfront development).

Environmental politics involves regulatory, distributive, and sometimes even redistributive policies. Although conventional wisdom normally assigns the environment (in a general sense) to the category of public goods, adjudicating any given environmental question involves a political struggle over the boundaries between public and private. The actors likely to become involved will not only prefer different outcomes but will define the situation differently. Which actors will become involved in shaping the definition may well vary according to the arena in which the conflict is located[13].

Most Latin American states lack resources, qualified personnel, and inter-institutional agility. With the economic crisis of the last decade, institutional lacunae have become worse; moreover, the state-shrinking exercises mandated by countless adjustment programs have often obeyed a political rather than a technical logic, meaning that survivors in government jobs may have had the best connections rather than the best qualifications. Remaining state capacity is strained by new responsibilities for environmental protection and for ensuring sustainability in development projects.

This is all the more true in that development projects that are most attractive politically tend to be expensive, externally funded mega-projects which most governments are ill-equipped to manage. For example, current development projects based on agro-ecological economic zoning plans in the Brazilian states of Mato Grosso and Rondônia are obliging the implementing agencies to borrow personnel from a variety of other state organs. When the project periods end, these people will scatter to their original posts, dispersing as well what institutional memory and learning was gleaned from the experience. Mega-projects have the advantage, however, of having as a rule more (and more physically dispersed) components, thus providing political leaders with more to distribute. Clientelism has not disappeared with the crisis of the Latin American state, but there are fewer spoils to distribute. Attempts to endow sustainable development projects with a technical rationality run headlong into the political logic of system maintenance[14].

What do we need to understand about a country in order to recognize when, and in exchange for what, will political leaders promote sustainable development alternatives and their followers will support them in (or even for) doing so? Most analyses of environmental policy concentrate on the environment as a separate sector of political life. The history of environmental institutions is certainly relevant, as are the costs and benefits of particular policies given a country's developmental situation. Even more relevant, given the interpenetration between public and private in the environmental arena, is the more general configuration of public and private spheres in a country's political life. At least as relevant as the existence of an environmental secretariat in Brazil is Brazil's tradition of clientelistic politics, non-responsible and fragmented parties, weak judiciary, labyrinthine legalism, and the countervailing *jeitinho*. Although successive Brazilian governments, military and civilian, have presided over what they considered the national interest, they have done less well as convincing guardians of the public good.

After the 1972 Stockholm conference, Brazil instituted an environmental secretariat at the federal level, under the auspices of the Ministry of the Interior, and São Paulo biologist Paulo Nogueira Neto was named the first environmental secretary[15]. In the late 1970s and early 1980s, environmental organs were established in most Brazilian states as well. The first broad federal environmental legislation was passed in 1981 and enabled in 1983. A national environmental council (CONAMA) was established, with members drawn from federal ministries, state organs, sectoral organizations within civil society, and environmental organizations. In 1986 CONAMA passed a resolution requiring all major development projects to include an environmental impact statement. In most instances, however, environmental organs remained institutionally quite weak, owing largely to their inability to influence the early stages of decision making in more powerful federal and state organs whose projects had significant environmental impacts; Nogueira Neto claims that their major role was putting out fires that had already started[16]. Although important regulatory legislation was passed at the federal level and in some states, the gap between law and implementation of the law was substantial.

During the 1980s, democratization of political institutions and the rapid growth of environmental organizations (and organizational life in general), especially in the more industrialized and wealthier states of the Brazilian southeast, helped narrow this gap. The environmental and health disaster caused by petrochemical industries in Cubatão, São Paulo, is a good example. The case mobilized local movements, the Brazilian scientific community, and a number of politicians; upon taking office in 1983 Governor Franco Montoro decided to make cleanup of this area a priority of his administration — a process that was accelerated by a pipeline explosion and fire in the area in 1984. The first "opposition" governor elected in São Paulo, Montoro reinforced the technical and planning capabilities of the major state environmental organ (CETESB)[17], and CETESB functionaries worked closely with local organizations. For its time, it was an unusual example of successful collaboration among these different sectors — a collaboration facilitated by the visibility of the problem, a sympathetic state government, the existence of identifiable technical solutions, and the availability of World Bank funding to cushion the financial impact of implementing pollution controls.

The facilitating conditions of the Cubatão cleanup represented an unusual conjunction of favorable circumstances. Although success stories exist, environmental legislation in Brazil is still implemented unevenly. This is not surprising, as the same holds generally for regulatory laws in Brazil. Part of the problem lies with the institutions (primarily at State level) charged with implementation: their capacities vary from State to State generally, and also within States over time. In addition, although the number of environmental organizations in Brazil has shot up since the beginning of the 1980s, few of these groups have the organizational capacity to monitor and influence this process, and those that do have done so inconsistently.

Environmental organizations participate in State-level environmental councils, as well as the federal CONAMA, but these councils have generally played a fairly weak role; not all States have them, and not all of them meet regularly. Although the 1988 constitution mandates public hearings on the environmental impact statements for large projects, few environmental organizations have the expertise or organizational capacity systematically to take advantage of these critical opportunities to raise their concerns. Many in fact choose not to do so, claiming that the hearings are always packed by project proponents and that environmentalists are shouted down.

There is incipient promise in the passage in 1985 of the Diffuse Interests Law (Law no. 7347/85). This measure extends to legally constituted organizations concerned with protection of the environment, historical patrimony, or consumers' rights (as well as to government organs and the public prosecutor's office — *Ministério Público*) the right to sue those esteemed to be producing damage by commission or omission. An important aspect of this law is its recognition of the right to sue for entities that have not been personally damaged by the violation in question. Nonetheless, in part because of lack of confidence in the judiciary and in part because of fears of being saddled with the costs, few organizations have sued on their own; generally they refer perceived abuses to the prosecutor's office in the hope that it will bring the suit[18]. Even in São Paulo, where it is likely to be better off than in most States, the *Curadoria do Meio Ambiente* has been grossly understaffed and underequipped.

Environmental politics potentially involves a multiplicity of actors and instruments. Where environmental and equity questions are joined, the panorama becomes even more varied. Overlapping jurisdictions, at the same and at different levels of the state apparatus, encourage this variety. If the conflict involves international actors and is (or can be) incorporated into international agendas, this affects the strategies of the domestic actors involved in the conflict. Strategic behavior around conflicts related to deforestation, for example, addresses foreign organizations and publics as much as Brazilians; with urban environmental issues this is rarely the case. The breadth of the potential arenas in which conflicts can be addressed can determine which social and political actors are likely to become important; internationalized conflicts bring in more intermediaries (individuals and organizations).

Civic organizations — both explicitly environmental movements and social movements organized around other kinds of issues (neighborhood services, housing, or demands for access to land) — play an important part in bringing environmental questions to public attention. These groups vary enormously in their goals, their form of organization, their degree of institutionalization and their durability, the kinds of alliances they make, and the resources upon which they can call. They also vary in terms of where they seek resources. There are few options. In a political culture with scanty traditions of voluntary organizations, few groups even try to collect membership dues. That leaves essentially governmental and foreign sources. The number of small environmental organizations in Brazil that finance their activities at least in part through consulting arrangements (*convênios*) with municipal or State (and sometimes federal) authorities is striking, particularly in view of the stress that virtually all of them place on their autonomy from the state. The most common *convênios* involve formulation and implementation of environmental education programs. Foreign support is generally available only to more institutionalized non-governmental organizations, discussed below.

The continuing prevalence of a "small is beautiful" ethic in the environmental movement — in Brazil as well as in the developed world — means that a great many, perhaps most, environmental groups do not want to become large or complex organizations. Most do not have formalized memberships, leadership is often self-selected, and very few have even minimal infrastructure. Nonetheless, many of these local organizations have a history of struggle over particular environmental issues, during which their members have won a certain legitimacy as spokespersons in this area. Even very small organizations often have more institutional resources than are initially evident. In particular, many have access to state resources through members who hold responsible positions in government or as parliamentary aides and who are able to use telephones, mailing privileges, photocopiers, computers, and the like, to serve organizational ends.

Over the last decade, an increasing number of intermediary organizations with broader popular education or grass-roots development missions have become involved in Brazilian environmental politics, responding both to donor incentives and internally to the resonance of the Chico Mendes/Acre rubber tappers case. Thus IBASE and FASE, among others, have begun to play an important role (and in fact are seen as interlopers by a number of more traditional environmental organizations as well as former close allies like AS-PTA).

The term NGO (non-governmental organization) will be used for these professionalized organizations that have relatively clear organizational missions, paid staff, headquarters and organizational infrastructure, and fund-raising capacity. Normally in Brazil they have international connections and are financed primarily from abroad; they also have a relatively high degree of access to and ability to process information. These two factors are their key political resources.

While some environmental organizations in Brazil should be classified as NGOs[19], most are more informal, volunteer organizations having substantially less access to information *as organizations*, though they may have members (scientists, for example) whose professional links do provide such access. Some NGOs promoting grass-roots development also play an important role in environmental organization[20].

These organizational distinctions matter because these groups play different roles. NGOs can help to aggregate grass-roots movements of different kinds and from different localities, bringing their concerns to national or international agendas. They mediate between grass-roots movements and national or foreign actors — governmental, non-governmental, and inter-governmental — and they are particularly visible in more internationalized conflicts. Their international connections make them the privileged interlocutors of foreign actors, and they can bring local struggles to the attention of these actors (or choose not to do so). Unlike grass-roots movements — the measure of whose effectiveness is the ability to mobilize their communities — or membership organizations, NGOs are not accountable to a constituency; they are accountable to their own organizational leaders and to their donors. There are no democratic mechanisms by which to hold them accountable before the larger society.

The big environmental organizations tend to be conservationist and/or research-oriented. There is normally a clear distinction between these and advocacy organizations, and the two rarely work together. There are exceptions: *SOS Mata Atlântica* in São Paulo, for example, was formed with the explicit intention of bridging the conservationist-advocacy gap. Most depend heavily (some exclusively) on funding from foreign foundations or development agencies, and there is little prospect of their sustaining themselves with domestic funds any time soon; the Brazilian tax code grants no fiscal advantages to corporate or individual donors to such organizations. As funding is normally project-specific, staffing — especially of technically qualified personnel — is always a problem, as most collaborators need to maintain primary employment elsewhere. Virtually all environmental organizations are heavily identified with and dependent upon the commitment of a small number of individuals. International environmental organizations (Greenpeace, WWF) have only just begun to establish themselves in Brazil, although Friends of the Earth has had a small Brazilian affiliate for many years.

In most cases, the pattern of interaction between social movements and the state around environmental questions is consistent with general patterns of Brazilian politics. Social movements seek direct contact with sympathetic individuals within the state bureaucracy in an attempt to have their grievances addressed. Failing this, they may move toward more dramatic forms of protest, but their protest is normally directed at bureaucratic organs. It is much more rare for political parties or the legislative branch to be a major focus of activity (except insofar as legislators can facilitate contact with bureaucratic organs or can help to publicize protests).

Some organizations, loosely grouped under the NGO rubric when environmental politics are being discussed, are more accurately referred to as organizations representing corporative interests — business associations, labor unions, agricultural cooperatives of various kinds. The missions of these organizations differ from those discussed above in that they are explicitly dedicated to defending the interests of an identifiable membership base. However much they might want to appeal to transcendent principles, if their leaderships are seen to pursue policies that injure their memberships, those leaders will surely not remain in office long. The circumstances under which it is possible for corporative leaderships to call upon a long time horizon in order to bring environmental (or sustainability) concerns into their day-to-day programming are probably somewhat rare.

Access to information and the ability to make it circulate rapidly and in a form that can be acted upon is a crucial political resource for the internationalized politics of the environment. This is where NGOs excel, and it is what explains their influence in a setting where others inevitably can bring more traditional political resources (wealth, political connections) to bear on a conflict. NGOs must be able to manage two information streams: one coming from the outside in (needed to keep abreast of developments relevant for domestic activities), the other going from the inside out (providing case materials in the testimony of local people about environmental damage, or local knowledge about botanical properties, etc.). The technologies of international information flows are the facsimile machine and the computer network; the language is English. These requirements limit those able to participate in information exchange, transforming those that can into brokers (and in some cases making them far more visible internationally than locally).

It is the fashion these days to see NGOs as the solution to the double bind of internationally financed development projects: how to cut through the bureaucratic layers and chronic inefficiency of state institutions and how to ensure the participation of socially relevant groups in the process. NGOs are seen as closer to the ground and more agile than the state, and (perhaps especially) they do not belong to the state. The growing desire to bring NGOs into project implementation represents a kind of privatization process in the social area. The problem is that it also implies a privatization of accountability that serves neither democracy nor the long-term *political* sustainability of environmentally sensitive development policy. Unwittingly, NGOs have had two contradictory effects on environmental politics in Latin America: on the one hand, they have stimulated environmental activity and organization; on the other, they have probably helped to insulate environmental questions from democratic politics, thus eliminating the necessity of developing mass support for environmental measures.

Preventing deforestation in Brazil and preserving biodiversity in Costa Rica

Two Latin American cases that are well known internationally will serve to illustrate the points made in the preceding section. Over the last decade, Brazil and Costa Rica have been portrayed as the negative and positive images of the environmental conservation story in Latin America; on an intuitive level, reasoning that a more equitable society is less likely to mine its natural resources, we would expect this to have something to do with Costa Rica's history as a democratic welfare state. Surprisingly, though, on several counts the cases are quite similar. Both countries have highly internationalized environmental politics, at least as concerns preservation of natural areas; both had serious foreign debt crises and have experienced a significant erosion of state capacity over the last decade. The issues of deforestation in Brazil and biodiversity in Costa Rica both raise thorny questions about who guards the public interest best (and how and by whom that should be decided).

Tropical deforestation became an issue on the international agenda in the first place because of its extent in Brazil. The Brazilian government's decision in the early 1970s to accelerate colonization and development projects in the Amazon alarmed scientists and provoked a letter of protest in 1972 from the presidents of the IUCN and WWF to President Médici[21]. In early 1974, the IUCN sponsored an international meeting in Caracas to discuss guidelines for economic development in tropical forest areas of Latin America[22]. By August 1974, the IUCN and WWF were calling tropical rain forests "the most important nature conservation program of the decade". In 1975 WWF launched a drive to raise $1 million, equivalent to half of its entire 1974 project budget, for rain forest conservation projects.

At the end of the 1970s President Carter and the US Congress joined the chorus, putting pressure on the UN General Assembly and on UNEP to take action[23]. Those initiatives foundered on two counts: the Reagan administration's lack of interest in pursuing the issue and the unwillingness of several of the most important tropical forest countries (including Brazil, Zaire, Colombia, Venezuela, and Burma) to participate in UNEP meetings on the subject.

In the late 1980s, as global environmental problems like climate change and the disintegrating ozone layer gripped the public imagination, Brazil became a scapegoat among developing countries. Deforestation in Amazonia was already a centerpiece of the international (but Washington-based) NGO campaign to add or reinforce an environmental dimension in multilateral banks' lending practices. When new satellite pictures of burning rain forest, the hot northern summer of 1988, and the murder of Chico Mendes followed each other in quick succession, it was easy to demonize Brazil, and in Chico Mendes sustainable development advocates had their first martyr.

The morality play that the Chico Mendes story became and the stress placed by international institutions on sustainable development and its relation to equity granted a privileged role to populations pursuing traditional livelihoods in Amazonia. New development projects in the works for the western Amazon were intended to take into account the views of these "defenders of the forests". Accordingly, particularly in Rondônia, where a sequel to Polonoroeste based on an agro-ecological and economic zoning plan was being prepared, a variety of NGOs brought people from rubber tapper and indigenous communities together with small farmers from the colonization projects and formed a deliberative council for the project. Several members of this council have participated actively in the formulation of various project components. From a technical standpoint, there is no doubt that their participation has been constructive.

NGOs brokered the interaction. NGO representatives in Rondônia owe their presence on the deliberative council (and indeed its existence) to pressure from foreign NGOs on the World Bank; they owe their interaction with the State government primarily to the World Bank. Their interlocutors are other NGOs, the state, the Bank, and donors. To some extent they have become involved in environmental policy at a national level, through Ibama or through the congressional commission on the environment. An extremely well-documented case, demonstrating that despite agreements and statements to the contrary INCRA (the federal land institute that controls most public land in Amazonia) was still issuing titles on the basis of deforestation in 1993 and was ignoring Rondônia's zoning plan, was presented to the environmental commission of the federal congress, the World Bank, foreign NGOs, and various high officials of the Brazilian government. It is striking that no effort was made to mobilize around this issue in Rondônia itself. No one had to. It was possible (and probably more quickly effective) to leapfrog local political arenas and move directly to higher ones where conditions were more favorable; in the same way, these NGOs and the social movements or populations with which they work managed to gain representation on a council deliberating about the State's development without having been elected, and in fact without having built much of a local base.

Local politicians, however, have a different set of expectations: once the money begins to arrive the role of these organizations will diminish significantly, and a political logic will be reimposed on the process. If the politicians are right, the NGOs and their allies will have a difficult time intervening, because they have not built a base in local political interactions. If the politicians are wrong, and the process remains tightly controlled by technical personnel with NGOs providing international cover, the likelihood increases that opponents will organize, and the policy's political sustainability may be jeopardized. This dynamic is discussed in the Conclusion.

If Brazil has been the environmentalists' showcase of what to avoid, Costa Rica has been their star. Over 20 per cent of Costa Rica's land is designated for some kind of conservation, and ecotourism is the third-highest income earner in the country, after coffee and bananas. Outside of park programs, however, deforestation remains a major problem. The example that best illustrates the profound political ambiguity of much current environmental policy is precisely the one to which outsiders point as Costa Rica's shining experiment in sustainability[24].

The agreement between the US-based pharmaceutical company Merck and the Costa Rican environmental NGO INBio (Instituto Nacional de Biodiversidad) to finance collection of biological specimens for a period of two years was touted as a model of a new kind of arrangement, in which Third World countries would receive the compensation they deserved for developed world exploitation of their resources. Under the terms of the agreement, signed in September 1991, Merck paid INBio $1.1 million up front, with a promise of royalties if commercial products were developed as a result of the specimens collected under INBio's auspices. Half the royalties would go to the Costa Rican government for conservation programs; of the original $1.1 million, INBio handed over $100 000 to the government for park conservation. At the same time, the government gave INBio's specimen collectors the right to prospect for species in national parks. The idea of the project was to train local people in taxonomy so that they could do this work; 15 people have been trained. The project has been enormously successful in increasing the number of known species in Costa Rica. Whether it will be commercially successful remains up in the air; product development to the point of producing royalties would take an estimated 15 years[25].

It is important to recognize that conservation activities in Costa Rica have been increasingly privatized in recent years; as the state was forced to shrink, it handed over more and more park maintenance functions to NGOs. The results have been relatively effective park management in Costa Rica, but a lack of a broader "public" policy context.

The concentration of effort on individual areas, particularly parks and their surroundings, leads to success at a micro level. But what of the macro-level need for national policy advocacy? Decentralization has led to atomization and a certain disconnectedness between individual projects and any collective program or plan for the long term. The struggle for funding in the context of a weak state also means that the professionals actually doing the conservation work, whether it be research, education, or legal advising, live hand to mouth, working in discontinuous bursts for diverse organizations. In short, NGOs suffer "projectitis" in Costa Rica because the focus of effort is on *proyectitos*[26].

However much NGOs have contributed to the conservation of the country's natural areas, the INBio agreement to a large extent privatizes what are, by any stretch of the imagination, public goods. The institute is not accountable in any way to Costa Ricans in general; they have no say over how the money received for the species specimens is spent, nor over what areas are "prospected". The mining analogy, while useful in pointing up the parallels in private appropriation of naturally occurring substances (frequently on public land), has some limits. These limits are evident in that the Merck-INBio agreement, when spoken of informally in discussions of environmental politics and sustainable development, is generally referred to as the agreement between Merck and Costa Rica.

The intent here is not to question the motives or behavior of INBio, or those of any other NGO referred to explicitly or implicitly. Rather, it is simply to claim that if the concept of sustainable development is to mean more than the payment of royalties to non-profit organizations, then it must include the creation of a public space for deliberation over and building support for a different kind of development.

Towards political sustainability

Trying to get past the vagueness that normally attaches to the notion of sustainable development, environmental economist John Dixon of the World Bank suggests desegregating the concept into ecological, ecosystemic, and economic dimensions of sustainability. The first measures maximum ecological viability; the second, "maintenance of ecosystem capacity to produce natural resources"; and the third, investment opportunities[27]. This essay suggests that a fourth dimension — political sustainability — must undergird the others. To imagine what might constitute political sustainability of environmentally sensitive development policy, we must first examine some reasons for the narrowness of the support base such policy currently has.

First, except in rare instances policy is initiated within small groups (usually though not necessarily in the state) which subsequently need to find allies for their proposals. Allies can be sought in the state, in civil society, or in international institutions. Although obviously not mutually exclusive, each set of alliances has political costs and benefits. Policy initiators may or may not care about these. Lack of attention to building political support is often justified with reference to *environmental crisis* — the notion that degradation is moving so fast that anything that works to stop it is worthwhile.

Second, owing to the collective-action problems involved in both support for and opposition to environmental policies, it is important to know whether the beneficiaries and costs of a policy are concentrated or diffuse. Unfortunately, while it is frequently easy to identify who will pay the costs of a policy, the beneficiaries tend to be more diffuse — and may even be unidentifiable as individuals (as in the case of policies intended to benefit humanity, or future generations). Environmentally sound policies whose proponents can appeal to an identifiable and concentrated constituency are likely to be more "sustainable" than those which cannot. The flip side of this set of questions is whether individuals will benefit over the short term from non-compliance with a policy. This is particularly likely to be true where frequent changes occur in policy or the seriousness with which it is enforced — as is the case in many Latin American countries.

Just as individuals in civil society may have strong incentives for free ridership, so too may individual policymakers have incentives to seek short-term individual or collective gains, material or political, instead of "optimizing" behavior over the long run[28]. Building a political base, rewarding supporters, repaying patrons, hedging against the risk of losing office after the next election (to say nothing of lining one's pockets) — all these are powerful reasons to ignore a technical rationality that offers little beyond civic virtue as an incentive to play by the rules.

States need sufficient autonomy from distributional pressures to implement policy effectively, but this does not mean that they must remove policy from the realm of democratic deliberation; rather, they need institutional arrangements that provide them with adequate support. This varies among and within Latin American countries. It helps to have party systems in which parties do not constantly seek to outbid each other; predictability (regularity and stability of political interactions) also helps. In some parts of Latin America the implantation of a consistent rule of law

— producing binding contracts, clear property rights, tax collection, and security of persons — would be an enormous step forward. In fact, a great deal could be accomplished by promotion of what used simply to be called "good government".

Removing responsibility for public goods from the domain of the state is not the solution, however inadequate the state's current fulfillment of that responsibility may be. NGOs can help to empower civil society and constructively to challenge states, but they are not a substitute for either, nor (in the main) do they purport to be. If policy is to be technically responsible then it must be politically responsive — and responsible — as well. Although building real support in state and society for environmentally sound development policy will likely seem too slow for those who believe that ecological collapse is imminent, anything else is likely to be unsustainable, and hence illusory.

Notes and References

1. The research on which this paper is based was made possible by financial assistance from the following institutions: the Howard Heinz Endowment / Center for Latin American Studies, University of Pittsburgh, research grant on Current Latin American Issues; the Joint Committee on Latin American Studies of the Social Science Research Council and the American Council of Learned Societies, with funds provided by the Ford Foundation; and the John D. and Catherine T. MacArthur Foundation. The author has also benefited immeasurably from the invariably stimulating comments of the students in her research seminar "Environment and Development in the Third World" at Yale University.

2. World Commission on Environment and Development, *Our Common Future* (Oxford and New York: Oxford University Press, 1987), p. 43.

3. International Union for Conservation of Nature and Natural Resources (IUCN), *World Conservation Strategy: Living Resource Conservation for Sustainable Development* (Gland, Switzerland: IUCN, 1980).

4. United Nations General Assembly, *Development and Environment* (22 December 1971). UN Doc. A/Conf.48/10. The Founex report was also published in a special issue of *International Conciliation*, 586 (January 1972), with commentaries by Miguel Ozorio de Almeida, Wilfred Beckerman, Gamani Corea, and Ignacy Sachs.

5. For an overview see, for example, Ignacy Sachs, *Ecodesenvolvimento: crescer sem destruir* (São Paulo: Vertice, 1986), a collection of articles previously published in English and French. See also his "Estratégias de transição para o século XXI", in Marcel Bursztyn, ed., *Para pensar o desenvolvimento sustentável* (São Paulo: Brasiliense, 1993). Sachs' commentary on the Founex report was published in *International Conciliation*, 586 (January 1972).

6. Jim MacNeill, "Let's have some fresh thinking about 'development'", *Christian Science Monitor*, 6 July 1987, p. 14 (from Nexis).

7. João Augusto de Araujo Castro, "Environment and Development: The Case of the Developing Countries", in David A. Kay and Eugene B. Skolnikoff, eds, *International Institutions and the Environmental Crisis*, special issue of *International Organization*, 26:2 (Spring 1972).

8. William Ascher and Robert Healy, *Natural Resource Policymaking in Developing Countries: Environment, Economic Growth, and Income Distribution* (Durham, NC: Duke University Press, 1990), pp. 94-95.

9. This is why these institutions became the target of a major campaign by environmental NGOs to strengthen environmental conditionality in development lending. For a description of the campaign, see Pat Aufderheide and Bruce Rich, "Environmental Reform and the Multilateral Banks", *World Policy Journal*, 5:2 (Spring 1988), pp. 301-21; Bruce Rich, "The Emperor's New Clothes: The World Bank and Environmental Reform", *World Policy Journal*, 7:2 (Spring 1990), pp. 305-29; and Barbara J. Bramble and Gareth Porter, "Non-governmental Organizations and the Making of US International Environmental Policy", in Andrew Hurrell and Benedict Kingsbury, eds, *The International Politics of the Environment* (Oxford: Oxford University Press, 1992), pp. 313-53.

10. The term "grass-roots support organization" draws from Thomas Carroll's distinction between GSOs and MSOs (member service organizations) in classifying intermediary NGOs in Latin America. The distinction was made in a book written as a report for the Inter-American Foundation: Thomas F. Carroll, *Intermediary NGOs: The Supporting Link in Grassroots Development* (West Hartford, CT: Kumarian Press, 1992).

11. For example, see José Goldemberg, "Current Policies Aimed at Attaining a Model of Sustainable Development in Brazil", *Journal of Environment and Development*, 1:1 (Summer 1992), pp. 112-13.

12. Marshall Wolfe made this point very well in a slightly different context (discussion of the great variety of attitudes on environmental issues within countries, including developing countries) in "Perspectivas del medio ambiente en la palestra política", in Osvaldo Sunkel and Nicolo Gligo, eds, *Estilos de desarrollo y medio ambiente en la América latina* (México: Fondo de Cultura Económico, 1980), especially p. 327.

13. The notion of regulatory, distributive, and redistributive "power arenas", and of the centrality of how an issue is defined, are drawn from Theodore Lowi, "American Business, Public Policy, Case-Studies, and Political Theory", *World Politics*, 16:4 (July 1964), pp. 677-715. Lowi's categories were used to shed light on decision-making arenas in Brazil in Maria do Carmo Campello de Souza, *Estado e partidos políticos no Brasil, 1930 a 1964* (São Paulo: Editora Alfa-Omega, 1976), Ch. 1.

14. On patronage politics see Frances Hagopian, "The Politics of Oligarchy: The Persistence of Traditional Elites in Contemporary Brazil", Ph.D. dissertation, Massachusetts Institute of Technology, 1986; Barry Ames, *Political Survival* (Berkeley: University of California Press, 1988); and Ames' subsequent unpublished papers on clientelism and political bailiwicks in the Brazilian national congress.

15. The early institutional development of SEMA is well covered in Roberto Guimarães, *The Ecopolitics of Development in the Third World: Politics and Environment in Brazil* (Boulder, Colorado: Lynne Reiner, 1991).

16. Interview with Paulo Nogueira Neto, São Paulo, 11 April 1991.

17. Unfortunately for CETESB, the subsequent governor of São Paulo, Orestes Quercia, rolled back many of these innovations and weakened the organ institutionally, by cutting back technical programs and replacing technical personnel with political appointees. Particularly useful on environmental policy in São Paulo during the Montoro and Quercia governments were interviews with Heliana Feo Lins and José Antonio Nunes, São Paulo, 17 August 1990, and with Werner Zulauf, São Paulo, 22 April 1991.

18. According to the chief prosecutor in the environmental unit of the São Paulo public prosecutor's office, of the more than 1 000 environmental suits pending in 1991 in that office, fewer than 5 per cent were brought by environmental organizations. Interview with Edis Millaré, São Paulo, 10 April 1991.

19. This group would include such organizations as FUNATURA, FBCN, IEA, IPHAE, OIKOS, SOS Mata Atlântica, and perhaps a dozen others.

20. This group would include such organizations as CEDI, IBASE, and FASE.

21. "The Opening Up of Brazil", *IUCN Bulletin*, 3:5 (May 1972), p. 18. This article was the first in which the IUCN explicitly took on the tropical forest issue, which previously had been subsumed under a broader concern for wildlife habitat preservation. At the organization's September 1972 General Assembly in Banff, Alberta, it passed for the first time a resolution on the conservation and development of tropical rain forests; see *IUCN Bulletin*, 3:10 (October 1972). At the subsequent

General Assembly held in September 1975 in Zaire, tropical rain forests were the topic of the first substantive session.

22. The meeting, which took place at the Instituto Venezolano de Investigaciones Cientificas, 20-22 February 1974, included experts, representatives of government departments, and representatives of international agencies. It was co-sponsored by FAO, UNDP, UNEP, ECLA, UNESCO, and the OAS, and was financed by the Swedish International Development Agency, WWF, and UNEP. Reports on meeting preparations can be found in *IUCN Bulletin*, 4:7 (July 1973) and 4:12 (December 1973), and a brief report on the meeting itself appears in *IUCN Bulletin*, 5:3 (March 1974). A similar meeting was held in May 1974 in Bandung, Indonesia, to discuss southeast Asian tropical forests.

23. See US Congress, House of Representatives, Subcommittee on International Organizations of the Committee on Foreign Affairs, Report on Tropical Deforestation, 96th Congress, 2nd Session, 7 May, 19 June, and 18 September 1980. UNEP, together with the FAO, UNESCO, and UNCTAD, held a meeting of around 50 experts from 6 developed and 14 developing countries, 25 February-1 March 1980, that focused on conservation as part of sustainable use of tropical forests. See *IUCN Bulletin*, 11:5 (May 1980).

24. The author is indebted, for many discussions on this topic, to Rick Rheingans, currently doing agro-forestry research for a Ph.D. dissertation at the La Selva research station in Costa Rica; Lisa Fernandez, also of the Yale School of Forestry and Environmental Studies; and Marc Edelman of the Yale Department of Anthropology.

25. The Merck-INBio agreement has been widely discussed in the press. See Roberto Herrscher, "Latin America: Third world biodiversity is north's 'green gold'", Inter Press Service, 22 April 1993 (from Nexis).

26. Lisa Fernandez, "Non-government Environmental Organizations and the State in Costa Rica", Yale University, May 1993, unpublished.

27. Discussed in Marc A. Stern, Gail Sevrens, and Zachary Britton, "Economic Growth and Environmental Protection in the Americas: Interdependent Priorities for the '90s", rapporteurs' report for the Latin American Environment and Hemispheric Technology Cooperation Conference, Institute of the Americas, La Jolla, California, 17-19 November 1991, in *Journal of Environment and Development*, 1:1 (Summer 1992), pp. 178-79.

28. This and several other points in this section were influenced by a reading of Stephan Haggard and Robert Kaufman, "The State in the Initiation and Consolidation of Market-oriented Reform", Universidade de São Paulo, Programa de Política Internacional e Comparada, Departamento de Ciência Política, Série Política Comparada 4, Agosto 1991, reprinted in Dietrich Rueschemeyer and Louis Putterman, eds, *State and Market in Development: Synergy or Rivalry?* (Boulder, Colorado: Lynne Reiner, 1993).

Towards a Social Agenda

Teresa Albánez Barnola

The balance sheet of recent experience

Latin America and the Caribbean have been making significant progress in institutionalising democracy, reducing political violence, increasing participation and decentralising the state. The region can also boast some success in relation to the growth and modernisation of its economies. Social advances, however, have been very limited: the region continues to be characterised by pronounced and scandalous social inequality. Even in those countries which are generally quoted as examples of democratic stability and which are claimed to have introduced successful economic reforms, social inequality remains practically intact, where it has not worsened.

As recent experience shows — and in this respect reference to the Venezuelan case cannot be avoided — democratic stability, even with some optimistic results in the macroeconomic field, may constitute a passing illusion when its benefits are not transferred to the majority of the population.

Studies by international bodies and agencies show that in recent years the countries of Latin America have recorded positive economic growth rates, relatively high rates in some cases, while at the same time the number of households living in poverty has increased. If these estimates are correct — and there is sufficient evidence that they are — the observed growth is spurious and very fragile, and is also exacerbating the already very unequal distribution of income which historically has characterised the region.

This tendency is extremely serious. It constitutes an explosive charge which, sooner or later, will be reflected in an even greater radicalisation of political conflicts and in a sharpening of what has been called the problem of governance. The social polarisation generated by the deepening trend towards regressive income distribution is also causing an increase in urban violence, particularly among the young — a problem that is scarcely taken into account in strategies for social development, but that is experienced most acutely by the majority of the population, including those with few economic resources.

The traditional violence of Latin America was fundamentally of agrarian origin, and generally was a form of political and ideological statement, although a primitive one. This violence has not completely disappeared, but it is not the most fundamental type of violence at present. The new violence is mainly urban, linked to new forms of social exclusion, and at the moment is not making any political or ideological statement. It is the violence of a society dangerously polarised by the continually growing imbalance in income distribution and by the distance between fantasy and reality, emphasized by exposure to the mass communications media.

The issue of the media in countries where the educational level is low, where there are severe economic and social shortages, and where the population is predominantly young has neither been analysed as it should nor considered as part of social development strategies. Great importance should therefore be attached to the proposals on this topic made by Fernando Fajnzylber in the book *Strategic Options for Latin America in the 1990s*, which gathers together the papers from the 1991 Forum on Latin American Perspectives. Fajnzylber talks of the existence in Latin American societies of a "frustration gap", stemming, first, from the uniform growth in aspirations for access to goods, services and modern institutions (reflected in the mass media), and, second, from a reduction in the purchasing power of the low-income groups, who find that every day they have less real possibility of obtaining the goods and services which they desperately desire.

The frustration gap feeds social resentment, violence and delinquency, especially among the young, for whom the schism between fantasy and reality is wider than that suggested by the overall figures. It is estimated that in Venezuela over 1 million young people are outside the educational system and the labour market; they constitute what has been called the biggest "unarmed army" in the country. As Fajnzylber says, the drug boom could be linked to this explosive frustration gap, from the point of view of both consumers and suppliers: for the former, drugs offer a way of escape; for the latter, rapid access to the pleasures of life.

In societies like that of Venezuela, where the traditional political organisations seem to be less influential and less combative each day and where the community is still relatively weak, the mass communications media, especially television, tend to fill this vacuum, and frequently present an image of a community. It is no accident that, in the majority of Latin American countries, the new economic power (and sometimes political power as well) has been set up and organised on the basis of the control of the mass social communications media.

The media, especially television, have been the main driving forces behind this new fundamentalism which sees the state as the root of all evil, the market as the solution for all problems and the obtaining of greater material benefits as the major focus of life. On the basis of this viewpoint, anyone who criticises the content and orientation of the programming is told that the viewers (including children) are free to change channels, as if it were merely a question of changing the brand of some mass consumption product which is available in thousands of commercial outlets.

The increase in poverty and its causes

The methodologies used to estimate the extent of poverty are now sufficiently advanced so that today the percentage of the population in poverty can be determined with a fair degree of accuracy.

The poverty figures for the region show that approximately 50 per cent of the population falls into this category, and that 25 per cent live in extreme poverty. One should remember that these estimates use demanding parameters, which probably tend to underestimate the size of these phenomena. For example, in Venezuela today, the poverty line is fixed at around $300 a month for a family of five, and the extreme poverty line at half this figure. These income levels would not be acceptable in other parts of the world.

When poverty is measured using other methodologies, such as listing unsatisfied basic needs, the requirements are no less strict. In this case, for example, households in which the children attend school only between the ages of 7 and 12 are classed not as poor, but as normal. It is considered acceptable that children above and below this bracket be outside the educational system.

Although poverty in Latin America has been with us for a long time, it had been diminishing until the beginning of the 1980s. It then began to increase as a result, first, of the economic crisis of the last decade, and subsequently due to the initial impact of the economic adjustment programmes. The recent intensification of poverty has been determined principally by the decline in real family incomes (in Venezuela there was a drop of 47 per cent between 1984 and 1992) and the increasing deterioration in the provision of social services. Targeted social programmes, despite their positive impact, were clearly incapable of checking these tendencies.

The decline in real incomes and real wages can be explained by inflation, and by the fact that the effects of inflation are particularly serious for those with low incomes. Following a long period of moderate inflation, Venezuela experienced an increased growth in the cost of living during the 1980s. Between 1980 and 1990, the general price index went up eight-fold, and food prices sixteen-fold. Although these differences have tended to shrink over the last few months, at the time of writing the gap still stands at levels very close to those indicated. The repercussions of price movements, and of the fact that food prices have increased most, are most serious for low-income groups. Their expenditure on goods of this nature is proportionally greater than that of groups at other income levels, so this sector of the population suffers twice over. Whereas the consumer price index for the 25 per cent of the population with the highest incomes increased by 970 per cent between 1984 and March 1993, the increase for the poorest people was 1 300 per cent. That means that over this period the cost of living for those on low incomes went up by 34 per cent more than it did for the richest people.

People with few resources spend a very high proportion of their income on food, so they are subject to very severe restrictions when it comes to satisfying the rest of their basic needs, such as education, health and accommodation. Whereas in 1987 the average family's income represented 1.7 times the cost of the minimum reference basket of goods and services, in 1992 it covered only 0.9 times this figure.

That is, in 1992 the incomes of 62 per cent of households were below the cost of this basket. This situation has led many families to develop survival strategies, which include a growing tendency, not only for women, but also for children, to enter the labour market. What is more serious is that children are exploited and excluded from the educational system.

The need to combat inflation and avoid capital flight has led the financial authorities to raise interest rates to positive real levels — in some cases, to twice the predicted rate of inflation — thus stimulating speculative activities and generating a crisis in the productive sectors, which has a devastating effect on employment and wages. As has been demonstrated by some recent studies from ECLAC, there has been a shift of labour from high-productivity, high-income activities into other activities where productivity and income levels are lower. The trend of labour movement from less productive sectors to more productive sectors, which had prevailed since the post-war period, has therefore been reversed since the early 1980s.

External conditions have contributed to bringing this about. The persistent protectionism of the developed countries, despite unilateral measures by developing countries to liberalise trade and open markets, has not improved the situation. Paradoxically, the end of the Cold War seems to have increased the gap, and the tension, between the North and the South. In their struggle to maintain and enlarge their markets, the developed countries have hardened their trade policies and reduced their aid to developing countries.

There is no doubt that a world-wide market more open to Latin American exports would have a very significant impact on the well-being of the region. Agreement in the Uruguay Round, a reduction in duties or elimination of quotas on sugar and bananas — to cite only a few examples — would do more for the poor in some of these countries than an increase in international financing.

The agenda for democratisation and for the adjustments to be made should not be limited to the internal situation in the developing countries. International economic relations continue to be profoundly anti-democratic, and should also be subjected to a process of adjustment and correction. The international bodies, and especially the multilateral financial institutions, have a fundamental part to play in this task. Despite some recent changes, these institutions continue, especially through the strings attached to their loans, to press for economic reforms which, for the sake of the market, tend to benefit a few to the detriment of the majority.

Naturally, not all the responsibility falls on these institutions. The weakness of Latin American negotiators and the prevailing power structures in the region have led to the rapid adoption of reforms which favour the most influential and best placed, while other reforms, such as tax reforms, which would have made it possible to share the costs of adjustment, have been rejected or postponed.

The new social agenda

The structural adjustment programmes do not include any real social development strategy. The economic reforms have been laid out in reasonably detailed form, but the same does not apply to social reform. The strategy for social policy comes down to proposing a change from indirect subsidies to direct and targeted subsidies, not only because this form of compensation is considered more efficient and fairer, but also because it does not contradict the broad lines of economic policy.

In perspective — at least as regards the Venezuelan experience — it seems obvious today that the magnitude of social problems was underestimated when the adjustment programmes were drawn up. The hope that encouraging economic results would have a sizable impact on social questions in a relatively short time has proved unrealistic.

This experience means that a new social agenda must now be defined within the framework of a more open and competitive society, overcoming the over-simplistic disunity that sees only two choices: the orthodoxy that has prevailed in adjustment programmes, or recession. The problem is more complex, and requires the drawing up of much more active policies which take into account the experience accumulated in the last few years.

The fundamental components of the new agenda have been falling into place over the last few years: the linkage of social and economic policy, the creation of new forms of participation in consumer society, extensive reform of the state to improve the education and health services, the drawing up of programmes intended to address the most vulnerable people in society.

Adjustment with a human face, *transformación productiva con equidad*, human development, and other proposals and statements intended to call attention to the need to modernise our societies without leaving most people on the fringes — these have now passed into the language of the international bodies and the governments of the region. Yet there remains a considerable gap between what is said and what is done. It sometimes appears that, despite some exceptions, there has never been so much talk about poverty and so little being done to tackle it.

How can we explain the gap between words and action — a gap which is unquestionably of abysmal proportions? There can be many different answers to this question, but probably at bottom most of them will contain a common element — the absence of a real and sustained political will. Until now, vested interests and, on occasion, economic imperatives and economic policies have prevailed.

"Political will" does not mean only the will of governments, but also social and personal responsibility, and readiness to take the risk of opening up social policy and social programmes to participation by the people, even if some consider this participation to be disorderly, and even if it generates scepticism and apprehension.

The link between economic policy and social policy

The economic conceptions upon which the adjustment programmes have been based have brought about a separation between economic and social questions, leading to the formulation of a set of specific measures for the social sector. Naturally, not all types of measures come under consideration — only those compatible with the economic postulates for development do so.

The social policy which evolved from this restrictive model had to be targeted, compensatory and transitional: compensatory, because its basic aim was to mitigate the social impact of the economic reforms on the most vulnerable sectors of the population; transitional, because it was considered that, within a relatively short period of time, adjustment would generate inflation-free growth which would reach the entire population — the famous "trickle-down effect" — creating jobs in the modern sectors of the economy, raising incomes and making it definitively unnecessary to maintain the social programmes.

The dismal facts have given the lie to most of these illusions.

At the moment, an attempt is being made to overcome the view that social questions have a supplementary and transitional character in relation to economic policy. What is central and permanent is to "promote general welfare and social security; bring about the equal participation of all in the enjoyment of wealth, in accordance with the principles of social justice, and stimulate the development of the economy in the service of Man", as it says in the Constitution of the Republic of Venezuela. No doubt most Latin American constitutions contain similar provisions.

Within the framework of the restrictions which have been imposed by economic orientations and the magnitude of the problems to be tackled, some of the actions undertaken in the social area have played an important part and have done what they were basically designed to do: compensate for the impact of the crisis and the adjustment measures. Nevertheless, a social crisis with the dimensions of the one facing Latin America can not be tackled with any possibility of success if economic policy is not also made responsible for the people's welfare.

Economic policy should include among its objectives the restitution of incomes and wages, an active policy for reducing inflation (especially with regard to those goods which are strategic for those on low incomes, such as essential foodstuffs and medicines), reversing the trend towards deterioration in education and health services, and sectoral and regional policies which promote the development of sectors having greater capacity to generate jobs and social equilibrium.

The re-activation of small and medium-sized industrial firms and of agriculture — sectors which have been severely affected by the recent reforms — would not only have an economic significance but would also have a profound impact on provincial development and on the improvement of social conditions. The decentralised and deconcentrated nature of agriculture means this activity has a special capacity for generating a more equitable geographical and social distribution of income, owing to its geographical dispersion, its lower scale of production in relation to other economic activities, and its greater capacity to create jobs and cater to the population's consumption requirements.

Finally, one of the main factors responsible for making the population poorer in recent years and for the deterioration in the position of the middle classes has been inflation, especially the disproportionate growth in the prices of some basic goods. The state can not refuse the task of working out formulas to prevent any exaggerated growth in the prices of those goods which have a strategic effect on nourishment and health. Nowadays the state can not allow the market to be the only mechanism which determines who should have access to goods on which depends, not only the well-being of its citizens, but in some cases their survival.

Participation — a new social contract

The last few years have witnessed the entry onto the scene of social organisations. Citizens have organised themselves into groups to draw attention to their basic problems and to take part in solving them. This process is not only redefining the functions of the political parties, but filling an empty space and catering to the needs of the masses.

This new reality makes it necessary to facilitate a continuous dialogue between the state and the community, involving the organised sectors of the community in the preparation and implementation of social policies and programmes. This relationship is not always easy, but it is indispensable if social problems are to be tackled with any probability of success. For the rest, the magnitude of these problems requires the assistance of all the actors which can participate in their solution. This involves the development of a new concept and a new attitude in administrative practice — offering space so that the vocation to serve, to act and to resolve the problems of society can be stimulated and supported by the state and by the government.

For relations between the state and the community to be harmonious and fruitful, it is important to start by recognising the advantages and limitations of each. The state has tended to consider as an exclusive right what it should understand as its obligation. This tendency has been particularly marked in education, but has also been present in other areas involving the provision of social services. Thus the state has frequently resisted the contribution which non-governmental organisations can make, considering that these bodies are motivated only by special or ideological interests.

Although the importance of the community and of its organisations in tackling social problems can never be sufficiently emphasized, one should not fall into the extreme position of idolising them. They usually represent specific and particular interests, generally legitimate, but which, in some cases, may restrict their vision when they go beyond the environment in which they originated. Recognition of this reality does not necessarily constitute an obstacle, but it may help to establish more realistic and sincere relations.

The experience of recent years has made it possible to reduce the mistrust between the state and community bodies, and conditions have come to fruition which can act as a base for a new "social contract". On the part of the state, this contract implies an effort to bring about the gradual transfer of a set of social services — which it is now providing directly — to the social organisations. These organisations will act as intermediaries between the state and those whose resources are few. The state sometimes will remunerate these organisations for providing services, and will offer its technical assistance and support in the institutional and management areas.

Experiments carried out in Venezuela show the possibilities for collaboration between the state and the community organisations. These include a programme of day-care centres that provide services to the children of working mothers and of poor families. This programme has grown very rapidly in recent years, from 137 000 children in 1991 to 250 000 in September 1993. It is implemented entirely through non-governmental organisations — neighbourhood, civic, cultural and religious groups. The number of non-governmental organisations involved in this programme went from 60 to 373 this year.

Another important example is that of the programme for reinforcing the working-class economy through the development of urban and rural micro-enterprises, the majority of which are run by women and young people. This programme is entirely run through decentralised bodies established by the regional governments and municipal authorities, co-operatives and non-governmental organisations.

The food enrichment programme, while of a different nature than the previous examples, is co-ordinated by a national commission presided over by the Ministry of Family Affairs. The foodstuffs industry plays a very important role. The programme began with the enrichment of maize flour, the basic foodstuff for those on low incomes. Through the enrichment of maize flour alone, national deficiencies in the availability of the most important of the so-called supernutrients were substantially reduced: iron, 80 per cent; niacin, 83 per cent; thiamine, 78 per cent; vitamin A, 23 per cent; and riboflavin, 28 per cent. In this way, thanks to a co-ordinated effort from the governmental sector, and with the participation of the private sector, an immense barrier against malnutrition has been constructed, at very low cost and at very high speed.

Recently, under the auspices of the National Commission for the Enrichment of Foodstuffs, agreement was reached with the wheat industry to incorporate this industrial sector into the programme, enriching all the wheat flour used for making bread and a good part of that used for making pasta. In this way, the availability deficits for the majority of nutrients will be eliminated, with the exception of vitamin A and riboflavin.

Institutional reform

Prominent among the difficulties which confronted the design and execution of social policy were those associated with problems of an institutional nature and with the need for an extensive reform of the state. The modernisation of the social public sector should include the creation of a high-level governing body to provide for the continuity of social action, thus reinforcing the sector's technical capital, the allocation of sufficient financial resources and the advancement of decentralisation processes. Nevertheless, the implementation of the social programmes directed at the most vulnerable sectors cannot always wait for reforms of the state or of the social sector. Sometimes these programmes must go forward through existing structures, with the political endorsement required by the urgency of these actions. In this sense, the Mexican experience with Solidarity constitutes an important point of reference.

Unfortunately, the proposals for reform of the state which have been put forward within the adjustment programmes have centred on, and thus been limited to, the area of privatisation. Although this process is undeniably important, the reform of the state also implies the rationalisation of its administrative operations, the redistribution of functions within a process of decentralisation to the regions and the municipal authorities, together with the establishment of some new rules of the game in relation to the community.

In Venezuela, the institutional reform of the social sector has not advanced sufficiently either, despite having been considered by the national government as an essential component of social policy. Plans to modernise the social public sector, creating a Ministry of Social Development, have not been brought to fruition. This has left the social sector without strong leadership just when it needs it most. The government's own view has been short-sighted, and sometimes too concentrated on macroeconomic manipulation, a little self-absorbed and reliant on its successes in this area.

The decentralisation process, which was initially intended to encourage greater political democracy and transfer national skills to the provinces, has become a more important part of the policy of the central government, which has little by little been reducing its objections and relinquishing social programmes which have a direct effect on the population. In this way, decentralisation is being converted into a very important mechanism for improving the provision of social services and the efficiency of social programmes, making them easier to follow up and monitor — something which is extremely difficult to do at the national level. Moreover, the transfer of these services and programmes to the regions stimulates the development of local planning and implementation skills and improves the country's medium- and long-term capacities for tackling social problems.

Social protection

The most vulnerable sectors of the population, who are living in poverty — children, unemployed young people, pregnant and nursing women, and the elderly — cannot wait for the structural reforms being promoted in the areas of education, health and social security. Emergency programmes must be designed to meet the nutritional, health and training needs of these people. In Venezuela, since the end of 1989, programmes have been initiated for transferring money and foodstuffs directly to the poorest sections of the population. Such programmes are intended to compensate for the precarious family income which, as we have seen, in many cases does not begin to cover the cost of the minimum basket of goods and services.

These initiatives have been progressing rapidly, efficiently and transparently, despite the precarious nature of the institutional structures, and in a relatively short period of time have managed, through targeted efforts, to reach a high proportion of those living in poverty. Several social indicators demonstrate the positive impact of these social programmes. Naturally, these achievements should not obscure the gravity of the difficulties and the social problems still confronting this country, which it will need a great national effort to overcome.

Nevertheless, these difficulties and problems cannot be fundamentally attributed to the compensatory social programmes. On the contrary, without the programmes the deterioration would have been even greater. This deserves emphasis, because a tendency has evolved to criticise social programmes involving the direct transfer of money, foodstuffs or educational aids to poor families with children who are attending primary school. These initiatives are dismissed as paternalistic programmes, when they are not considered as a kind of alibi to preserve the status quo. The truth is that in many cases these programmes represent the difference between life and death for low-income families (though this may not mean sudden death). To eliminate them without providing any real alternatives, with no improvement in incomes and no significant recovery in the education and health services, would be not only an injustice but a provocation.

Other programmes have been put forward, the potential effects of which go beyond the limits of the moment and which are intended to have an influence on structural problems. This is the case for the Mother and Infant Health Care Programme, the Pre-School Facilities Expansion Programme, the programmes mentioned above which involve day-care centres and the reinforcement of micro-enterprises, and others which are similarly oriented and which, for this reason, are being given priority consideration at present.

Moreover, an attempt has been made to set out the bases of a system of social protection, which the most vulnerable sectors of the population lack. The following actions are oriented in this direction: ensuring that companies comply with their obligation to pay part of the cost of day care for their workers' pre-school children (for those workers who earn up to five times the minimum salary); reinforcement of training and employment programmes for young people and programmes for the prevention of adolescent pregnancy; and the programme for the nutritional enrichment of foodstuffs already referred to. All of these are of enormous importance, since they are targeted at medium-term and long-term effects.

Other countries in the region have also been drawing up and implementing social policies and programmes, some of them wide-ranging, which can stand as a reference for the actions required in this area.

Some final thoughts

The experience of the last few years has led to the conclusion that the real problem is not that of defining a social policy but that of defining the kind of society we want, and above all the kind of people we want to be. To this extent, the social question is not a sectoral problem but a national problem: not only the public sector but society as a whole bears responsibility here, especially those who have the most and who can therefore do the most.

Of all the components of society, the poor not only have borne most of the burden of maladjustment and of adjustment, but have made the greatest effort to adapt to the crisis. They have developed strategies that have allowed them to survive in an environment which is becoming continually more difficult, and yet they continue to provide society with ridiculously cheap labour.

The state has failed, above all because it has proved incapable of pushing through its own reforms for the improvement of services or for meeting the everyday needs of its citizens.

The community has also failed. Here the term "community" does not refer principally to the non-governmental bodies, still relatively weak, but to the more powerful private economic sectors which, like the state, have not done all they could, and which should do much more in future.

Despite these limitations, in recent years Latin American societies have shown signs of emerging from scepticism and apathy and of searching for new forms of organisation and participation. Rights which were violated for years are now forcefully asserted. In Venezuela, this has been reflected in the decentralisation processes, in the demand for a wide-ranging reform of the electoral system, in the increasing number of non-governmental bodies and also (why deny it?) in the current political crisis. Sometimes, the social forces which have been restrained for a long time break through impatiently and come to the fore, sweeping along even those who helped to open the flood-gates. Nevertheless, the changes taking place in citizens' organisations and participation have a positive aspect that allows us to take an optimistic view of the future, and they point towards a new reality, which we should go forward to meet.

Governance, the Transition to Modernity, and Civil Society

João Paulo dos Reis Velloso

The aim of this chapter is to show how the positive side of civil society's recent development can contribute to improving the conditions of governance in Latin America, and Brazil in particular, by defending true socio-economic modernity.

Governance and reforms

To place the theme in perspective, two statements are in order. First, the modernity exhibited by developed nations is at least threefold in nature: economic, social and political. Second, this "triple modernity" is the only basis for supporting the governance (in the sense of sustaining the existing regime) of any country in the long run.

The first statement evokes the well-known fact that in Europe after the Second World War there was a simultaneous consolidation of democracy (which in many countries had entered into a state of collapse in the period between the wars), development (through market economies in mixed regimes that combined government and private enterprise) and reasonable income distribution (among other things, through development of the welfare state). In earlier periods, one or more elements of this triple modernity still found themselves on fragile bases, despite the great progress made on several fronts in the late 19th and early 20th centuries: the advent of the second Industrial Revolution; improved living conditions for workers and at least a stabilized level of income concentration; and the beginning of the various mass movements (mass politics, mass education, mass consumption and mass culture). One may conclude that the Industrial Revolution begun in the late 18th century really achieved full legitimacy — in other words, participation of the great mass in modern, developed, democratic and social-minded capitalism — only in recent decades when threefold modernity became implanted in Europe.

Indeed, it is not just a matter of achieving triple modernity. This has to be of a global and indivisible quality, for modernity either exists in all dimensions (including the cultural, spiritual and ethical), or it quite simply does not exist at all. In the short and medium terms the most diverse relationships are possible between democracy, development and income distribution. In the long run, however, there exists an implicit solidarity among the three modernities. Not only does each one reinforce the others, but the inexistence of one of them (democracy, for instance) undermines the sustainability of the other two.

This leads to the second statement, which is so well illustrated by the failure of communist regimes in the former Soviet Union and Eastern Europe. It is often said in Russia that while Brezhnev slept, civil society was preparing a revolution. In the final analysis, the fall of the Berlin Wall was not a victory for capitalism; more precisely, it was a victory for civil society, which continues to stand at the forefront of events in those countries. In short, even communism, the only totalitarian regime hitherto considered unshakable, in the long run proved unsustainable.

These statements bear important implications for Latin America in the early 1990s. In the troubled 1980s the region managed to achieve a return to democracy, macroeconomic readjustment (still incomplete in Brazil) and a certain number of economic reforms. More recently, most countries have managed to emerge from the "lost decade" of debt crisis and begun to display reasonable prospects for expansion of GNP. All this is promising, but it is not enough.

On the one hand, democracy must be politically consolidated by gradual construction of a broader-based dominant coalition, reinforcement of the system of political parties, reform of the electoral systems and development of the political institutions generally. On the other, better conditions of governance are needed. Problems of governance have arisen in several Latin American countries, owing to economic crises, the state's inability to administer growing social demands and its difficulties in coping with the new functions that civil society has obliged it to assume. Examples are environmental issues, the problems of active minorities and demands for greater political participation.

To solve these problems, two tasks are considered as priorities: first, strengthening the socio-economic bases of democracy by finding new models of socio-economic development to replace the old "national-developmentist" model; second, strengthening the political bases of development through creation of a proper space for rational decisions within the state, to counter-balance the "client-wooing" and populist forces that pervade the region. Similarly, it is necessary to modernise the institutions responsible for reconciling mass politics and sound economic management: the executive, the national congress, the judiciary and organisations representing business and labour.

The recent history of the region shows signs that the problem has been recognised. One such sign is the tendency towards the shaping of a typology of new models of development: Chile's exporting model, Mexico's integration model and Brazil's model of complementarity between the internal and external markets. Another is the generalised awareness of the importance of reform of the state, whether to take into account the economic and political changes of the 1980s, to adapt to the demands of the new model of development or to show receptiveness to the new questions raised within civil society.

Yet another sign has to do with the growing importance of civil society in two developing tendencies: the normative "positive" tendency for development of new institutions outside the government sphere, taking on important representative responsibilities and functions, and the normative "negative" tendency for emergence of new visions, values and entities (with their respective pressures) that reveal the limitations of the conventional conception of the state[1].

Brazil's vicious circle

Brazil lags behind other Latin American countries in that it has not yet managed to bring about macroeconomic adjustment, implement economic reforms and emerge from the crisis. This is above all due to a vicious circle of stagflation — or more precisely, unsustained growth — which has continued since 1985. A second reason is linked to the lack of national direction: a national project — a strategic vision for the future of the country — is indispensable in Brazil, especially in view of the prevailing contingents of absolute poverty and extreme inequality.

These two economic phenomena are exacerbated by a similar backwardness in the intellectual and political transition begun in the late 1980s, which aims at economic and political modernisation (aggiornamento), the abandonment of old clientelist, populist practices and the search for a new model of development. Such a transition mainly consists in modernising both the right and the left in order to ready them for government, as in Europe. In Brazil, the transition is still in progress, and the resulting political instability is to a great extent responsible for macroeconomic instability (together with the series of heterodox shocks applied to the national economy after 1986). Emerging from the vicious circle calls for a minimum sense of national direction.

The difficulties in creating a national project are well known, especially since there is no new reference for the values and interests that should characterise it, and since there is still no dominant coalition capable of transforming the project into policies and programmes[2]. Nonetheless, the first elements of a new national project can already be discerned. In the first place, development can no longer be conducted by the state alone, since the state is itself going through a period of crisis and since the private sector and civil society would not accept such a role for it. The state will have to engage in partnerships, with private enterprise (and union federations), with States and municipalities, with the local community, or with several of these partners at the same time. The importance of acting through joint strategies, in both the economic and social spheres, is therefore manifest.

The second element of a new project is that development can no longer be conceived only in terms of building the nation, as in the period of "national-developmentism". It will also be necessary to build citizenship within the context of the development of civil society. The idea of "integral citizenship" exposed in Marshall's classic study is a distant, almost unreachable reality, especially for the masses who live in absolute poverty[3].

These masses exercise their political rights in the strict sense of being able to vote, but not in the broad sense of participating in the dominant social coalition and in the institutions of civil society. Few exercise their civil rights, since they do not have access to equal protection before law. Even fewer exercise their social rights, as they are largely outside the market economy and far from the social action of the state and community.

The National Forum and the attaining of modernity

In the last two decades, and especially in the last few years, civil society in Brazil has shown clear signs of development. Society in general is no longer willing to accept the tutelage of the state, particularly that of the federal executive power, which is traditional in Brazil and became exaggerated during the period of authoritarianism. A tendency towards decentralisation of powers has appeared, in favour of the national congress, the political parties, States and municipalities, and civil society.

Within civil society, interest groups and institutions independent from the state have begun to appear. Thus the trade-union movement has left aside its old corporatism and become independent. Employers' federations are developing, still partly associated with the corporatist spirit but also partly adopting an independent attitude. The press, universities and the church, with all their limitations and faults, have also begun to adopt an attitude of reasonable autonomy towards the state. A broad, associative spirit has developed, ranging from local residents' associations to social grassroots movements and the various forms of NGOs concerned with ecology, the defence of minorities and a range of other causes. To a large extent the state has lost its co-optive power over the other institutions. Indeed, the new danger is that interest groups and client-minded and populist forces will invade the state.

One manifestation of this activism on the part of civil society was the appearance, in 1988, of the National Forum, which is now institutionalised through the National Institute for Advanced Studies (INAE). From the start, the basic aim of the Forum was to contribute ideas and programmes towards the economic, social and political modernisation of the country within a pluralist vision embracing all non-radical political currents and all tendencies of economic, social and political thought. In short, the objective is the pursuit of the overall modernity which has guided European development in particular.

The Forum is mainly dedicated to two lines of action. The first is to promote dialogue among the leading groups of the nation. The annual meetings (the VI National Forum is scheduled for April 1994) and the other public seminars unite not only social scientists (economists, sociologists and political scientists), but also leaders of the national congress and representatives from business organisations, trade unions, universities and even the church. The second line of action refers to the promotion of closed workshops with the government for the presentation of concrete suggestions relating to principal national policies and themes, such as the stabilization programme, industrial policy, fiscal reform, constitutional revision and insertion into the international economy.

In the last two years — and this will continue in 1994 — the basic theme of the National Forum has been the shaping of a new model of development for Brazil, a model capable, above all, of answering two fundamental questions. One bears on economics: what lies ahead for Brazilian industry, especially in light of the new industrial and technological paradigm and worldwide tendencies towards globalisation and regionalisation? The other is social: what is to be done about poverty and inequality in Brazil?

To answer the first question, one must bear in mind that the Brazilian crisis interrupted not only growth but also, as a consequence, the formation of the mass consumer market that had begun in the late 1970s. At present the two pillars of that formation, employment and real wages, are weakening. To answer the second question, one must recall that Brazil has lately committed itself to a kind of "social activism"[4], namely the idea of concentrating maximal resources in the social area in an attempt to reinforce the traditional social policies of social security, medical assistance, education, housing, social assistance, etc. This commitment has come about as a reaction to two "false modernities": the authoritarian regime's simple emphasis on growth, and the promotion of neoliberal economic reforms associated with the Collor government. There can be no doubt that the problem of poverty and inequality — that is, of fostering social modernity — must be placed on the national agenda.

One must ask, however, whether "social activism" is not also a form of incomplete modernity, for two reasons. First, it has no priorities and does not constitute social reform. It involves spending in all directions, often on social consumption rather than on the social investment needed for the development of human capital in the country. It is merely a matter of "doing more of the same", along the whole line of traditional social policies which often prove highly inefficient and unequal (for example, the poor are not the main target of such policies). Second, spending is out of control. The social security budget alone jumped from 2.5 per cent of GNP in 1987 to around 5 per cent in 1993. This substantially exacerbates the structural financial imbalance of the government and, consequently, contributes to wild inflation, which impedes growth.

The economic and social questions must be answered at the same time. The fate of the poor, the victims of inequality in Brazil, is linked to the possibility of promoting modern growth in a sustainable form, once the vicious circle has been broken. Growth would then be modern in two senses: in allowing absorption of the new industrial and technological paradigm and in incorporating a new social strategy into the strategy for economic growth. The vision, then, is one of growth with redistribution.

A socio-economic strategy formulated in two movements is needed. First, an economic framework is defined, based on a bidirectional market model. In synthesis, this states clearly that the Brazilian model, unlike the pure, Asian-NIE export model for manufactured goods, depends on the internal market in order to win markets overseas. The logic of the model therefore lies in the complementarity between the home and foreign markets, simultaneously taking into account the country's continental dimensions and commitment to international competitiveness. This type of model is characteristic of continental countries, such as the United States, whose exports account for only 10 per cent of the GNP, despite their strategic significance. The same might be said of Brazil.

At this point, consideration should be given to the complex phenomenon of a continent-sized country dimensions. On one hand, given the abundance of natural resources, continental size allows for differentiated comparative advantages of both the traditional and the modern types and for use of the home market as a point of support for the export drive. (Brazil's GNP is equal to the sum of the GNPs of the four Asian tigers.) On the other, it gives a certain illusion of wealth (in the old sense of abundance of conventional materials), and may imply a certain lack of social cohesion. That is why George Kennan calls nations like the United States, Russia, China and Brazil "monster countries"[5].

From a strictly economic perspective, the model can be seen mainly as the integration of three axes: industrial restructuring (in order to develop the country's new dynamic competitive advantages associated with niches of high technology, and to recycle the advantages won in the previous industrial paradigm), acceleration of technical and scientific progress (to intensify the use of knowledge — innovation, in its broad sense — on behalf of economic growth and social progress) and insertion into the international economy (not only to expand exports and imports, but also, and especially, to form strategic alliances and absorb externalities in the areas of technology and management).

A point to be emphasized here is that absorption of the new paradigm (and herein lies the answer to the question on Brazil's industrial future) represents both a great risk and a great opportunity. The risk derives from the modern character of the new paradigm. It is a matter of pursuing a new type of wealth, through factors of production that depend on recent scientific learning, upgrading the country's human capital, and incorporating the generic technologies of the new paradigm (electronics and information technology, telecommunications, new methods of management) into economic activity across the board.

The opportunity comes from the country's comparative advantages in modernising those sectors prominent in the previous paradigm, and in niches of high technology (commuter aircraft, customised capital goods and electronic-based machine tools, offshore oil drilling, computerised systems for banks, software, and engineering in general). Furthermore, for manufacture of the new products, the country can rely on its broad, reasonably efficient industrial base to form strategic alliances and subcontracting networks.

The second movement entails building a socio-economic strategy. This is essentially a matter of incorporating into the strategy we have outlined a number of complementary lines that are social in nature but nonetheless foster growth. These lines represent, above all, a massive investment in human capital (chiefly education for modernity) as a central element in a new industrial paradigm and as a social objective in itself. Thus attention is focussed on social spending, with top (but not exclusive) priority's being given to the investment that is indispensable to modern growth: essentially education, public health, general sanitation (especially water), training of the labour force and child nutrition. This effort in the area of human capital includes dismantling mechanisms in the field of education and the labour market that perpetuate poverty and inequality.

A further complementary line would support the creation of networks between large and small firms, with a view to expanding employment as well as the entrepreneurial base (through micro and small firms). Another would foster the implantation of both rural and urban integrated models for the purpose of reducing the subsistence economy quickly. The experience of the models of integrated rural development (and schemes to support low-income farmers) should be reviewed in order to include the idea of a technological shock for small producers, either through agricultural firms or co-operatives from the centre-south region (without neglecting the rural extension system).

Finally, support should be given to the development of production and consumption of staple goods (meat, milk, corn and soybeans). In the long-term improvement of working-class living standards in today's developed nations, a crucial role was played by increasing the supply and lowering the real relative prices of these basic products. A first step in this direction would be to reduce the tax burden imposed on their production and transfer the reduced costs to the consumer.

We thus have a new vision of social modernity. Instead of emphasizing consumption transfers, social security benefits and *assistencialismo*, the idea is to incorporate into the economic model lines of social action that enhance the capacity of poor citizens to generate income, especially through increased access to employment, human capital formation and other forms of capital generation. The aim is to strengthen the poor citizen as a unit of production, income and consumption, and so to "teach him how to fish", as the saying goes. This focus makes an immediate contribution to the formation of the mass consumer market, to the reduction of poverty and, in the long run, to the improvement of income distribution by changing the profile of human capital in the country.

As one of its strategic connections, this socio-economic framework should be articulated with the institutional political regime, as it is vital to modernise legal and institutional instruments on both the economic and social levels. The relationship with the system must involve a continuous process of feedback to induce congress and the political parties, in addition to other forms of social representation, to participate in the integrated process outlined above[6].

Principal requirements of the proposal

In view of the scope of certain suggestions made and the fact that we are using an unconventional concept of what is "social", we must be aware of the limitations and obstacles to the implementation of this proposal. This set of reforms must be introduced gradually. It is impossible to sweep off the table the existing structure of bureaucracy and traditional clienteles, but, for that very reason, it is necessary to act with determination.

From the economic-financial point of view, carrying out the socio-economic strategy will hinge on success in obtaining resources for the integration, in one single process, of industrial restructuring, techno-scientific progress and education for modernity. This includes resources from the federal government, the BNDES (National Development Bank) and the international financial institutions that support Brazil's development.

This requirement means, in the first place, control of "autonomous budgets", such as those of social security, costs of federal administrative staff and current costs of state-owned companies. Further ahead, it will mean having access to public savings (which at present are non-existent). From the political-institutional point of view, implantation of the strategy and social reforms will depend on reform of the social model of the state at all levels: federal, State and municipal. On the federal level, the first major change is the reformulation of the obligations of the nation with respect to ministries such as education, health, regional integration and social welfare, in order to transfer the responsibility for essentially local projects to the states and municipalities. The counterpart of this transfer should be to consolidate normative and co-ordinating structures within the same ministries.

Another problem to be faced is the creation of financial mechanisms. Federal funds cannot be distributed to programmes (those that continue to receive federal support) through the bureaucratic bodies of the administration. Experience has shown that this results in misapplication of funds and corruption. Therefore, just as the economic area has official banks, the social area likewise needs mechanisms to finance projects: for instance, a social-development company, which could even be a subsidiary of the BNDES.

In the three spheres of government, and especially on the State and local levels, the basic task should be to reformulate the structures of implementation. If there is decentralisation, local structures must be more efficient, and the whole process more transparent and more subject to internal and external control. This underlines the importance of such reforms as strengthening the career system through promotion by merit, re-assessing the system of incentives, increasing receptivity to the requirements of the economy and society, and gaining autonomy in the face of political pressures and the influence of clienteles and interest groups.

Conclusion

The transition that Brazil is currently going through is complex and difficult, but common concepts and language are gradually emerging to articulate a vision for the future which is realistic and motivating, general and specific, political and practical. The National Forum, within its possibilities, seems to be playing a formative role in developing this national project by bringing together the major groups in Brazil with power to affect the future. We can only hope that the emerging consensus will continue to engage broader segments of society, and that progress will continue to be made in the specific projects which derive from the articulation of the national project. Finally, if this process works in Brazil, perhaps it can serve as a useful experience for other countries struggling with similar challenges.

Notes and References

1. These tendencies are identified by Colin I. Bradford, Jr., in the Introduction to this volume, "Redefining the Role of the State: Political Processes, State Capacity and the New Agenda in Latin America".

2. Luciano Martins, "Projeto de desenvolvimento, sistema politico e a crise do Estado-Nação", paper prepared for the V National Forum, 1993.

3. T.H. Marshall, (1950), *Class, Citizenship and Social Development*, 1950; republished by Greenwood Press, Newport, 1973.

4. The concept of "social activism" is presented in a slightly different form by Ricardo Hausmann, "Sustaining Reform: What Role for Social Policy?", in this volume.

5. George F. Kennan, *Around the Cragged Hill*, W.W. Norton, New York, 1992.

6. For a more extensive presentation of the new model, see João Paulo dos Reis Velloso, "Innovation and Society: The Modern Bases for Development with Equity", in Colin I. Bradford, Jr., ed., *The New Paradigm of Systemic Competitiveness: Towards More Integrated Policies in Latin America*, OECD Development Centre, Paris (forthcoming).

Recasting State-Union Relations
in Latin America

J. Samuel Valenzuela

In the closing decade of the 20th century, after the most severe economic crisis since the early 1930s, Latin America is in the throes of a new phase of development, with new departures in the economy, politics and social institutions. The new phase is characterized economically by a greater opening to the international market, by an increased emphasis on private rather than state investment and initiative as the motor of economic growth, and by a reliance on market signals and incentives as the key mechanism for economic coordination among agents. Politically, there is once again a shift to fragile democracies after a wave of transitions out of military and other forms of authoritarian rule. The states of the area, in response to their recent fiscal crises, have sought to limit their participation in the economy, resulting not only in privatizations of state enterprises but also in a reformulation of social security, health, educational and housing programs, giving greater weight to the private sector in these areas. The changes toward this new phase of development are far from complete, and some countries have gone farther into it than others, particularly in terms of economic opening and privatizations.

The challenges that lie ahead in this new phase are formidable. It is imperative for Latin America to grow economically at a rapid pace. The gap between the region and the advanced industrial economies has only increased during the 20th century, and it is high time to reverse the trend. The region must also deepen its new or re-established democracies and reinvigorate its older ones. To this end, aside from reaffirming its democratic political institutions, it must enhance the governability of its national societies. If the poverty that prevents so many from participating fully as citizens in national life is to diminish, growth must be accompanied by increased equity. Parties, interest groups, community organizations, labor unions, business and professional associations can — or should be able to — flourish under the democratic settings, permitting the development of channels for expressing demands and of mechanisms for negotiating compromises over the numerous differences and conflicts that are the normal expression of free societies. The richer the texture of such organizations, the stronger will be the daily affirmation of citizenship rights, and the greater the chances for the development of civic cultures that will, in turn, enhance the social basis of consensus necessary for the secure functioning of the area's democratic regimes.

The new phase of Latin American development contains a mix of political and economic factors that no late developers have attempted to combine in the same way before. Prior cases, including most recently the Asian newly industrialized economies (NIEs), relied heavily on state directives for their growth. The Asian NIEs also developed since the early 1950s largely under authoritarian regimes that prevented the formation of autonomous and freely acting labor unions, interest organizations and community groups; democratization has only recently and tentatively begun to make its way in the area. The question therefore becomes: Is the new Latin American model viable? Is it possible to have high growth, greater equity, trade liberalization, a reliance on private initiative, and at the same time to advance in the consolidation of democracy, which grants its citizens not only the right to vote but also the freedom to form and/or strengthen all kinds of organizations, some of which, as is the case with labor unions, can have an impact on markets?

This question obviously cannot be answered fully in the context of this brief chapter, nor would it be easy to do so in a longer treatment of the matter. The purpose here is to address it from the perspective of the relations between labor, business and the state, while keeping the overall context in mind. In particular, how could the enhanced labor rights and the possibly stronger union movement that normally go hand in hand with political democratization contribute to the success of the new phase of Latin American development? What kind of labor organizations does this require, and what role should the state play in forging new labor relations?

This chapter is organized around six themes, for each of which we can only touch on complex issues and hint at optimal scenarios.

Democratic governance: states and civil societies

Democratic regimes are much more stable, orderly and consensual when their governance is located to a significant extent in decisions and actions taken directly in civil society rather than by the state, even if the state may at times be indirectly involved as rule-maker or guarantor of rights and procedures. If religious differences are an important fault line in the national societal fabric, it is all the more necessary for religious leaders to build strong ecumenical institutions, in which the problems that arise can be discussed in order to reach the appropriate understandings and arrangements to resolve them. The same is true for ethnic, linguistic and interest group conflicts. The encouragement of the state may be needed for such institutions to emerge, but they will usually fail to do so if the state actively discourages their formation. The greater the capacity of such social institutions to bridge differences, the less potential conflicts need to be resolved by the government, and the less such conflicts are politicized. Democratic stability is much more solid when it also rests on fluid relations among social groups rather than only on the ability of political organizations to "represent" and "channel" demands and interests to the legislative and/or executive spheres of government, where conflicts are presumably to be resolved. The processing of conflict and the building of democratic consensus therefore rests on two pillars: civil and political societies.

This is not intended to suggest that civil societies are an autonomous primordial source for building overall national stability and governance. As O'Donnell indicates, there is no easily determined borderline between the state and civil society — contrary to what is suggested in static and succinct definitions of the state that emphasize its location in permanent offices, its monopoly of force, and its function as the source of legally based and binding decisions for people living in a given territory. The legal apparatus — and as O'Donnell notes in particular, the formal rights of citizenship — enacted and enforced by state officials often provides an essential base for the formation of, and the relations between, organized groups and even individuals in civil society. As such, the characteristics of these groups and their relations already reflect to some extent the nature of the state and its laws[1]. Taking an extreme example, forms of work organization that are based on slavery are incompatible with democratic citizenship rights.

The laws may also establish procedures that groups in civil society must follow to resolve their disputes, and state officials may be involved in overseeing their operation. Yet this involvement should facilitate, not impair, the expression of conflicting positions and the substantive search for agreement among groups. Changes of regime also lead, or should lead, to many changes in the way the state operates and becomes implicated in the daily workings of civil society. As a result, processes of regime consolidation after transitions have much to do with the way in which relations between the state and civil society are altered. We may speak of the instauration of democratic regimes when the formal political and constitutional elements required are in place, with elected governments, but a deepening of such regimes involves a more or less slow structuring of civil societies in a manner that reflects a new form of state action (or inaction).

Labor-employer relations are a fundamental component of any civil society. The degree of conflict or consensus between these two agents can have a significant impact on the governability of national societies, on the relative success or failure of economic growth, and on democratic stability. Invariably, the state through its laws, regulations, and officials is much more obviously involved in the formation of the interest organizations of these two segments — especially of labor unions — than of other social groups, and it is much more present in structuring their relations. This involvement began with the escalation of labor conflict as workers sought to overcome prohibitions on their collective action that were contained in most 19th-century legislation, rooted as it was in liberal ideologies that enshrined individualism. The question since then is not whether the state should be involved in shaping industrial relations, but what form this involvement should take.

Following the premise that conflicts are best resolved directly in civil society, firm-level industrial relations should be set up in such a way that business and labor organizations are led to resolve their differences with a minimum of directive interference by state or government officials. State enterprises should be managed independently of government officials, and should use the same rules as the private sector in negotiating with their employees. Only public functionaries, including teachers and health workers in state-run institutions, would engage government ministries directly.

A series of conditions must be present if the negotiations between labor and business are to contribute veritably to governability. The state can be instrumental in establishing these conditions through laws and their application. The characteristics of labor organization will be discussed in more detail later; suffice it to say here that labor — and where relevant, business — organizations must have leaders whose mandates are subject to renewal following procedures that are clear-cut and transparent, giving them the necessary legitimacy to enter into binding agreements. Labor organizations must have their own sources of funding, such that their autonomy is not compromised. The laws that apply to the creation of business and labor organizations as well as the relations between them must be viewed by both sides as being generally fair, even if specific minor aspects are unsatisfactory. If they are not, one side or the other will seek to change the rules, usually *de facto*, rather than to concentrate on using them to build agreements with its counterpart.

The laws should be strictly enforced under state oversight, which is all the more reason why they should be accepted by both sides as fair; if there are aspects that are not appropriate, the laws should be changed following the normal procedures for legal reforms, rather than circumvented or violated. Relations between labor and business groups cannot be properly built upon the basis of norms that are only partially applied. There is nothing more frustrating, in particular to unions and their leaders, and — in historical perspective — more radicalizing of labor movements, than legal rights and advantageous procedures that exist only on paper. It is better for laws to be overly restrictive, and applied fully, than generous in the concession of rights and privileges, but applied only haphazardly.

Looking back over the past century, it is possible to find innumerable instances in which these basic conditions, seemingly so simple, have not been present in Latin America. Labor organizations have often not been autonomous from state (and sometimes employer) interference and political manipulation; as a result, labor leaders have at times not been viewed as fully legitimate by their bases, by employers, and even by the authorities themselves. Government officials have often intervened to settle labor disputes through any number of means, such as repressing labor leaders and forcing workers to accept conditions they do not like, or forcing employers to agree to pay workers at a higher level in exchange for tax breaks, direct subsidies, or tariff protection. Labor laws have been violated repeatedly, and labor rights, sometimes loftily stated as in the Mexican constitution of 1917, have existed principally on paper. State interventions have bred systems of industrial relations in which the parties press many conflicts to the point of obtaining the attention and resolution of government officials. Political exchanges become then unavoidably built into labor relations, favoring disproportionately the larger and stronger sectors of unionism, and a significant divorce sets in between legal norms and actual practices[2]. Once the way for the politicization of labor relations has been opened, this aspect of civil societies will fail to develop fully its potential ability to forge social consensus and to enhance democratic governability apart from substantive state interference.

Latin American government authorities have often viewed intervention in labor (and even business) organizations, as well as in labor relations, as a normal tool of state power to be used to enhance their objectives, whether these be to facilitate economic policies, or to enhance political control and mobilization in favor of the government and its party or parties. Permitting social organizations to flourish independently and to establish a capacity to forge opinions, to convoke concerted action, and to negotiate over matters that have an impact over the national economy certainly implies letting spaces of authority in society to escape *direct* state influence. Such limitations on the use of state authority are an essential building block of mature democracies, and should be valued intrinsically for this reason.

This does not mean that government planners should not seek, if necessary, to convince labor and business organizations to follow certain guidelines in resolving the substantive issues before them. In doing so they would be trying to reason with independent agents, rather than imposing a view on pliant organizations; there is a fundamental difference between these courses of action. Moreover, in addition to being able (with legislative approval) to change the legal framework that applies to labor and business organizations and to their relations, policy-makers have many resources to mold the socio-economic environment in which labor-management negotiations take place. As a result, they can exert a great deal of *indirect* influence over those negotiations. Opening the economy to the international market has, for instance, an enormous effect on setting the conditions under which labor/ management negotiations will take place. Creating an unemployment insurance program also affects the labor market, as it permits unemployed workers to hold off from accepting just any job that is offered to them. Hence, state policies can create incentives and disincentives for labor and business actors that will condition their negotiations and their outcomes. In the long run, direct state intervention in labor and business organizations and in their relations is probably less effective than such indirect means for instrumental state policy-making goals, and it has the negative effect of undermining construction of a self-replicating basis of consensus formation in this segment of civil society.

Certain forms of labor (and business) organizations are more conducive not only to forging consensus between the two parties, but also to doing so in ways that should contribute to economic performance in the new phase of Latin American development. States can also generate the necessary incentives for such types of organizations to emerge. These points require more detailed elaboration.

Strong or weak labor organizations?

Many political leaders, neo-liberal (or neo-conservative?) analysts and employers would prefer to have weak labor unions, if not to do away with unions entirely. They assume that this will help generate rapid economic growth, which they see, when and if they reflect on the matter, as the only means of enhancing the chances of reaching stable democracies in the future. They note that unions often support unrealistic, inflationary programs and demagogic populist politicians. They argue that unions also tend to undermine growth by raising labor costs, creating unnecessary conflicts and strikes, rigidifying the operation of the labor market (viewed from the perspective of interactions by individual agents), and interfering with managerial prerogatives in designing work procedures, rules and schedules; ostensibly, unions thereby deprive the enterprises of the flexibility needed to adopt new technologies and respond rapidly to changing markets. In this view, unions also tend to constitute labor aristocracies, and their pressures on wages and social services have generally regressive impacts on the distribution of income, since they favor middle to lower-middle income earners, not the poor.

While many enterprises, old and new, have been able to avoid the unionization of their work forces, no country has obliterated all traces of labor organization, even under the harshest authoritarian regimes. Moreover, the current phase of Latin American development includes political democracy among its mix of ingredients. Transitions to democracy and the deepening of democratization are associated normally with a strengthening of unions and labor movements, although this effect may, in specific cases, not be visible because of the coincidental presence of union-debilitating factors such as high unemployment, a decline of heavily unionized sectors of industry or mining, or peculiar political circumstances associated with the transition. Citizenship in a democracy permits by definition the organization of interest groups; moreover, workers can vote, thereby becoming important potential constituencies for political leaders, and union leaders and militants should be able to act without fearing gross abuses of their human rights through the action of overt or covert state agents, or private ones acting with impunity — an elementary fact of civilized life that has too frequently been missing in Latin America. Where in the past unions lost autonomy owing to authoritarian regimes' efforts to control labor through its leaders and organizations, they should become more able to act independently; and where the scope of unions was curtailed by limitations on affiliation and by circumscription of collective bargaining, they should be able to use the new freedoms to attempt to recoup their losses[3]. In sum, Latin American countries cannot count on following models of development that obliterate unions, and unions can currently be expected to become more — not less — relevant as national actors than in the recent past. The much discussed crisis in unionism, as Campero indicates, is not a symptom of the disappearance of unions as social actors; rather, it reflects the growing pains of a new model of union organization, which in turn reflects the changes associated with the new phase of Latin American development[4]. But how strong can Latin American unionism be?

The notion of union strength is much more complicated than it appears at first glance. Density of affiliation in the total salaried labor force (the most common indicator) does not convey the extent to which the union membership may be concentrated in key segments of economic activity, the degree to which members are active or simply passive participants in union affairs, the extent of the audience union leaders can command at critical moments beyond their affiliated members, the connections labor leaders may have with important parties that can magnify their influence, or the disproportionately greater or lesser presence of unions in principal cities, such as Lima-Callao or Montevideo, which are centers of all walks of national life. Each one of these considerations adds to or detracts from relative union strength. Nowhere in Latin America, however, can unions even hope to reach the levels of union affiliation and strength found in northern Europe. At best Latin America has labor movements of medium strength.

Returning to our earlier assumptions, does strengthening unions really have significant political and economic drawbacks? This need not be so. In some cases labor movements were prey to populist appeals, given the prior failure of business and the state to permit the development of normal industrial relations and union rights. *It is precisely the weakness of the pre-existing union organizations that created the context for labor manipulation by populist leaders.* How different the social and political history of postwar Argentina would have been if autonomous unions with regular patterns of collective bargaining with employers had gained a solid foothold in civil society under democratic government by the mid-1930s!

Unions can also make important direct and indirect contributions to economic growth. This depends on the type of economic development, on the organizational characteristics of unions, and on the way industrial relations fit into democratic politics. The following section will depict an admittedly ideal, but not unrealistic, scenario of how these elements may be combined in the new phase of Latin American development.

What kind of development?

Two national economies may well have similar levels of economic growth, as measured by per capita income figures, and may be equally open to the international market, but their growth may be based on entirely different underlying processes. In one it may take the form of increasing the production and export volumes of goods requiring little elaboration; in the other, that of upgrading the value added of what is produced. In the long run it is safe to assume that the second country is on a more solid route to development. Unless the first economy can continually find new export markets for the increased volume of its primary goods production — and that of course has its limits — it will eventually stagnate; the prices for its products are unlikely to rise enough to compensate for the saturation of its markets, and its terms of trade are likely to deteriorate. As a cushion to compensate for this effect and for unexpected oscillations in demand, the primary goods economy will have to put a cap on labor costs, as it is viable only if wages are relatively low. Labor costs are main ones over which export producers have some control, and since the enterprises in the field will tend to have conservative estimates for the future prices of their goods, they will strive to retain low labor costs in order to ensure profitability even with those prices. This pattern of development has every probability of leading to severe labor conflicts if workers are able to unionize, and if levels of unemployment decline.

Export producers are very vulnerable to organized workers' pressures, given their need to meet international sales contract obligations within specified periods, and there will frequently be a significant mismatch between labor's and management's estimations of future profits. Moreover, since the state will normally depend for a significant portion of its revenues on the profitability of the export enterprises, its authorities will often tend to side with the enterprises' calculations. Twentieth-century Latin America contains many examples of the severe, sometimes bloody, conflicts and dislocations that can emerge in these situations. Under these conditions, employers will prefer to have weak and pliant unions, but as they are located in the central axis of the national economy, to produce such weakness would require state interference. Needless to say, these conditions have little affinity with the kind of civil society arrangements delineated above.

139

While relatively low wages will be one comparative advantage in international markets (and in the internal markets of open economies) of a type of development based on increasing value added, it should nonetheless be possible to raise them progressively as well as to enhance working conditions. This second type of development will produce goods of increasing complexity (permitting a broader range of points where productivity can be enhanced) and a broader variety of goods that can command higher prices. It will also increase the technological sophistication of its productive apparatus, and therefore generate better jobs and require a greater diversification of skills. The second economy is also more likely to have a more equitable pattern of growth than the first type, and the union movement that develops is more likely to spread across the economy with a more even level of strength instead of concentrating in the high-stakes primary export sector. Obviously, this form of development is to be preferred over the previous one, as it not only augurs better growth in the future but also provides a better basis upon which to ground labor relations.

Most Latin American economies contain a mixture of both forms of development, and a key to the future is the continual growth of the second one. Although its success in the current phase of development depends on the response of private investors, national and foreign, state policies should be geared to facilitate it. This includes making sure that firms can count on the infrastructure and advanced communications needed to move products rapidly to markets; that exchange rates remain well in line with the currencies of major trading partners; that interest rates be reasonable; that tax incentives be offered for investments that upgrade technologies or for firms that do their own research, design, and development; that assistance be available to new producers who could place their products in export markets; and so on.

The second type of development is favored, not hindered, where there is a *moderate* upward pressure on wages. The investment climate should not attract investors who depend on the current wage levels to produce goods that other economies with even lower wages can easily make in the near future, or those who need to compensate — via low wages — for higher production costs that stem from the use of obsolete technologies. New investments should contemplate higher wage costs — which should nonetheless be lower than those of advanced countries given the lower wage levels in Latin American economies — to produce goods that are equal in quality and in design to those of the most competitive producers in the international economy. Wages would still provide a cost advantage to Latin American economies, but over time, as development proceeds, their levels should be increasing, narrowing the gap with more developed economies. Naturally, this form of development will succeed only if producers in Latin America respond to upward pressures on wages or to the saturation of the markets for their less sophisticated products by innovating technologically and by switching their production to new and more upscale products. Business must face up to this challenge. The long-run development of the area cannot be secured if investors consistently look to the state to secure lower labor costs and/or subsidies and protection from imports, which will simply compensate for their own failure to invest and to update facilities and technologies. These solutions to a lack of competitiveness can only be adopted as exceptional temporary measures after a strict commitment to restructuring programs.

The upward pressure on wages should be moderate enough for enterprises to adjust to the new costs, and the overall economy to the new levels of consumer spending. As long as labor unions contribute to that type of pressure, or to the perception that this pressure exists, they are doing nothing but assisting in creating the type of investment climate that is most conducive to long-term development. Yet, there is an additional condition for labor unions to have this general effect.

If an economy is to undertake a rapid form of development, using more productive technologies to produce a wider variety of goods with higher value added, it must engage in a permanent process of investment and restructuring. As a result, the skills of many workers will lose value, work places will often be in a process of acquiring new procedures and technologies, and some enterprises will trim the size of their work forces. If unions were to oppose these changes systematically, the result would not only be increased labor conflict; unions would stand in the way of the flexibility needed for these forms of continual restructuring.

Such union attitudes are defensive responses that can certainly be minimized if the necessary measures inducing workers to act differently are in place. This means, first, that labor legislations should not permit managers to carry out drastic changes in work places without at least informing employees in due time of their plans, allowing them the necessary time to adjust. Latin American enterprises have generally resisted fiercely any provisions that would impinge on their ability to organize work at will, but they must at least advise workers of the changes they are about to make. Second, it is absolutely fundamental to have an adequate unemployment insurance program, preferably funded by employer and employee contributions and administered by, or with the oversight of, business and labor representatives. State finances should not be burdened, except perhaps as the ultimate guarantor, with unemployment payments that may cause or inflate fiscal deficits. Moreover, if employer and labor representatives fund and administer the system, there is a better probability that it will not be abused by those who draw funds while hiring or working clandestinely. Third, it is crucial that workers, old and new, have access to proper training programs at only nominal cost to them. The jobs that they lose sometimes took years of skill acquisition to perform adequately, and if new technologies do away with them, they should have a chance to update their abilities in order to find new forms of employment. Training programs should focus on preparing workers for the kinds of jobs that the next phase of development in the economy will presumably require. The existence of a qualified work force is a powerful incentive to lead investors into establishing new firms, or into changing existing production lines. Training programs should also be run, or at least overseen, by business and labor representatives.

The often visible conservatism of unions — in the sense that they seek to preserve their current jobs, job rights, and work procedures — can be diminished if workers see alternatives to taking defensive actions against restructuring, and if union organizations have a presence in the institutions that tide workers over during periods of unemployment. Whether these institutions exist depends on state initiatives, as they must be set up by enabling legislation. Much labor conflict can be avoided through these means, and union resistance to technological innovations can decrease noticeably if not disappear altogether. After all, Latin American workers stand to gain in the long run by facilitating industrial restructuring — a point that, given current wage levels, is less clear in highly advanced economies. Unions can then focus much more easily on the requirements of production and the logic of investment planning by firms, and can locate the defense of worker interests not narrowly in individual firms, but in the labor market as a whole.

The economy can obviously not be transformed overnight. Many jobs will continue to be in lower-wage sectors. If they are also export sectors, labor pressures, as noted above, can be very strong. In some countries groups of relatively well-paid workers (although not by developed world standards), as is the case in oil and in some mining industries, will remain in a basic axis of the national economy, with considerable power to affect through their actions its performance and fiscal revenues. In all these segments, once a fair level of compensation for labor has been determined and reached, labor restraint is needed, limiting wage increases to productivity gains and concentrating union vigilance on working conditions and job safety.

Labor restraint in these and, when needed, in other sectors can best be reached if labor movement leaders become, together with employer association representatives, regular participants in dialogues with economic policy makers over trends in the national economy, its export markets, and its macroeconomic equilibria. This leads to the fourth theme.

The importance of macroeconomic equilibria

How can the above-mentioned "fair level of compensation" for workers be determined? Obviously, beyond the most blatant inequities in which labor costs represent minute proportions of enterprise profits, as has occurred in some Latin American primary export enterprises[5], this level is very hard to determine, and unions, enterprises, government, and independent observers will disagree over the matter. The simplest solution is to rely on the operation of the external labor market, but this is a less neutral mechanism than appears to be the case, for the following reason.

In less developed countries, national and foreign investors normally demand higher returns on their investments than those that they would consider reasonable in advanced economies, given what they perceive as the higher risk involved. Leaving aside the political uncertainties that may affect this higher risk, it is largely due to the fact that the national and export markets are more precarious, and the macroeconomic conditions impinging on their success much more variable. Interest and exchange rates can change drastically, and the levels of inflation can vary by large amounts from one year, even one month, to the next, producing large losses — or large gains. Investors consider extraordinary gains a just reward for the greater risk they have taken, and a cushion for the large losses that are also possible at another moment.

One way to minimize the risk is to control one of the costs over which firms have greater certainty, namely labor costs. If these are kept appropriately low, profits can be obtained even when other variables do not turn out to be particularly favorable. As this form of cushioning firms from the possible adverse effects of unforeseen variations is multiplied across the economy, the labor market tends to reflect these decisions, producing employment at lower wage levels than would otherwise be the case. Consequently the labor market is affected by the perceptions of investor risk, and this introduces an additional bone of contention in labor relations. What is "fair compensation" from the perspective of labor unions does not include this extra margin, which frequently turns out not to be necessary anyway; labor leaders look at the bottom line of their firms rather than at wage levels in the external labor market.

In this context, labor/management relations would certainly be smoother in the medium to long run, and wage levels higher, if the macroeconomic environment were relatively stable. Business would then not have to try to minimize risks by calculating labor costs so conservatively, and labor leaders could press for wage levels and other compensations that produce a better distribution of the fruits of the enterprises. These calculations apply to all sectors of the economy, but they are especially important where technological gains or product enhancements are unlikely to raise wage levels.

While the preservation of macroeconomic equilibria is primarily a concern for government policy makers, labor and business organizations should also develop a capacity to analyze the national economy as a whole, and should participate in discussions with each other and with state planners over economic trends. It is best if all sides agree to collaborate in taking the necessary measures to reduce the risks of macroeconomic disequilibria. If necessary, labor should contribute wage moderation to restore lost equilibria. Such a strategy should pay off in the medium to long run, as any attempt to advance wages rapidly above expected inflation levels will only induce other economic agents who can respond to market signals more rapidly to recoup their own losses, with even greater detrimental effects on real wages. However, policy makers should not force labor and the popular sectors generally to bear single-handedly the cost of restoring the equilibria, as occurred in Latin America during the 1980s[6]. There is no lack of policy instruments to ensure that the burdens are distributed more fairly.

Unfortunately, labor leaders in Latin America have not paid sufficient attention to the importance of macroeconomic equilibria, and few labor movements have the capacity to analyze the national economy as a whole. State authorities should take the initiative in convoking labor (and business) leaders to such discussions, and over time labor organizations should begin to have more sophisticated approaches to this matter. In the end, a more equitable distribution of the resources generated by enterprises should be possible.

The special case of public sector unionism

Organized government employees, including teachers and postal, health, social and municipal service workers, constitute a special case within national union movements, and they require a brief separate comment. Given that they are on the fiscal payroll, government policy makers expect them to respond readily and favorably to demands for wage restraint to conserve fiscal resources, to set a pattern for the rest of the economy, and to help maintain or restore macroeconomic equilibria. Yet, in many Latin American countries public sector workers are among the most active participants in strikes (even where they are prohibited by law from striking) and protest movements, and they have some of the strongest unions. The result is that some of the most acrimonious labor relations today concern the public sector.

It is very difficult not to sympathize with the demands of these employees given the erosion of their real wages and of their working conditions as a result of the retrenchments of the state sector since the late 1970s and early 1980s[7]. It is not possible to retain a sense of purpose and a commitment to public service among these employees, many of whom are professionals with strong vocational callings, when they are unable to meet even the basic necessities of a lower-middle-class life style. The quality of indispensable state-run services for the proper functioning of national economies and societies depends in part on the motivation of its employees. It is hard to retain that motivation if salaries fall to such low levels[8].

It is impossible to correct this situation rapidly, but plans should be drawn up to redress the salaries and working conditions of state employees in stages, negotiating the details with representatives of the various public sector unions. It may be difficult to avoid new conflicts, but at least a new effort is required to revalue public sector employment, and its workers should see some light at the end of the tunnel. Where public sector workers have job security and favorable pension and other benefits, they should also be willing to make every effort to forgo strike actions.

It should be noted emphatically that no program intended to rekindle a sense of commitment to public service, with what will always be, even after adjustments, relatively low salaries, will succeed if corruption runs rampant among high-level politicians and state and government officials. Ministers and sub-ministers cannot ask for wage restraint and sacrifices from their employees for the broader public good if their colleagues (if not they themselves) are widely perceived as making illicit gains at taxpayers' expense. Honesty from public officials is an essential component of governmental legitimacy and a prerequisite for proper labor relations in the public sector.

The characteristics of labor organizations

National labor movements are composed of organizations from at least three levels: in work places, union locals or workers' committees with strong union participation; at the occupational or industrial branch level, either unions with a national scope or federations of unions — depending on the nature of the lower-level organizations; and at the peak, national and confederal level. Strong labor movements normally have vibrant organizations at all three levels. Those that are weaker, given low densities of affiliation or less than favorable political connections, may have their "organizational weight" — so to speak — located primarily at one or another level, at two of them, or may have a good distribution of organizations at all three levels.

State policy makers should encourage the formation of labor movements with the latter characteristics, no matter how weak the overall levels of affiliation. It is very difficult for national union movements whose organizational weight is located heavily at the plant or, at best, the enterprise level, not to act mainly in a defensive way in response to local conditions. They do not normally develop the overall vision of the economy which is necessary for unions to act in ways that favor macroeconomic equilibria, or to facilitate technological innovation and restructuring by attempting to defend workers' interests in the labor market as a whole rather than simply in the existing jobs and work procedures within specific plants. The incentives for labor leadership careers in union movements that are heavily structured at the plant level revolve around what amounts to a conservative defense of local worker interests, a form of action that — when it hinders innovation and restructuring — is in the long run detrimental to the interests of the working class, as it slows economic modernization and development.

This is not to say that local organizations should be phased out. National union organizations without a plant-level presence become excessively weak, and union democracy suffers. Union weakness is likely to lead eventually to attempts to mobilize workers around local concerns in order to strengthen the labor movement, creating precisely the right incentives for the development of labor leaderships that generate plant-centered defensive actions. Such movements almost invariably provide a base for more radical labor and political leaders. Instead of weakening the local bases, the links between them and the federal and top national organizations should be strengthened, to the degree that the upper levels of labor leaderships acquire more of a directive capacity over the movement as a whole, while having their mandates emerge from a stronger participation (direct or indirect) of affiliates at the base. While this would give more power to the top labor leaders, it is, nonetheless, an unavoidable consequence of trying to forge industrial relations in ways that will contribute to national economic goals under democratic regimes. Labor movements must act in ways that take into account a view of the economy as a whole, as well as the production-enhancing requirements of firms, and this result can be obtained only if labor organizations are engaged in viewing workers' interests within the broader national and even international context.

Each rung of union organization should retain distinct functions, despite the co-ordination between them. Collective bargaining should take place at whatever level employers and workers agree to have it. In most areas of Latin American economies, where there is a wide disparity between the capitalization, working conditions, and productivity of firms and offices, the almost unavoidable result is that collective bargaining engages primarily local union leaders and organizations. Any attempt to do otherwise will be excessively detrimental to employees in the leading firms, and the result will simply be to revert eventually to localized bargaining. Nonetheless, branch-level organizations could try to establish minimal wages and working conditions in agreement with employers, and lead workers in opposing subcontracting by firms to smaller units if the latter employ obsolete procedures and rely on lengthy working hours and substandard working conditions to compensate for their lack of productivity. While such subcontracting may reduce labor costs in the leading firms, it becomes a mechanism to avoid investing in more competitive technologies, and lowers the modernization of the economy as a whole.

Branch-level organizations could also target collective bargaining on a typical firm, and use the agreement which is obtained as a model for others to follow. They should also co-operate with employer associations in managing the training programs for their area, conduct labor leadership training seminars, prepare periodic studies of conditions in their labor markets, and develop contacts with similar organizations in other countries.

The national level of union organization should participate in discussions with employer associations and the government over minimum wages and pensions — and over macroeconomic equilibria — for which it should develop the necessary technical capacity to suggest countermeasures to those prepared by its interlocutors. It should represent workers in negotiations with governments, employers, and legislatures over changes in labor legislation, and prepare to take part in legal suits over violations of labor laws in order to ensure that all the relevant legislation is fully applied. It should participate in discussions over national health, social security, housing and educational policies with a view to defending popular sector interests. It also should participate in the administration of the unemployment insurance funds.

Only if their functions are strengthened will the higher levels of union organization be able to exercise a directive role over the labor movement as a whole, preventing it from developing the negative and defensive culture that can easily grow in times of rapid change among localized organizations. The state should therefore encourage this type of union organizational development, even if it means strengthening the capacity of the unions to develop alternative proposals to those of policy makers and business leaders, and to oppose their initiatives. There will be disagreements, sometimes serious ones, and there will be conflicts; but that is what can be expected in a democratic society. The conflicts will occur, however, in a setting that contains the leaderships and the means needed for negotiations and, ultimately, for building social consensus over fundamental issues of national life by key actors in civil and political society.

Concluding comments

Can labor organizations and state, labor, and business relations in Latin America evolve towards the model depicted here? The governments of the area would have to foster it initially, and continue to play, where necessary, their part in maintaining it, and labor leaders and employer associations would have to commit themselves to making it work.

It is hard to be sanguine about its chances. Fundamental changes, albeit different ones from case to case, would be needed in most countries. Nowhere do union structures have a proper balance between their different organizational levels, and in some cases, primarily at this point in Mexico, they lack the necessary autonomy. Political, ideological, religious, and even personality divisions also affect the ability of labor organizations to develop the necessary internal consensus to present a single common position vis-à-vis governments and employer groups. Employers are also often divided into various organizations, and frequently no organization is considered fully representative even of the sectors it is supposed to represent. Governments would have to stimulate changes towards the model depicted above by working with several labor and employer organizations, hoping to initiate greater co-operation among them and more representativity on the part of those whose legitimacy is questionable.

Government officials may also be unwilling to risk enhancing the power and visibility of labor and/or business leaders they dislike by opting to press for this model. Indeed, some such leaders may have great difficulty in seeing beyond the narrow interests of their current members, despite their relatively high leadership positions.

In the end, the failure to advance toward this model means that labor/management relations in Latin America will continue to be characterized by conflicts resulting from defensive and bitter union attitudes that, given the proper incentives, are avoidable. As a result, this aspect of Latin American societies, which has been politically problematic in the past, will continue to be so in the future. It will be much harder to combine liberal economic policies, market discipline, and private initiative with social consensus — and therefore democratic stability — in the new phase of Latin American development than could otherwise be the case. While employers may derive some short-term benefit from the current relative weakness of unions, as labor gains strength it may well have the capacity to exert a significant influence, by which time it may manifest a negative and defensive posture that will generate otherwise needless conflicts. Yet, with the efforts of governments and the willingness of labor and business leaders to try forging a new future, the prospects could be much brighter, especially if care is taken to stimulate the formation of well balanced labor organizations that can become engaged at different levels of national life.

Notes and References

1.   For a preview of Guillermo O'Donnell's pioneering work on this subject in connection with problems of democratization, see his *On the State, Democratization and Some Conceptual Problems (A Latin American View with Glances at Some Post-Communist Countries)*, Kellogg Institute Working Paper, No. 192 (April 1993), Section 1.

2.   The notion of "political exchange" was developed by Alessandro Pizzorno in his seminal "Political Exchange and Collective Identity in Industrial Conflict", in Colin Crouch and Alessandro Pizzorno, eds, *The Resurgence of Class Conflict in Western Europe Since 1968*, Volume 2: *Comparative Analysis* (New York: Holmes and Meier Publishers, 1979), pp. 278-297.

   For a description of a system in which labor conflict is pursued by union leaders in ways designed to force government officials to intervene, see James L. Payne, *Labor and Politics in Peru: The System of Political Bargaining* (New Haven: Yale University Press, 1965). The book refers mainly to the period between the fall of Odría in 1956 and the early 1960s.

3.   The strategies of labor containment by authoritarian regimes and their consequences for democratization are discussed in J. Samuel Valenzuela, "Labor Movements in Transitions to Democracy: A Framework for Analysis", *Comparative Politics*, 21, 4 (July 1989). A revised Spanish translation of this paper, "El movimiento obrero en la transición hacia la democracia: un marco conceptual para su análisis", can be found in *Desarrollo Económico: Revista de Ciencias Sociales*, 30, 119 (October-December 1990).

4.   Guillermo Campero, "Sindicalismo en los 90': Desafíos y perspectivas", *Economía y Trabajo* (Santiago), 1, 2 (July-December 1993), pp. 25-44.

5.   Fruit production in Chile during the 1980s is a recent case in point, although greater inequities could be found in past Latin American experiences with sisal, rubber, and banana exports. The Chilean fruit enterprises were highly profitable, but most workers earned on average about \$3.25 to \$3.50 a day in 1988 according to figures in O. Daniel Rodriguez and L. Silvia Venegas, *Los trabajadores de la fruta en cifras* (Santiago: Universidad Academia de Humanismo Cristiano, Grupo de Estudios Agro-Regionales, 1991), p. 107. These incomes have increased in the early 1990s as a result of tighter labor markets, higher minimum wages introduced by the Aylwin government, and more extensive worker organization.

6.   There was a strong decrease in real wages and in popular sector incomes as a result of the economic adjustments in most of Latin America during the 1980s. Given the fact that upper incomes generally did not decline, the result was a sharp increase in inequality. See World Bank, Technical Department, *Latin America and the Caribbean:*

Poverty and Income Distribution in Latin America—The Story of the 1980s (Washington, D.C., March 1993).

7.   This observation coincides with Guillermo O'Donnell's comments in his contribution to this volume.

8.   The bitter and long-lasting teachers' strike at the end of 1993 in Ecuador was basically due to a pay dispute. Teachers asserted that their average salary was about $130 per month. They demanded a 50 per cent increase, while the government offered 15 per cent. See *Latin American Newsletters: Informe Latinoamericano,* 2 December 1993, No. 93-47, pp. 556-557. In Chile, the Aylwin government raised starting salaries for teachers to about $200 per month in 1991 to begin to redress the erosion of their incomes.

Third Part

ECONOMIC POLICY

Inequality, Exports and Human Capital in East Asia: Lessons for Latin America

Nancy Birdsall and Richard Sabot[1]

The extraordinary success of a group of economies in East Asia in the last 40 years should be measured not only in rapid rates of economic growth, but in the unusual degree to which that growth was distributed across all income groups. This paper focuses on a key component of the East Asian success story of truly equitable growth: human capital — the rapid accumulation of human capital through the educational system, and the efficient utilization of that human capital in the labor market.

Two critical aspects of overall economic and social policy in East Asia helped ensure success in the accumulation and utilization of human capital (Figure 1). A set of policies that can be labelled "shared growth" included a concentration on bringing education to all groups, especially the non-elites. The export push ensured efficient allocation in the labor market of an increasingly skilled work force. Most countries in Latin America have not emphasized policies of shared growth nor, until recently, of exports. There has been reasonably rapid growth of education, but inequality has risen (in part owing to growing wage disparities between the skilled and the unskilled), and dual labor markets with large low-productivity (informal) sectors have emerged. Although growth was rapid in some countries of Latin America before the 1980s, no countries have had the sustained growth that East Asia has known for more than three decades. Even after major economic reforms, many are still growing only slowly and are plagued with high levels of income inequality.

Growth with declining inequality in East Asia

From 1960 to 1985 the economies of East Asia grew significantly faster than those of any other region in the world. GDP per capita growth was concentrated in eight high-performing Asian economies (HPAEs): Japan; the "Four Tigers" (Hong Kong, the Republic of Korea, Singapore, and Taiwan); and the three newly industrializing economies (NIEs) of Southeast Asia (Indonesia, Malaysia, and

Thailand). GNP per capita in each of these HPAEs grew faster than in any country in Latin America except Brazil, whose growth rate for the period exceeded that of Thailand through 1985 (Figure 2). When countries are ranked by GDP growth (from highest to lowest), six of the top seven are HPAEs, and all eight of the HPAEs are in the top 20 fastest growing countries. In contrast, Latin American countries, with the exception of Brazil, rank in the lower middle and below[2].

Although conventional wisdom has held that rapid growth is accompanied by increasing inequality of incomes, inequality fell in the HPAEs (comparing the 1980s to the 1970s)[3], while it increased in much of Latin America[4]. Figure 3 illustrates the difference between the two regions. It combines information on inequality (the ratio of the income share of the richest to that of the poorest 20 per cent of the population in the mid-1980s) and GDP growth rates. The HPAEs, clustered in the top left corner, had low inequality and high growth, while Brazil, Mexico, Colombia, Peru, Chile, Venezuela, Bolivia and Argentina, all in the bottom right portion, had high inequality and relatively low growth.

Shared growth and human capital accumulation

Post-World War II East Asia did not, it is true, face the vast and deeply rooted inequalities that have historically beset Latin America. Initial differences in inequality, however, cannot by themselves explain the difference between the regions today; policy differences throughout the postwar period must also be taken into account. The HPAEs introduced specific policies and programs to ensure that the benefits of growth would be extended to all parts of the population, including the non-elites. These mechanisms of "shared growth" arose in part from political concerns[5]. The new postwar regimes of Korea, Taiwan, Singapore, Hong Kong, Thailand, Malaysia, and Indonesia faced a formidable challenge from the communists, some externally and virtually all internally, at least for some period. Their leaders therefore developed and implemented various programs to create and strengthen support from the working-class non-elites: land reform in Korea, Taiwan and China; housing programs in Hong Kong and Singapore; massive investment in rural infrastructure in Indonesia; credit and export guarantee programs for small and medium-size enterprises (SMEs) in Taiwan, China and, since the 1980s, Korea (where the SME shares in manufacturing employment and value added had risen to 51 and 35 per cent respectively by 1988); and legislation to ensure access of ethnic Malays to universities, public sector jobs and investment opportunities in Malaysia. Finally, the centerpiece of shared growth in all these countries was strong support for public education at the primary and eventually at the secondary level.

In addition, a matter we will return to below, these countries managed labor relations aggressively in order to suppress radical political activity, and as a result avoided the conflation of social policy with labor policy or workers' rights[6]. In Korea, Singapore and, to some extent, Malaysia, the labor movement was actively managed by government, and in Thailand and Indonesia labor unions were routinely suppressed for fear of communism. As a result of rapid growth and rising productivity, wages rose, generally in line with — but not ahead of — market forces. The mechanisms that elsewhere permitted a group of privileged workers in the formal sector to reap high rents through unionized pressure or interest group politics were not allowed to take hold[7].

Three aspects of this policy stance of shared growth in East Asia seem to have been key: first, the emphasis was not on direct transfers but on improving opportunities — this was not a populist approach; second, the distinction was not between the poor and the rest, but between the elites (which in Latin America could be said to include privileged public sector and public enterprise labor as well as industrialists and large landowners) and the rest[8]; and third, the process was managed by the government, usually in a manner that did not contravene the market, but rather ensured participation by non-elites in the market[9].

Rapid gains in education throughout East Asia were in part the result of the emphasis on shared growth, i.e. on reaching all parts of the population. Some countries, such as Korea, already had some education infrastructure in place and relatively high levels of education among workers in 1960; they continued to support and expand their investments. Other countries, such as Indonesia and Malaysia, had much less in 1960 but expanded their educational systems dramatically. By 1987, all of the HPAEs except Thailand (with 95 per cent enrollment) had achieved universal primary education, and all had secondary enrollment rates that were above international norms for their incomes (again, except Thailand) (Figure 4). Rapid educational growth in the HPAEs was in part due to rapid income growth, which increased the resources available for education, and to slower growth of school-age cohorts, as fertility declined (especially in the 1970s) compared to other developing regions.

Policy also played a role. The universalist (or saturation) emphasis on reaching all segments of the population, in the face of scarce resources, in effect meant that governments were induced to concentrate their resources originally at the level of primary schooling, where unit costs are lower — and where, of course, the non-elites are more likely to benefit — and gradually to expand the secondary level. The average percentage share of spending on education for developing countries in general is similar to the figure for East Asia (roughly 3.4 per cent of GDP), but in East Asia most of that public spending has gone to primary and secondary education, with about 15 per cent going to university education, compared to 24 per cent in Latin America and South Asia, and more in parts of Africa. Korea and Venezuela provide an extreme example of the contrast. In 1985, though public expenditure on education was higher in Venezuela as a percentage of GDP (at 4.3 per cent) than in Korea (at 3 per cent), 43 per cent of public education spending went to higher education in Venezuela compared to 10 per cent in Korea. The result: almost twice as much (as a percentage of GDP) was available for primary and secondary education in Korea.

By expanding the number of people enrolled at the primary and secondary levels, the HPAEs directly served the poor and the middle class (upper-class children already attended school). If the HPAEs had expanded higher education, the upper classes would have filled the majority of the newly created spots, and the non-elites would have gained little. This has been the case in Latin America, where educational investments have focused more heavily on higher education, prior to universalization of lower levels (Table 1).

Table 1. **Budget allocated to higher education, 1985**

(percentage of overall education budget)

HPAEs	
Hong Kong	25.1
Malaysia	14.6
Singapore	30.7
Thailand	12.0
Indonesia	9.0
Selected Latin American and Caribbean Countries	
Argentina[1]	30.8
Brazil	19.6
Chile	20.3
Colombia	22.2
Costa Rica	41.4
Dominican Republic	20.8
Ecuador	17.8
Honduras	21.3
Mexico	17.6
Nicaragua	23.2
Peru	2.7
Uruguay	22.4
Venezuela[2]	43.4

1.   Argentina: figure for 1986.
2.   Venezuela: figure for 1984.
Source: UNESCO, *Statistical Yearbook*, 1993.

Ironically, total enrollment rates, private and public, are higher in East Asia than elsewhere at the tertiary level, as the private sector has expanded to absorb the high demand generated by the much larger pools of graduates of good public secondary schools[10]. Countries in East Asia have not neglected higher education, but public spending has been motivated by strategic concerns about increasing such skills as engineering, the hard sciences and public administration. In contrast, spending on higher education in Latin America has been driven largely by the political impetus to subsidize the elites (and more recently the upwardly mobile middle class); as a result, far more public resources have gone to education of the upper classes in law, business and the humanities.

Similarly, countries of Latin America have not neglected primary and secondary schooling; indeed, the record is relatively good, at least with respect to enrollment rates[11]. However, expansion of enrollments, often driven by populist goals poorly backed by resources, has been faster than expansion of spending per child on books, equipment and teacher training (number of teachers employed and salaries have grown in some countries, but often teachers are not qualified). The result, as spending per child has fallen (from an estimated $164 in 1980 per primary school child to $118 in 1989[12]), has been high rates of repetition — the highest rate in the world — and dropout, almost certainly due to a decline in quality.

156

In contrast, the HPAEs saw quality rise, in part because expenditures per child rose — for example, by 355 per cent in Korea between 1970 and 1989 compared to just 38 per cent in Mexico[13]. Primary school completion rates (i.e. the percentage of children starting primary school who complete it) are a proxy for quality and illustrate the contrast between the two regions. Completion rates rose in Korea from about 35 per cent in 1955 to over 95 per cent in 1966); they have declined in Brazil from about 60 per cent in 1960 to probably half that in 1980[14]. Improvements in the quality of public school benefit the non-elites disproportionately, as they are the most likely to attend schools of relatively low quality in the first place and the most likely to leave school when the returns to spending time in school are low due to poor quality.

Perhaps the best measure of quality is output. East Asian students have gained a reputation for superior scholastic performance, particularly in mathematics and sciences. Recent international comparative studies show that Latin American students compare poorly. One study ranked Venezuelan nine-year-olds last in reading. In another, Brazilian 13-year-olds were outscored by every country but Mozambique in mathematics and science. In a third study a number of Latin American countries, when excluding elite schools, scored well below average for mathematics and sciences[15].

Finally, an additional benefit of the universalist emphasis on schooling was the rapid incorporation of girls into schools early in the postwar period, with the result some years later of reducing fertility (as well as large benefits for children's health and nutrition). The resulting early declines in fertility compared to other regions meant that by the 1970s, countries of East Asia were able to concentrate comparable educational resources on relatively smaller cohorts[16].

Over time, more rapid expansion of education and reductions in income inequality have reinforced each other in East Asia; Latin American countries have not exploited the benefits of this virtuous circle. On the one hand, a more equitable distribution of income contributes to more rapid expansion of education, particularly for the non-elites. Where income disparities are smaller, poorer households are relatively less poor for a given average income, and will therefore have higher demand for education; and those who are not poor are generally more willing to support public education where their relative tax burden associated with spending on non-taxpaying households is smaller. The poorest households in East Asia in the 1980s had higher incomes than their counterparts in Latin America, even where their respective countries' average incomes were similar. For example, while the per capita income of Brazil in 1983 slightly exceeded average incomes in Malaysia in 1987, households in the bottom income quintile received 4.6 per cent of total income in Malaysia, but only 2.4 per cent of total income in Brazil. As a consequence, the absolute incomes of the poorest income group in Brazil were only 52 per cent of the incomes of the corresponding group in Malaysia. Very poor households often do not seek or take advantage of educational opportunities for their children — for example if children are needed at home to work, or income is not available for books or uniforms[17]. Birdsall and Sabot (1993), assuming an income elasticity of demand for schooling of 0.4 (a conservative assumption), estimate that were the distribution of income as equitable in Brazil as in Malaysia, enrollments among poor Brazilian children would be more than 40 per cent higher[18].

At the same time, a broader base of education in a population brings greater income equality. Comparing Brazil and Korea, Park, Ross and Sabot (forthcoming) found that rapid increases in the availability of educated workers in Korea drove down the wages of skilled workers closer to those of the unskilled and reduced income inequality from the 1970s to the 1980s. In Brazil, with educational opportunities expanding more slowly and more at the top than at the primary and secondary levels, the gap between the wages of the skilled and unskilled did not decline, nor did inequality[19].

A policy of shared growth in East Asia thus contributed to a universalist, broad-based approach to education, emphasizing public spending at the primary and secondary levels. The broad base of education in the work force, in turn, contributed to reducing income inequality and, through household demand, encouraged continuing growth in education.

Emphasis on broad-based education to reach non-elites has been only one of a number of programs of shared growth in East Asia. As noted above, housing, credit for small businesses, and heavy emphasis on rural infrastructure (resulting for example in far greater access to electricity and clean water in the rural areas of Indonesia, Malaysia and Thailand than in Argentina and Brazil in the early 1980s[20]) were others. More fundamentally, overall economic management ensured broad-based labor-intensive growth, which encouraged efficient utilization of an increasingly educated work force. A critical ingredient of both broad-based growth and efficient use of human capital was the export push.

Export push and human capital utilization

Korea and Taiwan placed heavy emphasis on manufactured exports as early as the 1960s. The export push arose in part as a result of their drive to achieve economic and thus political independence from the West (and from their large neighbors), and their resultant compelling need for foreign exchange. Recognition that in the absence of natural resources, their comparative advantage lay in efficient use of their most plentiful resource, labor, almost surely also played a role. In contrast to many other economies, including some in Latin America, which tried to conserve foreign exchange by reducing imports, Korea and Taiwan, and eventually the other HPAEs, concentrated on exports.

All the HPAEs did not adopt identical trade regimes in their drive to export. While the trade regimes of Hong Kong and Singapore were close to free trade, Korea, Taiwan and Japan taxed and restricted imports, but also ensured free access to imports for their export industries; through countervailing subsidies, the promotion of exports coincided with protection of the domestic market. In the 1980s, Indonesia, Malaysia and Thailand adopted policies to encourage exports, including financial and institutional support for exporters, while gradually reducing protection from imports for local industries[21].

In all cases, however, governments have been clearly and fully committed to the export-push strategy, supporting exports not only through liberalized foreign exchange rates and devaluations when necessary to ensure export competitiveness, but through financing, help with marketing and information and so on. Sectoral policies, including access to credit and public infrastructure investments, were also geared to exports. The consistent and credible commitment to exports meant that in East Asia even producers in protected domestic industries knew that sooner or later their time to compete in global markets would come.

The contrast to policies in Latin America is marked. The exchange rate has often been used as a nominal anchor in fighting inflation in Latin America (with inflation itself rooted in lack of fiscal discipline), despite the penalty to exports from persistent overvaluation. Sectoral policies — including access to cheap credit, to scarce foreign exchange, and to fiscal incentives — have generally favored capital-intensive, import-substituting industries, further discouraging exports. Finally, and perhaps most important, Latin American governments stayed with import substitution well into the 1980s, owing in part to persistent ideological resistance to change; in contrast, the HPAE governments were highly flexible in their adaptation of policies and thoroughly pragmatic in promoting export growth, quick to modify any unsuccessful approaches.

The share of the HPAEs (excluding Japan) in world manufactured exports rose dramatically between 1965 and 1990, from about 1.6 per cent to 9 per cent; their share in developing-country manufactured exports rose from 14 per cent to almost 75 per cent[22]. While most Latin American countries experienced healthy (though lower) rates of export growth in the 1970s, export growth declined in virtually all of them during the 1980s. In Mexico, average annual export growth declined from 13.5 per cent during the 1970s to 3.5 per cent in the following decade; Brazil, Chile, Ecuador, Argentina, and Uruguay experienced similar declines[23]. Furthermore, while the HPAEs dramatically increased their share of world manufacturing exports, Latin America's share increased by only 0.9 per cent (to a total of 2.1 per cent) from the early 1970s to late 1980s[24]. In recent years, growth in Latin American exports has surged as trade and exchange rate reforms have dismantled the traditional anti-export bias.

The export push in East Asia meant that demand for labor was high. Obviously it is not sufficient for economies merely to accumulate human capital. Although the former Soviet Union and Egypt developed large supplies of human capital, the lack of sufficient demand for and inefficient utilization of this capital led to zero (or negative) marginal productivity and exercised a substantial drain on the government and economy as a whole. The HPAEs avoided both the problem of limited domestic demand and the inefficiency problem through emphasis on exports. High labor demand in export industries (which tend to be more labor-intensive than import-substituting industries[25]) was complemented by growth of agricultural output and productivity, itself the effect of much lower direct and indirect taxation of agriculture than occurred in Latin America[26]. Export industries were labor-intensive, so that the export-push strategy reinforced the tendency to rely heavily on the most plentiful factor of production, and to minimize the anti-labor bias associated with protecting capital-intensive industries.

Not only was demand not restricted by the limits of domestic consumption, the imperative to compete in international markets helped ensure efficient use of labor. The requirement to export meant that wages could not rise above market rates; there was no room for the kinds of rents awarded in much of Latin America to workers in the formal sector, particularly in the public sector and in public enterprises. Nor were the same labor-market rigidities, such as hiring and firing restrictions, created in East Asia (reflecting in part the suppression of labor movements referred to above, generally for political rather than economic reasons.)

Market-determined wages in fact rose rapidly, reflecting efficient use of labor and reinforcing the capacity of industries to avoid wages above market-determined rates. The rapid and sustained rate at which wages, a proxy for the productivity of labor, have increased in the HPAEs is historically unprecedented. In the first stages of rapid economic growth, aggregate output and the demand for wage labor increased steadily, but real wages changed very little. As output continued to grow, however, there came a point when increments to labor demand exceeded increments to labor supply and real wages began to rise rapidly. Real wages in Korea, for example, have grown more than 15 per cent per year since 1970, a pace which increased real earnings six-fold between 1966 and 1990. While wage growth in the other HPAEs has not been quite so dramatic, it has been strong and consistent. Wage growth in Latin America has been considerably more erratic, smaller, and sometimes negative during this period (Table 2).

Table 2. **Annual percentage increase in real earnings**

	1970-80	1980-90	1970-90
HPAEs	10	6.3	8.15
Korea	20.3	9.8	15.05
Taiwan	3	5	4
Singapore	5	5.9	5.45
Indonesia	1	6.5	3.75
Thailand	2	3.2	2.6
Malaysia	6.4	4.4	5.4
Hong Kong	3.1	2	2.55
Latin America			
Argentina	-2.1	-0.8	-1.45
Bolivia	0	-4.8	-2.4
Brazil	4	7.1	5.55
Colombia	-0.2	1.7	0.75
Mexico	1.2	-3.9	-1.35
Venezuela	3.8	-2.9	0.45

Source: Campos (1993), based on *World Development Report* (various years), and *Taiwan National Statistical Data Set.*

While the HPAEs experienced rapid growth in wages, the wage gap between skilled and unskilled workers, as noted above, was relatively modest. The small wage gap did not result from minimum wage legislation or other traditional measures to protect labor, but rather from the simultaneous growth in the demand for unskilled labor and the supply of educated workers. The equalizing pressure that resulted was important in a number of ways. First, it reduced the incentive for educated workers to remain unemployed to look for a high-paying job, instead of filling a job slot at a lower occupational level. Second, it minimized pressures on the government to provide more high-wage jobs than was justified by the derived demand for labor. High rates of growth in public employment, characteristic of many developing countries, divert scarce savings from productive investment and often indicate a squandering of valuable human capital. The percentage share of the public sector in the increase of total wage employment in Latin America, and in particular Peru and Brazil, has far outstripped that in Thailand and Taiwan[27].

Thus the export push became another factor contributing to income equality. The relatively small wage gap between skilled and unskilled labor has contributed in itself to better distribution of income and a greater sense of shared growth. In contrast, dual labor markets emerged and have intensified in Latin America, where the gap between wages in the formal and informal sectors often exceeds 100 per cent (compared to about a 20 per cent gap in Korea and Taiwan between the wages of the unskilled industrial or agricultural worker, and those of the average worker in the late 1960s and early 1970s[28]).

The export push also contributed directly to raising labor productivity. Initially, HPAE exporters utilized the very cheap supply of labor to produce inexpensive goods, thereby developing their own niche in international markets. As production and the derived demand for labor increased, however, wages rose and firms had to find an alternative means of competing or risk losing their market segment. HPAE firms, exposed to international markets, responded by investing heavily in both capital and technology, and by changing and adapting manufacturing processes learned from customers they were supplying. The resulting transition from low to high technological complexity was critical to the HPAEs; exports required increasing quantities of skilled and flexible labor, thereby boosting the demand for human capital.

While the transformations in HPAE export production occurred in many of the traditional sectors of the economy such as textiles, the overall composition of exports in the HPAEs also changed significantly[29]. The share of manufactured exports in total exports more than doubled in most of the HPAEs between 1970 and 1991, so that by the end of this period exports in machinery and equipment dominated total exports. This shift is especially remarkable as other traditional sectors of the economy (such as textiles and apparel) still thrived and grew, maintaining the high demand for less skilled labor. This traditional sector growth, however, was completely overshadowed by the expansion of machinery and equipment exports. Production of these more sophisticated exports further strengthened the labor demand for educated workers.

The growth in exports and improvements in technology and productivity spurred the demand for educated labor. At the same time, the relatively high levels of human capital which already existed in the work force improved the ability of exporters to adopt the new methods of production necessary to growth and successful competition in world markets[30]. Finally, of course, increases in the demand for human capital raised the returns to education, further increasing the related household demand for education.

The HPAEs have had the highest rates of total factor productivity (TFP) growth in the world over the last three decades, and there is little doubt that the export drives contributed to this growth, by exposing firms to international competition and to information about changing markets and technologies[31]. High

TFP growth has contributed to the region's rapid rates of output growth. Recent empirical work indicates not only that high rates of education and of exports are associated with strong growth in TFP and in output, but that each contributes more to output growth when associated with the other[32]. By emphasizing education and exports less, Latin America has done less well in terms of both growth itself and distribution of the benefits of growth.

Lessons for Latin America

Human capital accumulation and efficient utilization have been at the center of at least two virtuous circles in the high-performing East Asian economies.

–   The policy of shared growth contributed to rapid accumulation of human capital, as governments ensured that education of good quality would be accessible to all. Human capital accumulation contributed to economic growth and decreasing inequality, and these in turn ensured another round of high human capital accumulation.

–   The policy of pushing exports encouraged adherence to market-determined wages, ensuring the efficient utilization of labor and of human capital by limiting distortions in the wage structure, and contributing to productivity gains reflected in rapid wage growth. Productivity gains led to further export growth as well as overall economic growth which, in turn, helped to reinforce market-determined wages.

In East Asia, basic economic objectives including the idea of shared growth and the emphasis on exports contributed to rapid accumulation and efficient utilization of human capital, creating an environment in which both growth and equity could and did flourish. Most countries of Latin America are presently engaged in an opening of their economies, through trade liberalization and related structural adjustment efforts. The message from East Asia is that this is the right direction; efforts to maintain and strengthen macroeconomic balance and to open economies are critical not only in establishing the credibility and stability needed to sustain investment and growth, but in providing the setting for export growth. Such growth is in turn the source of sustained long-term productivity gains, and of continuing demand for skilled human capital — and thus of new growth and increasing income equality.

Perhaps the most important lesson for Latin America, however, lies in the notion of shared growth. Emphasis on shared growth, reaching the non-elites, is key to the region's future. Human capital is fundamental to this effort, as it is an input not only to growth but to equitable growth. It may also be the key to long-run political stability, and through political stability, to the sustainability of the economic reforms which underline both growth and reduced inequality[33].

Notes and References

1. Nancy Birdsall is Executive Vice-President, Inter-American Development Bank. The views expressed here do not necessarily reflect those of the Inter-American Development Bank or of its members.

    Richard Sabot is John J. Gibson Professor of Economics, Williams College; Senior Research Fellow, Policy Research Department, World Bank.

    We have drawn heavily from ideas and data in Birdsall and Sabot (1993) and in World Bank (1993a) for which the former study, focusing on human capital issues, was prepared. Appreciation is due to Rebecca Foster for her assistance with this paper.

2. Moreover, unlike many Latin American economies which experienced periods of rapid growth (particularly in the 1970s) followed by years of recession, the HPAEs managed to sustain healthy rates of growth over the entire period.

3. Birdsall, Ross and Sabot (1993) suggest why income equality is good for growth and provide empirical evidence for the link.

4. Based on data on Gini coefficients published by World Bank. Ginis fell in all the HPAEs, and rose in Argentina, Chile, and Mexico; were stable in Brazil; and fell in Colombia, Peru and Venezuela. Even where the Gini coefficients fell in Latin America, the percentage of population below the poverty line rose. In East Asia, not surprisingly, the combination of high growth and low inequality ensured declines over the period in the percentage of the poor — especially compared to Latin America (based on data from World Bank, 1990 and 1993c). The percentage of people below the poverty line fell from 58 to 17 per cent between 1970 and 1987 in Indonesia, and rose from 34 to 41 per cent from 1980 to 1989 in Brazil. The few countries in Latin America that managed to keep constant or decrease the number of poor during the 1980s include Chile, the earliest structural reformer, and Costa Rica, a country recognized for its expanding broad-based social programs.

5. Campos (1993) has characterized and discussed the idea of "shared growth" in terms of the need for governments to secure legitimacy. See also World Bank, 1993a.

6. Hausmann (in this volume) points out that in Latin America, workers' rights and social policy have often been seen as equivalent — resulting in some places in a privileged unionized formal-sector labor movement.

7. This suppression of labor rights had high costs, of course, in terms of loss of human rights; the lesson is not necessarily that such rights should be suppressed, but that high wages, above market rates, need to be avoided if the benefits of growth are to be broadly shared.

8. Another characteristic of the approach was that the elites were also attended to — however, in a fully transparent way, with clear rules of the game, which reduced the benefits of rent seeking and raised its costs. See Campos (1993), for discussion of the effect in reducing rent seeking of deliberative councils in Japan and comparable arrangements elsewhere in East Asia.

9. Where there is a high correlation of economic and political power, the elites can use political power to increase economic rents (Birdsall and James, 1993). If this is the context, *laissez-faire* economic policy will allow the elites to avoid market discipline, and managing "shared growth" to reach the non-elites can be necessary to ensure a real market economy.

10. See Birdsall and Sabot, 1993; and James and Han, 1989.

11. Inter-American Development Bank, 1993.

12. World Bank, 1993b.

13. Birdsall and Sabot, 1993, estimate these figures from data on total public expenditures for primary schooling and the size of the school-age populations.

14. Data on completion rates were compiled by Barro (1993). His rate for Brazil in 1980 is 19 per cent, but is probably understated compared to 1960 as the definition of primary school changed in the intervening period and by 1980 included eight rather than four grades.

15. World Bank, 1993b.

16. For example, the school-age population as a percentage of total population in the HPAEs was roughly equal to that of other developing countries in 1965, but was substantially lower by 1989. If Korea, for example, had had the growth rate of school-age population of Mexico in 1989, it would have be obliged to spend 4.2 per cent of its GNP in 1988/89, 1.4 percentage points more than it actually did spend in that year (Birdsall and Sabot, 1993).

17. Other constraints which reduce the demand for schooling are imperfect information on the benefits of schooling, and the inability to borrow for schooling costs where capital markets are imperfect.

18. For evidence that more egalitarian societies have higher secondary school enrollment rates and higher rates of public expenditure on secondary education per eligible child, see Williamson, 1993. Williamson attributes nearly all of the 27 per cent difference in secondary school enrollment rates between Korea and Brazil in the early 1970s to the greater inequality in the distribution of income in Brazil.

19. See Park, Ross and Sabot, forthcoming, Table 4.

20. Birdsall and Sabot (1993) compile data from other sources to show, for example, that in the early 1980s, the percentage of rural populations served by electricity was 40 and 55 per cent in Thailand and Malaysia, compared to 5 and 19 per cent in Argentina and Brazil.

21. For a full discussion, see World Bank, 1993a.

22. World Bank, 1993a, Table 1.5, p. 38.

23. World Bank, 1990.

24. Inter-American Development Bank, 1992.

25. Squire, 1981.

26. Data on the rapid growth of agricultural output and productivity are summarized in World Bank, 1993a. Birdsall (1993) includes the low direct and indirect taxation of

agriculture in East Asia as another sign of "shared growth". Low indirect taxation was the result of relatively undervalued exchange rates and the lower degree of protection of domestic industries, which improved the terms of trade for agriculture in East Asia.

27. Gelb, Knight and Sabot, 1991.

28. Birdsall and Sabot, 1993.

29. There is evidence that the industrial policy of the HPAEs emphasized this change in export composition by promoting the development of high-tech industries. These policies, however, appear to have had a marginal effect on the changes which actually occurred. See World Bank, 1993a.

30. High levels of human capital in the work force also raised employers' returns to training programs. Training in firms is associated with level of technology and workers' education. See Aw and Tan, 1993.

31. World Bank, 1993a, e.g. Figure 1.10, p. 56.

32. Birdsall, Page, Ross and Sabot (1993).

33. The increased supply of human capital in the HPAEs served, via both higher growth and higher equity, to maintain political stability and strengthen previously insecure governments. In economies such as those of Latin America, which have had a high degree of inequality, governments have fluctuated between extremely conservative policies (which supported the upper class and the status quo) and extremely populist policies (which attempted to ease dissatisfaction and redistribute wealth). By limiting inequality, the HPAEs avoided these cycles of policy extremes and could not only implement longer-term policies but also sustain a higher degree of political and economic stability. Moreover, as access to schooling in the HPAEs grew, people felt that they were sharing in the benefits of rapid economic growth and tended to be more receptive to the government policies and technocratic institutions which led the growth. Without this support, the HPAEs might not have had the flexibility or capacity needed to implement policies critical to their success.

Bibliography

AW, B.-Y. and H.W. TAN (1993), "Training, Technology and Firm Level Productivity in Taiwanese Manufacturing", *World Bank Working Paper*, World Bank, Washington, D.C.

BARRO, R.J. and JONG Wha-Lee (1993), "International Comparisons of Educational Attainment", paper presented at the conference "How Do National Policies Affect Long-run Growth?", World Bank, Washington, D.C., February.

BIRDSALL, N. (1993), "Shared Growth and Adjustment to Reduce Hunger", speech for World Bank Conference on Overcoming Global Hunger, Washington, D.C.

BIRDSALL, N. and E. JAMES (1993), "Efficiency and Equity in Social Spending: How and Why Governments Misbehave", in M. Lipton and J. van der Gaag, eds, *Including the Poor*, World Bank, Washington, D.C.

BIRDSALL, N., J. PAGE Jr., D. ROSS and R. SABOT (1993), "Education and Economic Growth: Increasing Supply Is Not Enough", World Bank, Washington, D.C., processed.

BIRDSALL, N. and R. SABOT (1993), "Virtuous Circles: Human Capital, Growth and Equity in East Asia", draft manuscript.

CAMPOS, E. (1993), "Leadership and the Principle of Shared Growth: Insights into the East Asian Miracle", *Asian Journal of Political Science*, December.

GELB, A., J. KNIGHT and R. SABOT (1991), "Public Sector Employment, Rent Seeking and Economic Growth", *Economic Journal*.

INTER-AMERICAN DEVELOPMENT BANK (1992), *Economic and Social Progress in Latin America*, Johns Hopkins University Press, Washington, D.C.

INTER-AMERICAN DEVELOPMENT BANK (1993), *Economic and Social Progress in Latin America*, Johns Hopkins University Press, Washington, D.C.

JAMES, E. and J.P. TAN (1989), "Higher Education in Asia: A Proposal for Further Study", draft report, World Bank, Washington, D.C.

PARK, Y.B., D. ROSS and R. SABOT (forthcoming), "Education Expansion and the Inequality of Pay in Brazil and Korea", in N. Birdsall and R. Sabot, eds, *Opportunity Foregone: Education, Growth, and Equity in Brazil*.

SQUIRE, L. (1981), *Employment Policy in Developing Countries: A Survey of Issues and Evidence*, Oxford University Press, New York.

SUMMERS, L. and A. HESTON (1988), "A New Set of International Comparisons of Real Product and Prices: Estimates for 130 Countries", *Review of Income and Wealth* 34(1): 1-25.

UNESCO (various years), *Statistical Yearbook*, Paris.

WILLIAMSON, J. (1993), "Human Capital Deepening, Inequality and Demographic Events along the Asia Pacific Rim", in O. Naohiro, G. Jones and J. Williamson, eds, *Human Resources in Development along the Asia Pacific Rim*, Oxford University Press, Singapore.

WORLD BANK (1990), *World Development Report*, Oxford University Press, New York.

WORLD BANK (1993a), *The East Asian Miracle: Economic Growth and Public Policy*, Oxford University Press, New York.

WORLD BANK (1993b), *Latin America and the Caribbean: A Decade after the Debt Crisis*, Oxford University Press, New York.

WORLD BANK (1993c), "Poverty and Income Distribution in Latin America: The Story of the 1980s", draft manuscript.

Figure 1.

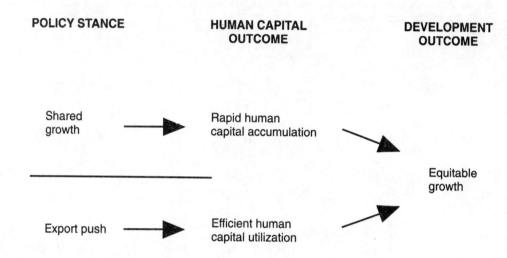

| POLICY STANCE | HUMAN CAPITAL OUTCOME | DEVELOPMENT OUTCOME |

Shared growth → Rapid human capital accumulation

Export push → Efficient human capital utilization

Equitable growth

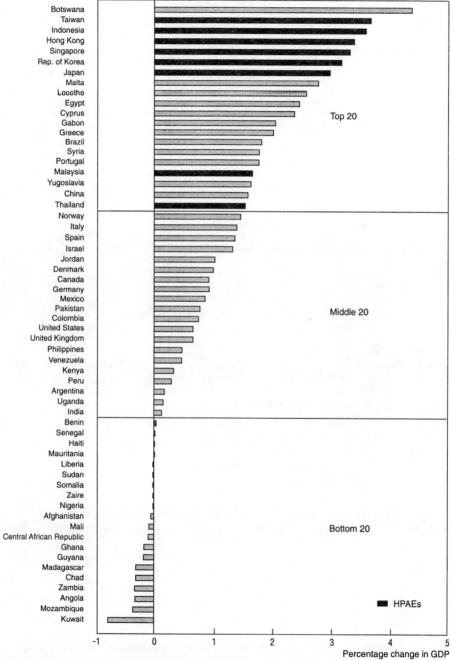

Figure 2. **Change in GDP per capita, 1960-85**

Source: World Bank, *The East Asian Miracle: Economic Growth and Public Policy* (1993), based on Summers and Heston (1988).

169

Figure 3. **Income inequality and growth of GDP, 1965-89**

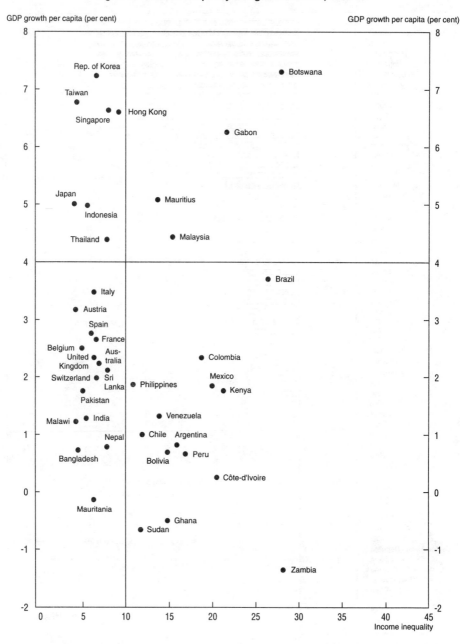

GDP growth per capita (per cent)

GDP growth per capita (per cent)

Income inequality

Note: Income inequality is measured by the ratio of the income shares of the richest 20 per cent and the poorest 20 per cent of the population.
Source: World Bank, *The East Asian Miracle: Economic Growth and Public Policy* (1993), based on World Bank data.

Figure 4. Cross country regression for secondary enrollment rates
1965 and 1987

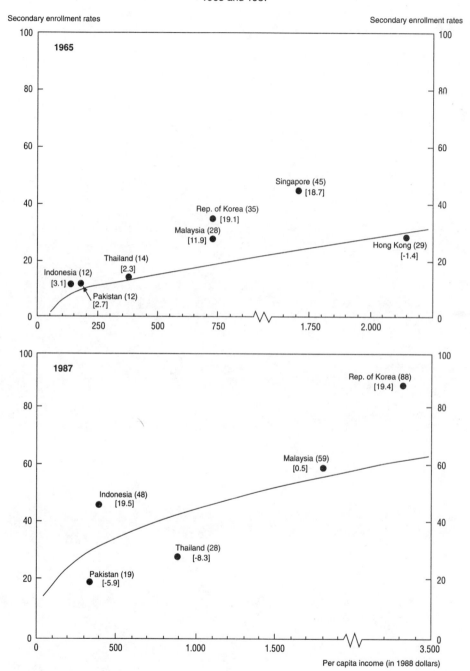

Source: Birdsall and Sabot, 1993.

Sustaining Reform: What Role for Social Policy?

Ricardo Hausmann

The perils of the new social activism

Most countries in Latin America have just undergone a major reform program. The catch-phrases and sound-bites of that process are well known: market orientation, trade liberalization, economic integration, fiscal discipline, privatization, financial reform, exchange rate unification, tax reform, direct subsidies targeted on the poor, decentralization of political power and responsibilities, democratic deepening.

The ideology of most of the reformers is that a streamlined state will concentrate the resources it can efficiently acquire through its power to tax on the sorts of things the market cannot do better. The process would reduce reliance on the regressive inflation tax and generate a permanent flow of resources that can used to improve the opportunities of the less fortunate. Fewer state-owned steel plants and more schools have characterized the sort of transformation that epitomizes the new conception. Social policy is no longer seen as the ambulance behind economic reform, simply in charge of mitigating the costs of the transition. Human capital has replaced natural resources as the most often mentioned source of comparative advantage, and there is increased acceptance of the idea that the fundamental development role for the government has to do with accelerating the rate at which human capital is accumulated. Governments should make sure that education and health empower people to be more productive. New theories of growth and international trade give intellectual currency to this view. Roads and other public goods can even be provided privately.

Implementing these ideas in the real world has been quite a bit more conflictive than it would seem from this epic agenda of efficiency and compassion. In most countries, it has implied a severe confrontation between the reformers in the executive branch and the representatives of the people in the legislative branch. In Peru and Russia, parliaments had to be unconstitutionally dissolved in order to move the agenda forward. In Venezuela, the stalemate between the powers has brought many reform initiatives to a halt. In Poland, voters have returned the former communists to power.

Political support for the agenda is weak. In Colombia, Venezuela and Brazil populism still carries an electoral appeal very well captured by the often cited Brazilian graffito: "enough of realities, we want promises". Attention is more concentrated on the so-called costs of adjustment, since the costs of disadjustment averted through the reform effort are counter-factual and hence unobservable, something much too abstract for electoral slogans. The reform is under political and ideological attack just when all major countries in the region face presidential elections.

The threat to economic liberalization has made political sustainability a new concern. The multilateral institutions are under pressure to find an amended Washington consensus[1]. This task has been defined as doing more on the social side so as to patch up the political and thus make the economic reform sustainable. This new social activism, based on political sustainability and not on development objectives *per se*, is dangerous for two main reasons. First, it misinterprets the reasons for the political strife in many reforming countries. It often assumes that the essence of opposition is caused by the lot of the poor, not by the fact that economic reform has threatened the livelihood of groups living off the quasi-rents generated by the now abandoned government interventions[2]. These reforms have also eliminated indirect subsidies that reach mainly the middle class in order to make room for direct subsidies scientifically designed not to reach the middle class. As in other aspects of life, the poor are usually too poor to become politically important.

Second, the new social activism assumes that fixing and improving the social services generates more political capital than it consumes. As this paper will argue, the required reform of social policy will be opposed by entrenched vested interest groups and by a middle class that has already been impoverished and is in no mood for solidarity. Moreover, the new activism does not emphasize the sorts of problems the region encounters in its social policy. Often one gets the impression that political opposition to reform has made the Washington consensus discover social policy. In Latin America, social policy is not new. It is more than 60 years old and it is in a terrible mess. If one forgets this fact and assumes that we can start from zero (instead of minus 100), one risks becoming a naïve archaeologist exploring a den of thieves.

This paper aims to define and explore what we may call "traditional social policy" and to elaborate on its shortcomings in order to set an agenda for reform. This is the course we followed before engaging in *economic* reform: analyzing the nature and consequences of our traditional policy, and through that process, generating the concepts that guided the reform effort. A new social activism that is not guided by a conceptual framework and is based only on dissatisfaction with outcomes can do much harm. To paraphrase Alan Blinder, there has been a lot of soft feeling, not much hard thinking.

The traditional approach to social policy

Latin America is the region with the worst income distribution in the world, comparable only to Africa's (World Bank, 1990). It has also been the one where populism has had the widest appeal and the greatest policy influence for the longest period. In many countries, policies have been shaped by what would be considered internationally as left-of-center parties such as the Radicals and Peronists in Argentina, the revolutionary parties in Mexico and Bolivia, the Liberals in Colombia, the Social Democrats in Peru and Venezuela, the Socialists and the Christian Left in Chile. Obviously, unequal income distribution tends to make equity dominant over efficiency as a political goal, thus prompting the appeal of populism. But why, after 40 to 80 years of government action in this direction, is income distribution just as unequal as it has ever been[3]?

There are many answers to this question, some of them related to economic structure[4]. The main cause explored here, and the one that seems to leave the most room for policy action, is the regressive distributive consequences of the social policies that have been adopted.

Traditional social policy has interpreted income distribution to be mainly determined by the confrontation between the two main factors of production: capital and labor. In the traditional approach these are seen as two social classes. Many government policy actions, such as price controls or labor legislation, were conceived of as means of regulating the clash between the classes or the ability of the capitalists to appropriate a larger share of the pie.

This conceptual approach is inadequate for two reasons. First, "capital" can hardly be assimilated to a class. Most of the "capital" in any modern society is life-cycle savings by the "workers". The fact that Chile's pension funds have accumulated $20 billion drives the idea home. Most companies are highly leveraged with the banking system, which draws its resources anonymously from quite a few people. Finally, the fact that most of the richer Latin Americans have parked a significant proportion of their assets abroad does not suggest that returns have been particularly attractive. Capital mobility prevents risk-adjusted returns from getting too far away from the international average.

Second, and more important, concentrating on capital and labor obscures an obvious fact: *Latin America has a very unequal distribution of labor income.* Take the distribution of income of the lower 80 per cent of the population in order to make sure you are not including either capitalists or professionals. Table 1 shows the ratio between the income of the fourth quintile of the population and that of the first quintile: it still looks very unequal. If labor income is unequally distributed, it is only a matter of time before capital income is also poorly distributed as the share of savings generated by the top echelons of the population will be much larger than that of the lower quintile.

Table 1. **Income distribution in Latin America, circa 1987**

	I	II	III	IV	V	**IV/I**	V/I
Brazil	2.4	5.7	10.7	18.6	62.6	**7.8**	26.1
Colombia	4.0	8.7	13.5	20.8	53.0	**5.2**	13.3
Costa Rica	3.3	8.3	13.2	20.7	54.5	**6.3**	16.5
Jamaica	5.4	9.9	14.4	21.2	49.2	**3.9**	9.1
Peru	4.4	8.5	13.7	21.5	51.9	**4.9**	11.8
Venezuela	4.9	9.7	14.3	21.9	49.3	**4.5**	10.1

Source: G. Márquez *et al.*, in Hausmann and Rigobon (1993), p. 152.

Studies on the determinants of labor income differentials find that the most important explanatory factor is the distribution of years of schooling [Psacharopoulos and Ng (1992), Márquez (1993)]. Not surprisingly, schooling is poorly distributed in Latin America, especially in countries, such as Brazil, where income distribution is particularly bad. When many individuals without primary education and few persons with university degrees try to find jobs, large wage differentials will logically ensue. Weak primary school systems and high subsidies for university education exacerbate this problem. In essence, the distribution of labor income is uneven because human capital is poorly distributed.

Most countries instituted massive programs of public education and health more than 40 years ago. The problems involved in the *provision* of these services will be dealt with below; here, some aspects affecting the *demand* for these services will be indicated.

Some descriptive characteristics of poverty in Venezuela bring the point home. As shown in Table 2, poor households have more children and hence a much higher dependency ratio. They also have less schooling. Teenagers from poor households tend to work more and go less to school.

Table 2. **Socio-demographic indicators of poverty in Venezuela**

	lower 30%	middle 40%	upper 30%
Years of schooling	5	7	10
Persons per household	6	5	4
Labor force participation ratio	37	51	63
Dependents per worker	3	2	1
School attendance rates of working teenagers[a]	35%	40%	54%

a.   Average school attendance by teenagers who do not work is 80 per cent.
Source: OCEI, Encuesta Social, processed by the World Bank.

Large families headed by a single parent with no primary education are bound to be poor anywhere in the world. The proportion of such households in many Latin American countries is large, however, and in Venezuela at least, the trend is not improving, owing to the rising incidence of teen-age pregnancies. Fourteen per cent of 16-year-old girls have had at least one pregnancy, and about a quarter of all women reach age 20 with at least one child. Table 3 shows the relationship between teenage pregnancy and years of schooling. Expectant mothers are required to leave the school system, which forces them to enter the labor market with few skills. Interestingly, the Social Survey of 1991 finds that the incidence of malnutrition in children of mothers with primary education or less is 3 times (13.9 per cent) that of children whose mothers have secondary education.

These observations clearly point out a strategy for action. Large households imply fewer resources per child. Teenage pregnancy implies fewer years of schooling, more children per mother and thus larger households. An educated mother can earn more money and can learn to take better care of her children, thus reducing the incidence of malnutrition. Keeping teenage girls in school and postponing pregnancy looks like a promising strategy that is currently being neglected. Failing to act on these issues creates households that are economically not viable and that will be with us for decades. Policy discussion on these issues has been notoriously absent in the region, for reasons that are known all too well.

Table 3. **Pregnancy and schooling of 20-year-old women in Venezuela**

Number of pregnancies	Years of schooling
None	11
One pregnancy, no births	9
One birth	8
Two births	6
Three births	5
Five births	2

Source: OCEI, Encuesta Social, processed by the World Bank.

The main elements of traditional social policy

Traditional social policy is composed of four main policy actions:

– centralized and public provision of health and education services;
– labor legislation;
– pay-as-you-go publicly provided social security;
– interventions in the price mechanism through controls and indirect (explicit or implicit) subsidies.

These policies shaped society, the economy and the state, and reforming them will have similar consequences. We will analyze each of these elements separately.

Centralized and public provision of health and education services

A recent World Bank education sector review for Venezuela (1992a) indicates appalling results in spite of reasonable budgets. Monie tend to go to bureaucracy and

177

higher education. Schools lack maintenance, books and teaching materials. Teachers are poorly educated and there is no in-service training scheme. Drop-out and repetition rates are high. Secondary school enrollment is amazingly low and entry to the free university system is unusually liberal. A similar World Bank study for the health sector (1992b) comes to very similar conclusions.

Why are the education and health systems in such a mess? Can this mess be somehow considered the equilibrium result of the system, given its structure? One can go a long way toward understanding the performance of the system by analyzing its structure. If the analysis is right, a very specific kind of reform is needed[5].

The main difference between economic and social policy is that the first is basically a set of rules while the second is mostly a sector of production. The Ministry of Education of Venezuela is by far the country's largest single employer, followed by the Ministry of Health and the social security system. If we exclude the armed forces, the state oil company Petróleos de Venezuela, which generates about 23 per cent of the country's GDP, comes in only fourth. If one thinks of the education and health sector as an important part of national output, which uses a very significant proportion of available resources, concepts of industrial organization immediately come to mind. A school and a hospital are after all production units. When social services are centrally and publicly provided, however, the structure of production and incentives takes a very peculiar form.

Consider the standard microeconomics-textbook firm. This is a hierarchical structure that relates in a particular way to its environment. For example, there is a relationship between output and cash flow, and a further link between the input mix and technology used in the production process and cash flow. It is the market, not just the costs of the inputs, that values the output of the firm. In fact, the difference between the two is profit, and there are people in the firm who would like to maximize this variable.

Profit maximization implies that there are incentives for cost reduction, which is achieved by choosing among the available technologies given the relative price of the inputs. It also implies choosing a certain quality that satisfies the market's price and quality tastes. To expand, the firm must convince financial markets of its long-term viability and profitability.

As time goes by, new technologies become available. New products can be used as inputs and others may come to act as substitutes for a given firm's output, thus luring customers away. Input prices may shift, calling for a change in the technological mix. To maintain its economic viability and to prosper, the firm must react quickly to these changes.

The firm is not the only way of organizing social production, but it is a good benchmark to understand how other forms of organization may differ. IBM has just about the same number of people on its payroll as Venezuela's Ministry of Education, but it faces competitive product and input markets and a highly exacting capital and financial market. These markets send signals that force the organization to change, often in a quite radical manner.

The centralized and public provision of health and education services implies quite a different structure. Production units — e.g. hospitals and schools — receive resources through a budget independently of the quality or quantity of output. These budgets can hardly be adjusted to meet changes in demand, be it between different medical services in a given hospital or between different school districts. They are more sensitive to political pressure: university students can burn buses, pre-school children cannot.

Budgets also imply that for each individual production unit, there is no relationship between output and cash flow. In a firm, if society wants more, it pays more, thus supplying the means with which to purchase additional inputs and expand production. With centralized and public provision, as a hospital tries to produce more, the budget becomes effectively tighter, causing more managerial headaches. In essence, this generates incentives to produce less: why perform 10 000 operations if you can perform only 100 with the same budget?

Budgets are usually itemized by input. Production units cannot choose the input mix. Schools are poorly maintained and have no books because these items have not been budgeted, not because the principal chose a particular technology. Technological change can hardly be incorporated.

Since the provision of these services is centralized, hiring is done directly by the federal government ministry. This has several important implications. A school principal or a hospital director cannot choose the people he works with, much less fire those he does not feel are adequate. This generates severe governance problems. Salaries are fixed at a national scale so they do not reflect the local conditions of the labor market. Thus, the production units often cannot hire the people they need, nor use personnel policy to achieve particular objectives.

On the opposite side of the market, teachers, doctors or nurses face a monopsonist: a single employer. They do not face a standard labor market where they can contrast the employment conditions of a given school district with that of a different one, or the salary offered by two competing hospitals. There is a single contract on a national scale which all units must offer. Under such conditions, it is obvious that even a Chicago School graduate would join a trade union or a professional association. It is the only way to have a say in the smoke-filled room where the single national contract is decided.

It therefore comes as no surprise that the education and health sectors have the largest and most conflictive trade unions and tend to undergo the largest number of strikes. The main element in the job description of a successful health or education minister is his ability to negotiate strikes. The presence of unions transforms the relevant labor market from a monopsony into a bilateral monopoly: teachers can work only for the ministry and the ministry can hire only union teachers. Theory tells us how inefficient and troublesome bilateral monopolies are. Reality, unfortunately, does resemble theory sometimes.

In the relationship between minister and trade unions, certain elements come into play which determine the outcome. The minister faces a total budget allocation which is difficult to change, since it must be approved by the full cabinet, composed of other spending ministers who also face budgetary problems, and by parliament. Reallocating expenditures within the ministry's budget is much easier to do. Thus, when faced with a strike, the minister will cut other expenditures to make room for the labor contract. This is in essence the mechanism whereby the input mix is decided. A school without working toilets and books is in equilibrium since, if funds had been allocated for such expenditures, there would be room for a successful strike.

The choice of the input mix is crucial in the determination of efficiency and quality. When the budget is cut 10 per cent, most reductions are made in all inputs other than personal emoluments. Hence, quality and output tend to fall more than proportionally because the input mix becomes even more inefficient. When an IDB or a World Bank team identifies high-return investments in the social areas, it is simply seeing the other side of the coin of an inefficient input mix. If the mix were optimal, the production unit would have, as the textbook says, equated the marginal value product of each input to its price. Hence, no increase in expenditures on any specific input would generate an especially large expansion in output. If in real life one finds that such an expansion is possible, the input mix is inadequate. The relevant question then becomes what went into determining that mix.

With centralized public provisioning, production units cannot choose the mix, which is allocated through a budget. They have no incentives to be efficient since resources are independent of output, and an explosive bilateral monopoly exists in the human resources market. Why would the mix be optimal? What would make an optimal mix sustainable over time?

Trade unions have a longer planning horizon than ministers. If a school or a hospital goes on strike, the cost to teachers or doctors is relatively low. Their budget will not be cut because of a strike and they will negotiate the payment of lost wages as a condition to stop the strike. On the other hand, having schools or hospitals closed represents a huge political pressure on the government. The minister, who on average lasts less than two years, will clearly prefer to give concessions today and defer the costs to the more distant future. Some of the concessions gained by the Venezuelan trade unions are the following:

- Teachers, doctors, nurses and all other employees in the social services are chosen not by the ministry but by the trade unions;

- There are no entrance exams to the service, nor are there any quality controls at any point in the career of these professionals. There are no established means of measuring quality of output;

- Through collective bargaining, the school year and the school day have been shortened substantially over time. Compulsory final exams were eliminated from secondary schools in order to shorten the effective academic year and reduce the work load;

- University professors retire after 25 years of service with full pensions. A year spent in an administrative post counts as two for the purpose of retirement. Most professors start their careers after a bachelor's degree and retire before they are 50.

The Venezuelan university system is a particularly interesting case of this form of organization. According to the University Law, the executive branch can only assign the total university budget to a single council composed of all the presidents of the national universities. These are democratically elected by the faculty and by student and employee representatives. Often, the qualities that make a professor a good trade union leader also get him elected as dean or president[6].

The budget is distributed by the council among the different universities. Professor's salaries are set at the national level, so universities have no means of competing for the good professors. They also have few incentives to do so, since they do not have to compete for students either. The National University Council effectively works as a cartel where budgets are distributed on the basis of past costs, not current output. Gross inequalities exist depending on each university's political leverage.

The structure of production makes the performance of the system unsurprisingly dismal. It also points the way to future reform. Budgets have become an entitlement of producers, not the purchase of a service on behalf of consumers. Universities often fight for a "just budget". Centralization breeds unionization and the consequence is a bilateral monopoly where the government is bound to be the weak member and will compromise the future to get over the present.

The solutions that this approach suggests are quite clear: give power back to consumers by empowering them with choice and by making resources enter production units as a function of output, not budgets. In education, the solutions are theoretically easier. Decentralizing the system will create more employers, and hence more competition in the market for teachers, unless unions impose national negotiations. Giving school directors the power to hire and fire will effectively restore governance and further spread market decision making. A voucher system is probably the neatest alternative structure. Expenditure on university education should be made a function of student enrollment, not employee payrolls. Competition should replace cartels, and quality premia should be introduced.

The theoretical simplicity of these solutions does not translate into political ease. Such reforms would be considered today as tantamount to a declaration of war. This makes us return to one of our original questions: is there a political pay-off to improving social policy?

The case of health is theoretically much more complex. Most medical expenditures are not predictable by individuals: they are the consequence of unforeseen contingencies. Insurance is involved, and it is well known that important distortions tend to occur in these markets: moral hazard and adverse selection problems become pervasive. With free, centralized public provisioning there is no price mechanism to limit demand to available resources, so the system adjusts through queues and poor service until the quality differential with full-price private provisioning convinces the richer individuals to leave the system. The equivalent of a voucher system in education would be a fee-per-service payment to hospitals by the government, but the distortions generated by such a scheme, exemplified by the US system, are clear. Since neither doctors nor patients face the true costs of the service, the system can become very expensive.

Here the concepts of choice, competition and empowering consumers must be complemented by schemes that make some people in the system face its true costs. Health maintenance organizations (HMOs) are such schemes: as production units that are paid not for actual output but for their commitment to provide certain services if needed, these institutions end up making money when people are healthy. Once a patient goes in for surgery, a dollar well saved by the HMO is a dollar earned. A dollar unwisely pinched will generate future costs to the HMO, in terms of additional services it will have to provide to cure the patient, without being able to charge for them. HMOs have a greater incentive to offer preventive care than do regular fee-per-service hospitals. In the absence of severe malpractice legislation, however, it is conceivable that HMOs have incentives to let a patient die if saving him is too costly.

Reforming health care is thus conceptually more complex than economic or educational reform. The discussion around the Clinton plan for reforming the US health system is just one example. The desire to make health care equally available to all members of society in spite of differences in income requires government action. The fact that most medical interventions are contingent creates the need for insurance and thus creates problems of adverse selection and moral hazard. Market failures must be weighed against government failures. (We shall return to these issues when we deal with social security.) A solid basis for reform can be formulated, however, by distinguishing between the financing of health insurance and the actual provision of medical services. A significant role for the public sector should remain in the first domain, while the market should take care of the second.

Labor legislation as an instrument of income redistribution

Traditional social policy sees the distributive problem as a confrontation between the two main social classes — capitalists and laborers — which meet in the production process. Hence, intervening in the labor contract through legal means is considered a way to bring some balance to social relations. The process is seen as cumulative. Workers gain *conquistas* or *revindicaciones* which become social rights and can therefore not be renounced by any individual worker[7]. As time goes on, society becomes a better place as workers gain the right to more days of paid vacation and maternity leave, higher severance payments, more closed-shop legislation and non-working paid union representatives.

Latin America has much more "advanced" labor legislation than does the United States or Canada, something that the protectionist lobby in the United States found out when searching for arguments to stop the North American Free Trade Agreement. The fact that wages in the south are a small fraction of those in the north could well be a consequence of the "advanced" labor legislation.

The principal problem with this approach to social progress is that it forgets that the labor contract is a mutually voluntary relationship: "it takes two to tango". Ways of shifting the implied costs of the legislation to be shifted back to workers are legion, making the effective incidence of the benefits less than obvious. For example, the law can say that workers have the right to receive not 12 but 15 months of salary per year, as a consequence of paid vacations and end-of-year *utilidades*, but it obviously cannot determine the monthly wage. Hence, companies will decide what yearly wage they are willing to pay for any given worker and will split it into as many months as the law tells them to. There should be no durable benefit to workers from this measure.

The labor contract has also been used to address problems which should ideally be more widely socialized. For example, the Venezuelan Labor Code has tried to deal with pensions, unemployment insurance, paid maternity leave and pre-school education through the individual labor contract. The first two have been implemented through a highly distortionary severance-payment scheme which is based on the seniority the worker has accumulated in his current job. For pensions it means that the worker does not accumulate resources during all his life but only during each individual working relationship. For example, construction workers, who have a high turnover, find the last severance payment inadequate to sustain a pension. When unemployment compensation is a function of seniority in the worker's last job rather than of the duration of unemployment, it is obviously inefficient. Moreover, these severance-payment schemes are highly distortionary since they affect labor mobility, governance and incentives to invest in worker training.

Maternity leave and pre-school education are interesting examples of the problems faced in addressing social problems through a private labor contract. The new Labor Code grants women the right to 140 days of paid maternity leave, billed to the employer. It grants all workers the right to receive pre-school education for each child under six years of age, either through direct provisioning by the employer or as a bonus payment equal to about 40 per cent of the minimum wage.

What are the consequences of such legislation? Obviously, the attractiveness of hiring women of a certain age group is affected. Employers must factor in the expected cost of maternity leave and will incorporate it in the wage they are willing to pay. This creates a gap between male and female wages and makes finding employment particularly difficult for many women. Any resulting redistribution tends to be between women who are paid less than men but do not have children and those who do. This problem could have been avoided by socializing the cost of the maternity leave.

The case of pre-school education is similar. Imagine an employer choosing between two unskilled workers: one with two children under six years old and the other with none. The direct cost to the employer of pre-school education is 80 per cent of the minimum wage if he decides to hire the worker with children. Will he do so?

All these matters sound very hypothetical, but recent studies (Márquez, 1993) show that the gap between male and female wages in Venezuela is large and unexplained by differences in years of schooling, hours worked, sector of employment and the like. More important, the overall benefits of such legislation are unclear. Hausmann (1993a), using a general equilibrium model with a modern and an informal sector, argues that increasing the indirect costs of employment in the modern sector causes the equilibrium size of the informal sector and of unemployment to rise, aggregate output and real wages to decline and factorial income distribution to worsen.

In practice, the "advanced" labor legislation reaches less than 60 per cent of the work force in Venezuela. As shown in Table 4, unemployment and informal employment, both unprotected by the Labor Code, represent between 42 and 51 per cent of the total labor force of Venezuela. Equally revealing is the fact that since 1985, wages of informal workers have outpaced those of modern sector workers by 45 per cent (Hausmann, 1993b).

Questions must therefore be asked: Is this road to social progress paying off? Are workers receiving the benefits of the legislation or is it being shifted back to them in the form of lower wages? Do the distortions caused by the legislation affect the size of the large informal sector in Latin America? Is this labor legislation consistent with the creation of high-paying jobs in an open competitive economy? Is labor market deregulation a way forward in the road to social progress?

Table 4. **Venezuela: Workers unprotected by the Labor Code**
Unemployment and informal employment
(as a share of the labor force)

	Unemploy-ment	Informal Employment	Total
1981	6.1	36.5	42.6
1982	7.1	36.7	43.8
1983	10.3	37.9	48.2
1984	13.4	37.4	50.8
1985	12.1	39.1	51.2
1986	10.3	38.1	48.4
1987	8.5	36.6	45.1
1988	6.9	35.9	42.8
1989	9.6	36.7	46.3
1990	9.9	38.0	47.9
1991	8.8	37.5	46.3
1992	7.1	37.3	44.4

Source: World Bank, *Venezuelan Labor Market Study* (Washington, D.C., 1993), p. 14.

Pay-as-you-go social security

Social security systems were established in Latin America mostly in the decade of the 1930s. The systems usually provide pension schemes and health insurance. Pension schemes, whether by design or by the force of events, have become unfunded pay-as-you-go mechanisms, while health insurance usually implies direct provisioning of medical services.

In Argentina and Uruguay social security transfers exceed 10 per cent of GDP, causing serious fiscal strains closely related to the financial and inflationary instability of these countries. In Venezuela, as in other countries, the savings of formally funded schemes were squandered while inflation reduced the real value of pensions to minuscule levels. Eventually, when political pressure builds up, pensions are increased and the system becomes underfunded.

As for medical insurance, social security systems have tended to provide the service directly. In Venezuela, this service employs 70 000 persons and runs over 70 hospitals with an associated network of primary care centers. Like the Ministry of Health, it clearly shows the consequences of centralized public provisioning with its characteristic bilateral monopoly, bitter labor relations, perverse incentives and high inefficiency.

Social security systems are usually financed through payroll taxes. Consequently they can be extended only to the formal sector of the economy. This has a series of important implications. First, a large segment of the population is not covered, which forces the government to run a parallel health service encompassing the whole population. Once the two systems are in place, it is difficult to make sense of who pays for what. The social security system is forced to accept non-contributing patients while the ministry attends patients that pay their dues to the social security system without being reimbursed for the expenses incurred.

Second, the fact that taxes are paid by the formal but not the informal sector has distortionary consequences. As mentioned above, it increases the equilibrium size of the informal sector and reduces output, the capital stock and real wages. According to Hausmann (1993a), substituting a VAT for payroll taxes would have significant efficiency and equity benefits to the economy.

The reform of social security poses the question of the adequate use of the market and hence the relevant split between the public and the private sector. This issue requires quite a bit of care, since the market presents two important drawbacks: it tends to fail due to either moral hazard or adverse selection problems, and it limits the scope for redistribution. These problems present themselves quite differently in the case of pensions than in that of health insurance.

In the case of health, privatizing the provision of the service creates the problem of how to pay hospitals and doctors for the services provided. Here, fee-per-service eliminates incentives to reduce costs. Other forms such as HMOs or disease-related groups (DRGs)[8] may be quite complicated to manage. Privatizing the insurance itself entails adverse selection and equity problems. First, private insurance companies will have incentives to discriminate against people with high risk factors and may in fact reinterpret contracts opportunistically in order to deny coverage. Sectors of the population may also find insurance policies inaccessible. Second, private companies would at best charge the same price to all people. Financing health through taxes can be made more progressive, however, since payroll taxes are proportional to income while a VAT is proportional to consumption. Giving up a role for public financing means also eliminating this element of solidarity from social policy.

In the case of pensions, the problems are different. Privatizing the pension system forces it to become a fully funded scheme. Pensioners can receive resources only as a function of their individual contributions. This has important advantages and disadvantages. The main advantage is elimination of the perverse tendency of pay-as-you-go schemes to grant concessions that become absurdly expensive in the more distant future, such as reductions in the age of retirement. Most countries have a long list of horror stories of this type.

Privatizing also takes away the government's role as the guardian of the workers' savings. Experience shows that fiscal pressures make it very hard for the government to refrain from unduly sticking its hands into the honey pot. It may not do so often, but the time horizon involved in these schemes is long: dipping into the pension fund once a decade may be enough to damage the solvency of the system.

A notable disadvantage is that moving from a public pay-as-you-go scheme to a private fully capitalized system implies that today's workers, who will be accumulating financial assets for their own account, will no longer pay for today's pensioners. Hence pensioners become a fiscal liability, and the changeover has important fiscal implications. If the deficit is already high and if the government is having problems managing its internal debt, putting more pressure on the system may be unwise. In Chile, the shift implied fiscal costs of 3 percentage points of GDP per year[9].

Second, public systems allow for inter-generational transfers in a way that private schemes do not. If society becomes richer, it may decide to be more generous with today's pensioners. A private system would not do that. The other side of this coin is that today's workers may decide to give themselves a hefty retirement, passing on the bill to yet unborn future workers.

Most social security systems in the region are in deep trouble, and reform must be put on the agenda. Coverage must be extended to the whole population by incorporating it as taxpayer and user, so that the system does not become financially explosive. Hence, alternatives to payroll taxes must be explored. Direct provision of medical services must be phased out, but the alternatives are unclear and complicated. A major challenge for the future is to define roles for the public and private sectors so as to achieve results that so far have proved unreachable owing to market and government failures.

Intervening in the price mechanism

Price interventions in the markets for goods and services in Latin America have been very common. Such interventions — the examples treated here are direct price controls, explicit indirect fiscal subsidies and implicit subsidies through low prices for the output of state-owned firms — have lost much of their intellectual appeal, but a recent study (Hausmann and Rigobon, 1993) shows that significant resources are still being allocated through them.

Price controls

Price controls have tended to go hand in hand with import-substitution policies. Through trade restrictions, the government usually granted significant market power to a few companies in each market. Pressures to impose price controls are usually prompted by the tendency of these policy-supported oligopolies to exercise their market power. As Naím (1993) argues, the Industrial Policy Division of the Ministry of Development would create the monopolies that the Commerce Division would try to control.

Price controls create incentives for potential competitors to collude on prices in order to improve their power to negotiate with the government. In fact, governments often promote this behavior since it is simpler to negotiate prices at the industrial level than at the firm level. Firms thus have incentives to devote more attention to lobbying through their trade associations than to improving their competitive performance. Moreover, insofar as controls effectively depress prices in the short run, they affect investment and medium-term supply, causing larger price increases in the future. As price negotiations are staggered through time, they also cause shortages and stock-outs as the public accelerates purchases and suppliers postpone sales before the next price increase is expected to take place.

186

Indirect subsidies

In many countries, indirect subsidies are still pervasive[10]. Explicit subsidies that appear as such in the fiscal accounts are becoming less common, but the price policies for the goods and services provided by state-owned companies are constantly under political pressure, generating implicit subsidies that can easily become large. Implicit subsidies to electricity, gasoline and water amounted to some 3 percentage points of GDP in Venezuela in 1993, an amount roughly equal to twice the budget of the Ministry of Health and three times the expenditures on primary and secondary education. Moreover, these subsidies are very regressive. As shown in Table 5, the richest 25 per cent of the population receives between four and five times more in subsidies than the lowest quartile.

Table 5. **Distributive impact of indirect subsidies on gasoline and electricity (1991)**

(Bolivars per person at 1986 prices)

	I	II	III	IV
Electricity subsidy per person	451	626	799	1 721
Gasoline subsidy per person	177	347	517	886

Source: G. Márquez *et al.*, in Hausmann and Rigobon (1993), pp. 166 and 202.

Indirect subsidies also tend to be diverted and to distort resource allocation. Gasoline is illegally exported; the indirect subsidy to milk, now eliminated, used to be diverted to the production of cheese; in Peru, flour was used to mark football fields.

More important than the straight diversion of the subsidized products to other uses are the efficiency costs due to resource misallocation. Venezuela's highly complex system of multiple exchange rates, implemented between 1983 and 1989, had a preferential rate for agricultural products at half the official rate and between a fourth and a sixth of the parallel rate. Feed grains were imported at this preferential rate, stimulating the production of pork and poultry to the detriment of cattle, a sector in which ample natural pastures give Venezuela a comparative advantage. The same exchange-rate subsidy allowed imported wheat to displace rice, a crop that is competitively grown in Venezuela.

The implementation of implicit subsidies through state-owned firms, usually by delaying price adjustments in an inflationary environment, tends to deprive them of the capital resources with which to guarantee adequate expansion of the services they provide. Current water prices in Venezuela are insufficient to pay for the electricity consumed in pumping water to the Caracas valley. The consequent lack of resources for maintenance and investment causes the quality of service to be extremely low: many sectors of the city receive an insufficient and unreliable supply. The Venezuelan telephone company CANTV used to invest less than $50 million a year, causing poor service and a great shortage of telephone lines. Since it was privatized in December 1991, it has been investing $650 million a year, thanks in good part to a legal commitment to maintain adequate real prices.

The reform programs carried out in Latin America have used the principle of pricing goods and services adequately and replacing indirect subsidies on goods by direct subsidies to targeted sectors of the population. As described by Teresa Albánez in her contribution to this volume, Venezuela instituted a system of transfers by targeting school children through the educational services and pre-school children through the primary care system. Both cash and food stamps are delivered through these schemes. These programs pay for half of the milk consumed in Venezuela, but do not lower by half the price to all consumers; milk is provided free of charge to some 4 million children, but other consumers must face the real price of the good. Hence, both the efficiency and equity of transfers is improved.

The convenience of this reform agenda does not translate into political enthusiasm. In Venezuela, support for the direct subsidy programs is lukewarm in most political circles, including the church. Realigning public-sector prices to their true economic costs is still a most explosive issue: the middle class prefers to keep the indirect subsidies that reach it and cares little for transfer programs that exclude it. Political pressures for "socially oriented" price interventions are certainly not dead.

Political obstacles to social reform

This essay began by criticizing the idea that doing more on the social agenda would improve the politics of economic reform. After description of the problems with our traditional social policy, it is easy to see the degree of political opposition that a serious reform effort would entail. The reform of health and education implies a confrontation with entrenched trade unions and professional associations that have accumulated "rights" that make the system inefficient and ungovernable. Regaining control of the hiring and firing process, strengthening the power of school directors, and charging tuition at universities in order to increase expenditures on pre-school and primary education are just a few samples from the political minefield ahead.

Reforming labor rights that are in fact paid for by workers (with an efficiency-related premium) through lower wages is always a hard sell. Social security reform, if it is fiscally sound, cannot be made politically easy. After all, it affects the allocation of resources between generations. Price interventions, for all their obvious inefficiencies and inequities, are a habit very difficult to overcome. Social reform must be attempted, but it will consume political capital and increase tensions. It is not a way to ease the pain of economic reform.

Traditional social policy, not the new economic strategy, is behind most of the social problems faced by Latin America. Strategies to make social reform politically palatable to the groups that matter are needed but difficult to come up with.

Although social discontent often affects both the poor and the middle class, most policy alternatives usually force a confrontation between these two groups. To understand why, let us define the middle class as the group of people who do not use public education (except universities), health services or transportation (they own cars). They have been impoverished by the consequences of the terrible economic performance of the 1980s, and many have abandoned public education and health because of falling quality. Proposing to them a tax reform in order to improve social services which they do not use is a non-starter. Charging for university education means taking away "their only remaining right". Financing targeted subsidies by

188

raising taxes or electricity prices is obviously not in their interest. In essence, improving the lot of the poor does not play well in the Latin American middle class. It has often been said that the middle class is the backbone of Latin American democracy. It should not surprise us that this has translated into a regressive social policy.

At a more fundamental level, keeping any social policy from falling into the chaos that has affected the traditional approach requires a change in the way the democratic political process is played. Until now, the interaction among the different players in the game has generated an *entitlement bias*. Each group imposes a right (really a privilege) on the rest of society. These entitlements are cumulative and once obtained become acquired rights, often enacted into law or signed into contracts: teachers earn the right to work short days and school years; trade unions gain the right to determine who gets hired; graduates from schools of journalism gain a monopoly over the right to write and read the news and even to interview people on television; agricultural lobbies gain the legal right to negotiate minimum prices; established pharmacies get the right not to have a competitor established within a radius of three blocks; university professors and employees obtain the right to have their children registered into higher education without an admission exam.

Entitlements are paid by the rest of society, but since they usually imply a distortion or a drag on fiscal resources, they end up costing more than the benefit they generate. That is, they imply a negative-sum game. Consequently, the value of the entitlements obtained by any group may well be lower than the cost to the same group of paying for the entitlements obtained by all other groups. A highly inefficient political equilibrium may be reached, but since no mechanism exists to exchange entitlements, each group has an incentive to ask for more in order to get even. Through this destructive game, the state loses its ability to achieve the social goals that justified the creation of the institutions it manages. These fall prey to the interest of those involved in producing the services, to the detriment of those who were supposed to benefit from them. Eliminating the entitlement bias may very well be the most fundamental of the reforms to be achieved.

Notes and References

1. The term "Washington consensus" was coined by Williamson (1991) to refer to the set of beliefs held by most multilateral and US policy agencies and think tanks located in Washington, around 1990. It does not deal with social policy. Although the name refers to a set of beliefs held by Washington agencies, it does not imply that the ideas originated in Washington or that the reform initiatives were led by the United States or the multilaterals. To a large degree, it is a Latin American consensus, led by intellectuals and policy-makers from the region.

2. The principal source of policy slippage in Venezuela since President Pérez was ousted has been an increase in tariffs and other forms of trade protection for agriculture, textiles and cars, hardly the sort of changes that stand high on the list of priorities for improving the well-being of the mostly urban poor.

3. How inequality affects growth has been recently studied by the new literature on political economy. See Alesina and Perotti (1992), Alesina and Rodrik (1992), Persson and Tabellini (1990). On the macroeconomics of populism see Dornbusch and Edwards (1991 and forthcoming). The Venezuelan experience is studied in Hausmann (1993c).

4. For example, Anne Krueger points out that the region is well endowed with natural resources and that this has perverse implications for the evolution of labor income over time, as the constant stock of "land" becomes less important relative to the other factors.

5. The new concepts of information economics and incentives have opened up a truly fertile way of understanding organizations. See Milgrom and Roberts (1992).

6. Recently, a candidate for dean in an economics department tried to win the student representatives' vote by offering to reduce the load of mathematics and microeconomics, which students often find hard.

7. Not allowing workers to renounce their acquired social rights is seen as a way of protecting them. An alternative view would see this as a restriction that limits the tradability of those rights and hence reduces their value. If a worker is allowed to trade one right for another, he cannot be made worse off.

8. DRGs are menus of standard costs, independent of how much the hospital spent on any particular patient. Hence, when a patient is admitted for a medical intervention, the hospital already knows what its revenues are going to be and consequently, a dollar saved is a dollar earned. Developing that menu of standard costs, however, is often extremely complicated.

9. A macroeconomist could argue that the transition entails no aggregate cost. The savings of workers in their individual accounts will match the deficit of the government

because of its new responsibility to pay for the pensioners. The government manages the transfer by issuing domestic debt. This assumes, however, that the government does not face an upward-sloping cost of funds, given the public's reasonable assumption that the government will use inflationary finance in order to service the debt in the future. Hence today's interest rates will rise as the stock of bonds grows.

10. Hausmann and Rigobon (1993) document the cases of the Dominican Republic, Peru and Venezuela.

Bibliography

ALESINA, A. and R. PEROTTI (1992), "The Political Economy of Growth: A Critical Survey of the Literature", mimeo, Harvard University.

ALESINA, A. and D. RODRIK (1992), "Distributive Politics and Economic Growth", *American Economic Review*.

BLINDER, A.S. (1988), *Hard Heads, Soft Hearts: Tough-Minded Economies for a Just Society*, Reading, MA: Addison Wesley.

CLARKE, G. (1992) "More Evidence on Income Distribution and Growth", World Bank Working Paper WPS 1064, December.

DORNBUSCH, R. and S. EDWARDS (1991), *The Macroeconomics of Populism in Latin America*, Chicago: Chicago University Press.

DORNBUSCH, R. and S. EDWARDS (forthcoming), *Stabilization, Economic Reform and Growth*, Chicago: Chicago University Press.

HAUSMANN, R. (1993a), "El impacto distributivo de las finanzas públicas", in R. Hausmann, ed., *Ajuste y pobreza: falsos dilemas y verdaderos problemas*, Washington, D.C.: Banco Interamericano de Desarrollo.

HAUSMANN, R. (1993b), "Ante el colapso de la política social tradicional: ¿qué hacer?", paper presented to the 17th Meeting of the Grupo Santa Lucia, 9-13 October, San José de Costa Rica.

HAUSMANN, R. (1993c), "Quitting Populism Cold Turkey: Venezuela's 1989 Big Bang Approach to Macro Balance", in Goodman, L.W., J. Mendelson, M. Naím and J. Tulchin, eds, *The Lessons of Venezuela*, Washington: Johns Hopkins University Press.

HAUSMANN, R. and R. RIGOBON, eds (1993), *Government Spending and Income Distribution in Latin America*, Washington: Inter-American Development Bank.

MÁRQUEZ, G. (1993), "Cui Bono?: Regulation and Outcomes in the Labor Market", in *Venezuelan Labor Market Study*, Washington, D.C.: World Bank.

MILGROM, P. and J. ROBERTS (1992), *Economics, Organization and Management*, Englewood Cliffs: Prentice-Hall.

NAÍM, M. (1993), *Paper Tigers and Minotaurs: The Politics of Venezuela's Economic Reforms*, Washington, D.C.: Carnegie Endowment.

PERSSON, T. and G. TABELLINI (1990), *Is Inequality Harmful for Growth?: Theory and Evidence*, NBER Working Paper 3599.

PSACHAROPOULOS, G. and Y.C. NG (1992), "Earnings and Education in Latin America: Assessing Priorities for Schooling Investment", World Bank Working Paper Series No. 1056, Washington, D.C.

WILLIAMSON, J. (1991), *Latin American Adjustment: How Much Has Happened?*, Washington, D.C.: Institute for International Economics.

WORLD BANK (1990), *World Development Report*, Washington, D.C.: Oxford University Press.

WORLD BANK (1992a), "Venezuela: Education Sector Review", grey cover, Washington, D.C.

WORLD BANK (1992b), "Venezuela: Health Sector Review", grey cover, Washington, D.C.

WORLD BANK (1993), *World Development Report*, Washington, D.C.: Oxford University Press.

Fiscal Reform, Structural Adjustment and the New Role of the State in Latin America

Guillermo Perry

Introduction

The structural reforms undertaken in most Latin American countries, and the emerging new roles of the state, demand significant fiscal reforms. Tax reforms in the region during the last decade were conditioned by both the necessities of short-run macroeconomic adjustment (to overcome the acute exchange and fiscal crisis that most countries suffered in the early 1980s) and by the needs of long-term structural adjustment.

Consequently, two parallel processes of fiscal reform took place in the decade. Although simultaneous in some countries, they came about sequentially in most cases. First, specific and generally temporary adjustments ("quick fixes") were undertaken to meet short-term stabilization needs. Both the initial crisis and these adjustments tended to worsen the quality of the tax system. Second, structural reforms were necessary in order to adapt the tax system to the wider objectives of long-term structural adjustment.

Relations between these two processes were complex. In many cases, the urgent need for fiscal stabilization led to postponement of structural tax reforms. The precise stabilization measures adopted frequently hindered structural fiscal reform later. In particular, this was the case in countries which initially resorted to increases in taxes on foreign trade, taxes on financial transactions and other minor, inefficient taxes, with negative effects on the competitiveness of the economy. Over time, however, the need to adapt the tax system to the requirements of more open and deregulated economies has become undeniable. These trends are traced below.

The schizophrenic process of tax reform during the 1980s

Fiscal reform and stabilization: the predominance of short-term and temporary adjustments

Most Latin American countries suffered acute exchange and fiscal crises during the early 1980s, owing to the superposition of external shocks (deterioration in the terms of trade, rise in international interest rates and, later, suspension of foreign credit by commercial banks) on increasing macroeconomic imbalances and on the accumulation of considerable foreign debt. The imbalances and indebtedness, in turn, were permitted by the wide availability of international financial resources during the second half of the 1970s. Governments reacted to the crisis with stabilization programmes of varying force and success. To date, a considerable number of countries in the region have succeeded in their objectives of stabilizing prices and obtaining fiscal adjustment, although not all of them have managed to overcome the effects of the crisis and of adjustment programmes on investment rates and economic growth.

Table 1 depicts an assessment of the magnitude of the fiscal imbalances and later adjustments in 13 selected countries in the 1980s. It shows that at some moment during the decade, consolidated non-financial public-sector deficits exceeded 4 per cent of GDP in all of these countries, 7 per cent in ten of them and 10 per cent in five (Argentina, Mexico, Bolivia, Peru and Uruguay). When the deficit originating in quasi-fiscal transactions is counted, the combined total exceeded 20 per cent of GDP in Argentina in 1983 and in Mexico in 1987. The magnitude of adjustment during the 1980s may be appreciated by noting that 8 of the 13 countries showed primary fiscal surpluses at the end of the decade.

A recent quantitative appraisal[1] draws the following conclusions. External variables had a considerable direct impact, both on the process of fiscal imbalance and on the subsequent adjustment. This was particularly marked for changes in the terms of trade of those countries in which public finances depend heavily on revenues from commodity exports (e.g. Chile, Mexico and Colombia). Similarly, the increase in international interest rates and the subsequent suspension of credit by commercial banks severely penalised public finances, especially in countries that had accumulated a large foreign debt in previous years.

Second, the economic crisis, suffered by most countries in the region as a consequence both of the superposition of external shocks on increasing macroeconomic imbalances and of the adjustment programmes themselves, also had a considerable effect on the behaviour of public finances. In particular, the acceleration of inflationary processes, recession, the shrinking of imports, the outflow of capital and in some countries the sharp real devaluation all had marked effects on real fiscal revenues. Internal financial crises and the rise in domestic interest rates also caused substantial quasi-fiscal deficits in various countries in the region (Argentina, Chile and Mexico), as well as considerable increases in the service of domestic debt (Argentina, Brazil and Mexico) and in subsidies to the private sector (Chile and Argentina). On the positive side, the ultimate success of price stabilization programmes and the start of economic recovery in some countries contributed substantially to the subsequent fiscal adjustment.

Table 1. **Surplus/deficit of the consolidated non-financial public sector**

(percentage of GDP)

		1980	Maximum deficit	Year	1990	1991
Argentina						
	Total surplus	8.0	-17.9	(83)	-5.1	-1.6
	Primary surplus	-4.6	-11.9		-2.0	0.4
Bolivia						
	Total surplus	-7.8	-26.6	(84)	-8.3[a]	
	Primary surplus	-5.2			-6.3[a]	
Brazil						
	Total surplus	-2.0	-7.4	(88)	-7.4[b]	
	Primary surplus	0.0			-1.1[b]	
Colombia						
	Total surplus	-2.3	-7.4	(83)	-0.7	
	Primary surplus	-0.8	-5.2		3.0	
Costa Rica						
	Total surplus	-9.3	-9.3	(80)	3.3[a]	
	Primary surplus	-3.1			9.6[a]	
Chile						
	Total surplus	5.6	-4.4	(84)	5.3[c]	
	Primary surplus	6.4	-2.0		7.5[c]	
Ecuador						
	Total surplus	-7.4	-8.5	(81)	-4.4[a]	
	Primary surplus	-4.3			-0.5[a]	
Guatemala						
	Total surplus	-4.7	-7.4	(81)	-1.3[a]	
	Primary surplus	-4.1			0.1[a]	
Mexico						
	Total surplus	-6.9	-16.8	(82)	-7.6[c]	
	Primary surplus	-3.4	-8.6		5.4[c]	
Paraguay						
	Total surplus	1.3	-4.9	(84)	-0.9[b]	
	Primary surplus	1.8			0.5[b]	
Peru						
	Total surplus	-3.9	-10.3	(83)	-5.5[c]	
	Primary surplus	0.8			-3.8[c]	
Uruguay						
	Total surplus	1.3	-10.4	(82)	0.7[a]	
	Primary surplus	1.8			3.2[a]	
Venezuela						
	Total surplus	7.3	-5.5	(88)	-5.5[b]	
	Primary surplus	10.8			-1.7[b]	

[a] 1987 figures.
[b] 1988 figures.
[c] 1989 figures.

Sources: *Estudio económico de América Latina y el Caribe 1990*, CEPAL.
Case studies.

Exchange rate policy played a major role in fiscal stabilization. Where the public sector is a net exporter of goods and services (e.g. Chile, Mexico and Colombia), real devaluations, required for the adjustment of the external sector, contributed enormously to the subsequent fiscal adjustment. The opposite happened in countries such as Argentina. This fact seems to have had a considerable effect on the differences in exchange-rate policy in the countries examined, particularly at the end of the decade.

Third, autonomous fiscal policy proved unable to react promptly to the fiscal imbalances caused by both internal and external shocks, owing to the lag between policy decisions and their effects and, in some cases, to expansionary fiscal policies early in the decade. This sluggishness accentuated the worsening of public finances during the crisis years or led to delays in fiscal adjustment.

Fourth, in the face of fiscal imbalance, governments initially reacted by cutting public investment (with the exception of certain countries such as Colombia) and by increasing prices and tariffs in the public sector, taxes on foreign exchange and financial transactions, and other minor taxes. These measures enabled a more rapid response and were politically more expedient. In contrast, the reform of income taxes and value-added tax (VAT), particularly the former, required complex legal and political procedures and did not generate immediate returns. In other words, the urgency of stabilization processes in almost all the countries led to deterioration of the tax system and made it difficult to carry out structural reforms directed towards greater economic efficiency.

Fifth, the system of taxes on domestic activity (in particular, income taxes and VAT) not only failed to contribute initially to the fiscal adjustment process, but generally aggravated the fiscal imbalance. Recession reduced tax revenues. Acceleration in inflation caused a fall in the real value of tax revenues, because of the lag between accruals and depreciated actual receipts (the so-called Olivera-Tanzi effect) and because the deduction of interest payments has greater weight in inflated nominal terms in non-indexed tax systems. Tax evasion increased considerably. Owing to variations in inflation rates, the process of demonetisation and greater informal-sector activities in some countries increased opportunities for evasion, making tax control more difficult. Reductions in tax rates, as a result of the political crisis that accompanied the economic crisis (as in Argentina in 1986) or for long-term structural reasons (as in Chile in 1984), exacerbated fiscal imbalances.

Sixth, for fiscal reasons some countries plunged into ambitious privatisation programmes. In particular, this was the case with countries that had incurred considerable debt (Argentina, Mexico); the revenue obtained from privatising public enterprises allowed them not only to avoid issuing additional debt to finance the deficit, but also to reduce the size of the current debt.

Finally, in the majority of the countries of the region, collection of basic taxes (income and VAT) was not reinforced until the late 1980s or early 1990s. This finally came about as a result of a growing conviction of the need for permanent and credible fiscal adjustment in order to balance an open economy, as well as the necessity of finding a substitute for tax receipts on foreign trade, which had been reduced as a result of trade liberalisation.

Tax reform and structural adjustment: trade, financial and structural tax reform

The majority of Latin American countries have undertaken (in some cases, simultaneously with macroeconomic adjustment) a series of structural reforms, directed towards achieving greater efficiency in the economy and in state actions and defining a new relationship between the state and the private sector. Trade and financial liberalisation, deregulation of internal markets, privatisation of some public companies and other state reforms have had important consequences for public finances.

The tax-reform process was of a structural nature and was characterised by the following features:

– decrease in rates and simplification of rate structures for income tax on individuals;

– lowering nominal tax burdens on capital incomes through integration of company-stockholder taxation, introduction of inflation adjustments, reduction of tax rates on business income, remittance of profits and, in some countries, elimination of taxes on the net wealth of individuals;

– widening of withholding systems, advances and at-source taxation;

– generalised adoption of VAT and continued widening of its coverage;

– elimination of a large number of exemptions in direct taxation; and

– increased use of presumed income systems.

The initial recourse to taxes offering high and prompt yields with easy control (taxes on foreign trade, energy and foreign exchange and financial transactions) gave way in the late 1980s and the early 1990s to a process of bolstering revenues from basic domestic taxes. These structural reforms obeyed the precepts of administrative simplicity, the influence of the concepts of "supply side economics" and, increasingly important, the requirements of more open and deregulated economies. Broadly speaking, the objectives of structural reform processes — in particular those of trade and financial liberalisation — imposed the necessity of increasing revenues from basic taxes on domestic activities (income and VAT).

It was increasingly recognised that macroeconomic balance in open economies required fiscal adjustment of a permanent and credible nature. A significant fiscal imbalance in an open economy has immediate consequences both on the current account of the balance of payments (a rapid rise in imports and service payments) and on the capital account. (Even if the fiscal deficit is financed domestically, there would be an increase in foreign debt as a consequence of the greater inflow of capital caused by the raising of domestic interest rates.) In a closed economy, these effects could be restrained, at least for a time, by recourse to greater quantitative restrictions on imports and inflows of private capital.

The need to increase or maintain investment in physical infrastructure and in human capital, required to improve international competitiveness, meant that fiscal adjustment could not continue to be based on additional cuts in expenditure and public investment. Consequently, a permanent increase in fiscal revenues was required. The temporary "fixes" used — recourse to capital income through privatisation and the use and abuse of minor taxes — also had an adverse effect on the efficiency and competitiveness of the economy.

Finally, there was a need to substitute revenues from domestic taxes for taxes on foreign trade, as taxing foreign exchange and financial transactions ran counter to the objectives of the trade and financial liberalisation.

In some Latin American countries, trade liberalisation did not initially reduce revenues from duties (thanks to the effects of real devaluation, along with the elimination of tariff exemptions and quantitative restrictions, and in some cases, the initial replacement of the latter by duties). In the late 1980s and early 1990s, however, in countries with such diverse experiences as those of Argentina, Chile and Colombia the trend was one of significant reduction in the ratio of trade taxes to GDP, in comparison to the highest levels reached during the 1980s. This process is inevitable with the trend towards a general reduction in nominal duties and integration agreements. Broadly speaking, the significance of taxes on trade will increasingly reflect the minor role they play in all industrialised economies[2].

Trade and financial reform have also largely determined the long-term modifications of the internal structure of direct and indirect taxation on domestic activities. Financial liberalisation, increased international capital mobility and the need to recover investment levels have led countries to encourage greater inflows of foreign investment and capital repatriation by decreasing the rates of direct taxes and reducing, through various mechanisms, the nominal tax burden on capital income, amongst other measures. In order to reconcile these requirements with the need for greater revenue, it became necessary to broaden the base of direct taxes, to reduce the number of exemptions and other privileges in favour of specific sectors, to generalise withholding systems, to make greater use of presumptive systems and to improve administration.

These realities and the objectives of trade liberalisation reinforced the tendency to introduce and strengthen VAT rather than other indirect taxes. VAT is almost the only indirect tax that allows absolute tax exemption on exports (with tax rebates, under zero-rating regimes) and, more generally, a greater compatibility with free trade — this is why the European Community (EC) required its members to adopt VAT instead of sales taxes. It is not surprising that Latin American countries have been increasing VAT rates at the same time as they reduce nominal tariffs.

Faced with the option of an extremely rapid rise in VAT rates, several countries have preferred to broaden their bases, reduce exemptions and improve their administration, as has been the case with direct taxes. In fact, one of the least expected consequences of the structural reform process in Latin America has been a growing conviction of the need to reduce the gap between high nominal tax rates and low effective revenues, a disparity due to the erosion caused by multiplicity of regimes, wide exemptions and privileges, evasion and weak administrations. The recent trend towards strengthening the tax administration and fighting evasion in Mexico and Argentina is very revealing in this respect.

Growth, efficiency and equity effects of recent tax trends

The long-term trend towards a greater emphasis on VAT and income taxes — as against taxes on trade and financial transactions, as well as excise and other minor taxes — is undoubtedly conducive to a more efficient and competitive economy, and thus, in the context of open economies, to higher growth. Recent quantitative exercises, using computable general equilibrium models, suggest that this trend also has positive distributive effects[3].

The effects of two other trends — towards a greater importance of VAT as against income taxes, and towards more "neutral", simpler and less progressive VAT and income taxes — are more open to question. From the point of view of growth it is clear that consumption-type VAT is preferable to income taxes, as it does not tax savings. Precisely for the same reason, however, there is little doubt that VAT has more regressive effects and income taxes more progressive effects, especially in the case of simple (single-rate), broad-based VAT.

A flat-rate, broad-based consumption tax is regressive because higher-income families save a higher proportion of their income and spend a higher proportion out of the country, thus escaping domestic taxation. In many Latin American countries an attempt is made to reduce the inherent regressiveness of the VAT by exempting basic consumption goods (e.g. foodstuffs) or taxing them at reduced rates, and charging a higher rate for luxury goods. The price is less enforceability, a more costly administration and reduced revenue. While a broad-based VAT, as in Chile, yields about 9 per cent of GDP, those in other Latin American countries, with differential rate structures and more exemptions, produce around 3-5 per cent of GDP. The political dilemma is not a simple one.

Flat rates were also criticised, for some time, from the point of view of a theoretical "economic efficiency". One of the best-known results of the so-called optimal taxation theory was that rates should differ according to demand and supply elasticities. Practitioners were never convinced of this prescription, partly because of the technical difficulties involved, but mainly because of the administrative costs it would entail. More recent work has shown that such a result no longer holds when theoretical models include, as they should, collection costs (both taxpayer compliance and administration enforcement costs)[4]. Curiously enough, the main legacy of "optimal taxation theory" seems to be a theoretical revendication of some old-fashioned excises (on alcoholic beverages, gasoline and the like), where elasticity and administrative-cost arguments go in the same direction.

Income taxes, in contrast, are definitely progressive in practice, since lower-income families pay no income tax. This advantage is lost, to some extent, due to the current trend towards broad withholding mechanisms, but this trend also reduces administrative costs, helps control evasion, diminishes the negative effects of inflation in tax collection and, as a consequence, increases the real yield of direct taxes.

The higher theoretical progressiveness attributed to the progressive nominal rate structure of personal income taxes was rarely translated into real collections in developing countries, as both evasion and the benefits of tax incentives and exemptions were usually concentrated in the top deciles. Indeed, higher marginal rates were usually accompanied by more exemptions and evasion — the higher the marginal rate, the higher the benefit of investing in evasion and lobbying for special exemptions, "incentives" or outright loopholes.

Such evidence changed the advice provided by experts: instead of the highly progressive rates characteristic of the 1960s and 1970s, they began to recommend "flatter" rate structures with fewer exemptions and loopholes. The actual political processes of such reforms have typically emphasized the high concentration of previous tax benefits (in a small number of large enterprises, economic groups and the very wealthy), which, if abolished, would allow reduced rates for most taxpayers with no loss of state revenue.

The topic of tax incentives deserves further discussion. Most previous work, in Latin America and elsewhere, had found evidence of slight effectiveness but high fiscal costs. Cases such as the "industrial promotion law" of Argentina became synonymous with fiscal waste. The discussion has recently been revived, however, by a monumental work on incentives[5], which found some evidence to the contrary in the Asian NIEs. A reasonable conclusion[6] may be that tax incentives work when they are well designed, specific, temporary and closely monitored (leading to an unavoidable, high administrative cost) and operate in a proper macroeconomic environment (so there is, among other things, fiscal equilibrium despite the cost of incentives). The political, macroeconomic and administrative preconditions for such good practice are yet to be seen in Latin America.

The previous discussion underscores the fact that there is no "free lunch" in tax policy. Trade-offs between revenue, growth, efficiency and equity objectives (as would happen in the case of "textbook case" tax incentives) are largely unavoidable, especially when collection costs (both taxpayers' compliance costs and the administrative costs of enforcement) and political economy considerations are fully taken into account. Current expert advice and recent Latin American trends (keep it simple, broad and general, and avoid using high marginal rates) seem to be a reasonable compromise. After all, the growth and equity objectives of government intervention may be better served by a tax system that generates high yields with low collection costs, and thus finances badly needed infrastructure and social expenditures without impairing macroeconomic equilibrium.

Some emerging topics of fiscal reform

Decentralisation and fiscal reform

Considerations of efficiency and democratic control have led to the transfer of greater responsibilities for public expenditure to the States, provinces and town councils of many countries in the region. At the same time, the focus on a small number of broad-based high-yield taxes has tended to concentrate revenues in the central state, as income taxes and VAT (and the former taxes on foreign trade) are very difficult to administer in a decentralised manner. In Mexico, poor results in the administration of VAT by the States led to the federal authorities' taking over in 1989, after which revenues increased significantly.

This divergence has two implications. The first is the need to bolster tax revenue at regional and local levels. In particular, property tax revenues are extremely low in the majority of Latin American countries. This largely explains the chronic financial problems of the majority of large Latin American cities, their poor physical and social infrastructures, and their dependence on national finances. Second, the imbalance noted above — between the high concentration of tax revenues controlled by the central government and the responsibility for expenditure under the control of the States, provinces and town councils — requires transfer systems or schemes for sharing of national revenues. Additionally, imbalances in the level of economic development and wealth between different regions and towns require a transfer system to support those which have a lower fiscal capacity or which are further behind in the provision of basic services.

The responsibility for supplying the most basic services (education, health, etc.) rests ultimately on the national or federal government, in many countries by constitutional mandate. Consequently, the national government may not affect ignorance of the problem and, at least, must guarantee suitable financing of the States, provinces or town councils in order to fulfill these obligations.

All these considerations require transfer or revenue-participation schemes. There are several problems associated with existing systems of transfers or co-participation. When transfers are entirely discretionary, regional and local bodies cannot properly plan their investments and programmes. The political procedure of annual appropriations is very costly and wasteful and, in general, does not lead to an efficient allocation of resources. When transfers are entirely automatic, they are generally applied by means of simple formulas that do not take appropriately into consideration either the real expenditure needs or the fiscal capacity of the different regional and local bodies.

Under both systems, some regional and local bodies will have low total resources in relation to their obligations whilst others have excessive resources, leading to waste and deterioration of fiscal efforts. For this reason, some countries have attempted to link transfers to regional and local fiscal efforts and administrative efficiency, but the experience has not been very satisfactory because, among other reasons, in such cases resources tend to concentrate on the most developed regional and local bodies.

In some countries, revenues from a few specific taxes have been used for transfers or co-participation. This has led to biases in tax-policy decisions: when the national government needs resources, it prefers to increase non-participatory taxes, thus often reducing the quality of the tax system. (This has frequently been the case in countries such as Argentina and Brazil.)

Lack of control over the indebtedness of the regional and local bodies has had unfortunate effects in some countries: the national or federal government's efforts towards fiscal discipline may be defeated by the expansionist policy of regional bodies, which are not responsible for overall macroeconomic balance (again, Argentina and Brazil are examples). In other cases, total and discretionary control by central government has prevented a more autonomous and efficient development of investment programmes in the regional bodies.

In summary, the topic of fiscal reform is closely related to overall state reform. The need for efficient redefinition of relations between the nation-state and regional, provincial and local governments is clear, but very little progress has been made in the majority of Latin American countries. This will be a critical item on the agenda in subsequent decades.

Stabilization of public expenditure vis-à-vis variations in revenues from main export commodities

In many countries of Latin America, total public revenue depends heavily (by more than 20 per cent, and in some countries by more than 50 per cent) on exports of petroleum and mineral products. This is the case in Bolivia, Chile, Colombia, Ecuador, Mexico, Peru, Trinidad and Tobago, and Venezuela. When public spending has followed the strong oscillations that characterise these revenues, it has induced or reinforced wide variability in the behaviour of the economy: recession and boom periods, periodical inflationary bursts, marked variations in the real exchange rate, and so on. These variations have contributed to weakening investment rates and long-term growth.

In boom periods, governments tend to increase their current expenditures (in terms of both number employed and salaries) markedly and to launch projects of doubtful economic and social return. During low periods, it becomes necessary to interrupt ongoing projects or programmes, to reduce real government salaries drastically and to dismiss large numbers of employees. The benefits and costs associated with these sharp variations are asymmetric and provoke great inefficiencies and trauma. The experiences of all Latin American petroleum-producing countries during the price boom of the 1970s and early 1980s, and their subsequent crises, exemplify these problems in a dramatic way. In some of these countries, the very high dependence of public receipts on oil and mineral exports partly reflects the lack of a strong and modern tax system, but it is also a consequence of their economic structure, and thus will not disappear any time soon.

The solution to this problem lies in suitable institutional schemes. Chile's recent experience with the Copper Stabilization Fund and Colombia's past experience with the National Coffee Fund indicate the importance of such schemes in moderating the inevitable political and social pressure on expenditures during boom periods, and thus in saving for times of crisis in a planned manner. This aspect of fiscal reform is attracting increasing attention from Latin American economists[7], and will probably have an important place on the political agenda in several countries in the 1990s.

The reform of social security systems

The financial crisis within the social security systems of several countries in the region has led to consideration or implementation of far-reaching reforms. In particular, several countries are introducing changes in their pension systems, following the Chilean example of the early 1980s. Such a reform includes shifting from simple pay-as-you-go systems to individual capitalisation funds and transferring responsibility from a state monopoly to private funds. Several objectives have been established: an increase in national savings, development of the capital market and long-term fiscal balance.

From the purely fiscal point of view, a rapid transition from one system to the other creates short- and medium-term problems. Government must meet existing obligations, contribute as an employer to capitalisation funds, and guarantee minimum pensions and a minimum return from these funds. The magnitude of the resulting fiscal deficits depends on the extent of the system's coverage and the initial level of reserves. In the case of Chile, this deficit has been estimated as equivalent to an average of 4.5 per cent of GDP per year over almost a decade[8]; in the case of Colombia, it has been estimated at about 2 per cent of GDP over a similar period. Such a deficit may be financed, at least in part, by the capitalisation funds themselves, but the accumulation of a large public debt *vis-à-vis* the funds (or the "sinceration" of the public debt, as it is called by the champions of the changeover) cannot avoid having adverse consequences for the capacity and terms of public sector financing.

Problems of a non-fiscal nature (the eventual concentration of economic power, the abandonment of traditional principles or solidarity) have also generated wide-reaching discussion in several countries in the region. As a result, it is obvious that the topic of social security will play a major role on the reform agenda in several Latin American countries.

Fiscal harmonization

Processes of economic integration in the region will lead to a growing importance of the topic of tax and fiscal harmonization, as has been the trend for some time within the EC. The debate, which is scarcely getting under way, has so far focused more on the need for harmonization of state subsidies, in order to avoid situations of unfair competition, than on tax harmonization. Nevertheless, as the sub-regional integration schemes (Grupo Andino, Mercosur, etc.) gain momentum, and should NAFTA approval by the US Congress lead to acceleration of negotiations directed at the formation of a hemispherical free trade zone, or to the integration of other countries into NAFTA, the topic of fiscal harmonization will gradually appear on the agenda for negotiation.

Environmental taxes and charges

The growing concern, at world and regional level, with the environment, and the need to reconcile economic development with environmental conservation, will put this topic on the agenda of fiscal reform in Latin America. For the present, the majority of the countries of the region are resorting more to "command and control" systems than to economic incentives. Nevertheless, sooner or later, the inefficiency of these command and control systems, fully proved and documented in industrialised nations, will lead to discussion and development of systems of taxes, charges and negotiable permits, as has already started to happen in the United States and some European countries.

The process will be a slow one, as a result of practical difficulties in the design and administration of these taxes and charges (although their theoretical attractiveness has been recognised, as the taxes would be few and would not imply "welfare losses") and the resistance of many militant ecological groups to the principle that "the polluter pays". Industries on which this financial burden is imposed unilaterally by their host countries object on the grounds that it undermines their international competitiveness; this objection would also have to be overcome. In fact, it is difficult to imagine a rapid development of these taxes and charges (except in highly localised situations: for example, where the pollution of water bodies is concerned) without some degree of co-ordination and compromise at the international level. As proposals such as that of an "ecotax", the carbon tax or the energy tax gather momentum in the industrialised countries, the issue will quickly move onto the agenda of fiscal reform in Latin America.

Conclusions

Two processes of tax reform were undertaken in the 1980s and the early 1990s: specific adjustments ("quick fixes"), generally of a temporary nature, to meet short-term stabilization needs; and structural reforms to adapt the tax system to the wider objectives of long-term structural adjustment. The stabilization measures adopted frequently hindered the later fiscal reform. In the end, however, it has become necessary to adapt the tax system to the requirements of more open and deregulated economies.

In particular, the objectives of trade and financial liberalisation imposed the necessity of increasing revenues from basic taxes on domestic activities (income and VAT). There was an increasing perception that macroeconomic balance in open economies required permanent and credible fiscal adjustment. Fiscal adjustment could not continue to be based on cuts in expenditure and public investment, privatisation and the use and abuse of minor taxes; all these had an adverse effect on economic efficiency and competitiveness. Thus there was a need to substitute domestic taxes for taxes on foreign trade and to avoid taxing foreign exchange and financial transactions.

Trade and financial reform have also largely determined long-term modifications of direct and indirect taxation on domestic activities. Financial liberalisation, increased international capital mobility and the need to recover investment levels have led governments to encourage inflows of foreign investment and capital repatriation by, amongst other measures, decreasing direct tax rates and reducing the nominal tax burden on capital income. In order to reconcile these requirements with the need for greater revenue, it became necessary to broaden the base of direct taxes, reduce the number of exemptions and other privileges in favour of specific sectors, generalise withholding systems, make greater use of presumptive systems and improve administration.

These factors and the objectives of trade liberalisation reinforced the tendency to introduce and strengthen VAT rather than other indirect taxes. Faced with the option of an extremely rapid rise in VAT rates, several countries have preferred to broaden the bases of VAT, reduce exemptions and improve administration, as has been the case with direct taxes.

In fact, one of the least expected consequences of the structural reform process in Latin America has been growing conviction of the need to reduce the gap between high nominal tax rates and low effective revenues, a disparity due to the erosion caused by multiplicity of regimes, wide exemptions and privileges, evasion and weak administrations.

Trade-offs between revenue, growth, efficiency and equity objectives are largely unavoidable, especially when collection costs and political economy considerations are fully taken into account. Current expert advice and recent Latin American trends (keep it simple, broad and general, and avoid using high marginal rates) seem to be a reasonable compromise. After all, the growth and equity objectives of government intervention may be better served by a tax system that allows high yields with low collection costs, which permit badly needed infrastructure and social expenditures without impairing macroeconomic equilibrium.

In addition to these trends in tax structure, several new issues of broader fiscal reform are emerging on the political agenda:

- the trend towards fiscal decentralisation and other problems in the financial relations between various levels of government;
- the need to establish expenditure stabilization mechanisms in countries subject to wide fluctuations in fiscal revenue, due to the dependence of public finances on the revenues from main export commodities (oil, copper and the like);
- the need to reform social security systems, owing to changes in fertility rates, in life expectancy and hence in the structure of population age groups;
- the growing need to harmonize taxes and subsidies in economic integration agreements; and
- the growing importance of environmental taxes and fees, as instruments for harmonizing development and environmental requirements.

Although many countries in the region have made some advances in tax reform during the 1980s and early 1990s, the fiscal reform agenda for Latin America in the next decade appears to be very demanding. The degree of success in this area will largely determine the possibility of developing an efficient new role of the state in the context of the more open and deregulated economies of the 1990s.

Notes and References

1. Perry and Herrera (forthcoming).
2. Tanzi (1990).
3. See, for example, Lora (1993).
4. Mihaljek (1992).
5. Shah (1992).
6. Bird (forthcoming).
7. See for example Meller and Engel (1992).
8. Ortuzar (1986).

Bibliographical References

ARELLANO, José Pablo, y Manuel MARFÁN (1987), "Veinticinco años de política fiscal en Chile", *Colección de Estudios CIEPLAN*, No. 21, Estudio No. 127, 129-162.

BAQUEIRO CÁRDENAS, Armando (1991), *El déficit del sector público consolidado con el banco central: la experiencia mexicana de 1980 a 1989*, Serie Política Fiscal, CEPAL/PNUD, Santiago.

BARTOLI, Gloria (1988), "Fiscal Expansion and External Current Account Balance", *IMF Working Papers*, Fiscal Affairs Department, IMF, Washington, D.C.

BIRD, Richard M. (1992), *Tax Policy and Economic Development*, Johns Hopkins University Press, Baltimore.

BIRD, Richard M. (forthcoming), "Tax Incentives for Investment in Developing Countries", in Whalley and Guillermo Perry, eds, *Tax Reform and Structural Adjustment*, Macmillan, London.

BIRD, Richard M. and Oliver OLDMAN (1990), *Taxation in Developing Countries*, Johns Hopkins University Press, Baltimore.

BLEJER, Mario I. and Adrienne CHEASTY (1988), "The Fiscal Implications of Trade Liberalization", *IMF Working Papers*, Fiscal Affairs Department, IMF, Washington, D.C.

BOSKIN, Michael J. and Charles E. McCLURE, Jr. (1990), *World Tax Reform: Case Studies of Developed and Developing Countries*, International Center for Economic Growth, Panama.

CEPAL (1991), *La economía de América latina y el Caribe en 1990; las finanzas públicas en la década de 1980. Estudio económico de América latina y el Caribe 1990, Volumen* , Santiago.

FAUS-FESCOL (1991), *Sistemas tributarios y ajustes por inflación en América latina*, Bogotá.

GILLIS, Malcolm (ed.) (1989), *Tax Reform in Developing Countries*, Durham, N.C., Duke University Press.

KHALILZADEH-SHIRAZI, Javad and Anwar SHAH (1991), "Tax Policy in Developing Countries", *World Bank Symposium*.

LORA, E. (1993), *Colombia Poverty Assessment*, mimeo, Fedesarrollo, Santiago.

MARCEL, Mario (1989), "Privatización y finanzas públicas: el caso de Chile 1985-88", *Colección Estudios 26*, CIEPLAN, Santiago.

MARCEL, Mario y Manuel MARFÁN (1988), "La cuestión tributaria", *Revista CIEPLAN*, No. 13, "Corporación de investigaciones económicas para Latinoamérica", Santiago.

MELLER Patricio and Eduardo ENGEL, (1992), *Shocks externos y mecanismos de estabilización*, CIEPLAN and Inter-American Development Bank, Santiago.

MIHALJEK, Dubravko (1992), "Tariffs, Optimal Taxes, and Collection Costs", *IMF Working Papers*, European I Department, IMF, Washington, D.C.

MITRA, Pradeep (1990), "The Coordinated Reform of Tariffs and Domestic Indirect Taxes", *IMF Working Papers*, IMF, Washington, D.C.

NEWBERY, David and Nicholas STERN (1987), "The Theory of Taxation for Developing Countries", *World Bank Research Publication*, The World Bank, Washington, D.C.

OCAMPO, José Antonio and Edgar REVÉIZ (1979), "Bonanza Cafetera y Economía Concertada", Centro de Estudios de Desarrollo Económico (CEDE), Bogotá.

OKS, Daniel F. and David DUNN (1991), *Forecasting the Primary Fiscal Balance in Mexico*, World Bank, Washington, D.C.

ORTIZ, Guillermo (n.d.), "Public Finance, Trade, and Economic Growth: The Mexican Experience", IMF Paper, IMF, Washington, D.C.

ORTUZAR, P. (1986), "La reforma previsional de 1980. Mitos y premoniciones", Centro de Estudios Públicos, Documento de trabajo 71, Santiago.

OSPINA SARDI, Jorge (1991), *Lecciones de la política fiscal colombiana*, Serie política fiscal, CEPAL/PNUD, Santiago.

PERRY, Guillermo and Mauricio CÁRDENAS (1986), "Diez años de reformas tributarias en Colombia", Fedesarrollo, Santiago.

PERRY, Guillermo and Ana Maria HERRERA (forthcoming), *Finanzas públicas, estabilización y reforma estructural en America latina*, Inter-American Development Bank, Washington, D.C.

PERRY, Guillermo E., Roberto JUNGUITO and Nohora de JUNGUITO (1981), *Política económica y endeudamiento externo en Colombia 1970-1980*, Centro de Estudios de Desarrollo Económico (CEDE), Bogotá.

PERRY, Guillermo and Jorge Armando RODRÍGUEZ (1991), "Las finanzas intergubernamentales en la constitución de 1991", Inst. de Economía, Universidad Católica de Chile, Santiago.

ROS, Jaime (1992), "Ajuste macroeconómico, reformas estructurales y crecimiento en México", paper prsented at the seminar: Red Latinoamericana de Macroeconomía sobre Políticas de Estabilización y Reforma del Estado, Inter-American Development Bank, Washington, D.C.

SADKA, Efrain and Vito TANZI (1992), "A Tax on Gross Assets of Enterprises as a Form of Presumptive Taxation", *IMF Working Papers*, Fiscal Affairs Department, IMF, Washington, D.C.

SÁNCHEZ, Manuel (1992), "Privatización en América latina", Inter-American Development Bank Report, Washington, D.C.

SARMIENTO, Eduardo (1991), "La política fiscal en Colombia", CEPAL, Santiago.

SHAH, Anwar, ed. (1992), *Fiscal Incentives for Investment in Developing Countries*, World Bank, Washington, D.C.

SHOME, Parthasarathi (1992) "Trends and Future Directions in Tax Policy Reform: A Latin American Perspective", *IMF Working Papers*, WP/9243, Fiscal Affairs Department, IMF, Washington, D.C.

TANZI, Vito (1987a), "Tax Reform in Industrial Countries and the Impact of the US Tax Reform Act of 1986", *IMF Working Papers*, Fiscal Affairs Department, IMF, Washington, D.C.

TANZI, Vito (1987b), "Fiscal Policy, Growth, and the Design of Stabilization Programs", *IMF Working Papers*, Fiscal Affairs Department, IMF, Washington, D.C.

TANZI, Vito (1989), "Fiscal Policy and Economic Reconstruction in Latin America", *IMF Working Papers*, Fiscal Affairs Department, IMF, Washington, D.C.

TANZI, Vito (1990), "Quantitative Characteristics of Tax Systems of Developing Countries", in Bird and Oldman, *Taxation in Developing Countries*, 4th edition.

TANZI, Vito, ed. (n.d.), *Fiscal Policy in Open Developing Economies*, IMF, Washington, D.C.

TANZI, Vito and Mario I. BLEJER (1986), "Public Debt and Fiscal Policy in Developing Countries", *IMF Working Papers*, Fiscal Affairs Department, IMF, Washington, D.C.

TANZI, Vito and Ke-young CHE (1989), "Fiscal Policy for Stable and Equitable Growth in Latin America", *IMF Working Papers*, Fiscal Affairs Department, IMF, Washington, D.C.

TAX POLICY DIVISION (1990), "Tax Policy and Reform for Foreign Direct Investment in Developing Countries", *IMF Working Papers*, Fiscal Affairs Department, IMF, Washington, D.C.

WIESNER DURÁN, Eduardo (1992), "Colombia: descentralización y federalismo fiscal", informa final de la misión para la descentralización, Presidencia de la República, Departamento Nacional de Planeación.

WORLD BANK (1992a), *Argentina: Public Finance Review—From Insolvency to Growth*, Latin America and the Caribbean Regional Office, Washington, D.C.

WORLD BANK (1992b), *Lessons of Tax Reform*, Washington, D.C.

Administrative Reform and State Capacity: A Comparative Study of Antitrust Legislation in Italy, Venezuela and Mexico

Luciano Cafagna

Introduction

This analysis assumes that democratic and capitalist systems are strictly correlated, and in particular that reinforcing democratic institutions implies strengthening capitalist ones. Indeed, the institution of a free decentralised market system can by itself serve to check the natural tendency of the state to encroach in the allocative process and can deprive the state of the ability to suppress opposition. In an economy characterised by a large public sector and heavily regulated markets, the state can more easily engage in strategic behaviour against political or economic interest groups that it considers adversarial by limiting their access to resources. In contrast, a capitalist economy affords opportunities for the political opposition to find employment, gather financing and channel its views[1]. In this context, the effectiveness of competition policy must be valued in so far as it can allow economic entities to engage in economic activities without fear of strategic interference from the state or from other special interest groups that control the state; the advocacy role of the antitrust enforcer thus becomes of paramount importance. Indeed, if this new power were applied in the political struggle persecution would take on a new meaning. Moreover, competition laws may reinforce the process of democratisation in that they follow or are contemporaneous with the removal of regulations restricting the rights of economic entities to go freely about their business and imposing limitations on property rights.

The potential conflicts of interest among antitrust, industrial and trade policies are not examined in any great depth here. These topics are treated only in so far as state efforts to bring together economic actors around different strategic objectives may create incentives and opportunities for anticompetitive behaviour. Given this potential conflict and the natural tendency for economic interests to appropriate supracompetitive rents in the transition from a controlled to a liberalised economy, the implication is that if the state wishes to implement a successful administrative reform it must create an atmosphere of credibility and transparency. This it can accomplish by distancing itself from special-interest-group pressures and reducing the probability of opportunistic behaviour. Consequently, the adoption of laws which establish transparent administrative proceedings for evaluating and restricting anticompetitive behaviour — by private and public sector economic entities — in markets undergoing transformations becomes integral to reinforcing democratisation and economic liberalisation.

The introduction of antitrust legislation in Italy, Venezuela and Mexico[2] reveals the desire to turn away from a reliance on industrial policy and direct government participation as the principal tools for stimulating economic growth. In part, this change originates in the realisation that direct state intervention in the allocative system has failed to develop an industrial structure capable of sustained long-term growth[3]. In this context, the adoption of competition policy is aimed at restraining the potential abuses that can arise, once markets are allowed to find their own equilibrium in the post-liberalisation era, and at eliminating the entry barriers and allocative distortions caused by existing oligopolistic market structures and anticompetitive laws. The broad objectives of antitrust policy are thus twofold: direct intervention in the private sector to influence the direction that market structure and performance take, and advocacy directed at the state to push for the implementation of legal or administrative reforms.

As defined by the three laws under consideration here, the purpose of the antitrust authority is not to identify and impose particular market configurations, but rather to determine which configurations are not acceptable, to attenuate their effects and where possible to eliminate them. The distinction is key because it ties in with the principle of removing from the state the power of actively determining how markets should allocate resources. Thus, if one accepts this proposition, state antitrust interventions should be limited to those areas characterised by market failures where prices have a tendency to rise above marginal costs and output is restricted below the optimal level. Whether this policy engenders new modes of production that are smaller, more flexible and more responsive to consumers remains a function of the peculiarities of the industries involved and the regulations surrounding them. The antitrust objective of eliminating supracompetitive rents may very well be compatible with high degrees of market concentration[4].

The contexts within which the three bodies of legislation have been introduced are dramatically different and thus pose a useful backdrop against which to judge the potential efficacy of the various policies in fulfilling their primary objectives. Indeed, the decision to choose Venezuela and Mexico as countries of comparison arises from the desire to analyse the potential impact of the different antitrust approaches on economic and political systems at different levels of development and regional integration. Furthermore, it is hoped that analysis of the experiences and legislation of countries facing different conditions will make it possible to draw important lessons for other Latin American countries and for Italy.

The similarities between the three countries also serve to validate the comparison since all three are engaged in extensive economic liberalisation plans and thus — to a certain degree — face the same conceptual problems. Indeed, the three countries share the difficulties associated with creating competitive markets in sectors previously characterised by a strong public presence and with controlling the practices of competitors in industries that have only recently faced market liberalisation and deregulation. In the first case, the antitrust authority's role of monitoring mergers will be crucial in avoiding the transformation of public monopolies into private monopolies; in the second, the tendency of competitors to collude on prices — even in the face of price liberalisations — can be of particular relevance especially if the industry has historically developed into a oligopolistic structure.

The historical evolution of market regulation in Italy, Venezuela and Mexico

The adoption of antitrust laws in the countries under consideration imposed a global framework that encompasses and in some cases supersedes the individual provisions dealing with market regulation which were previously scattered throughout the legal system in various laws, articles of constitutions and civil or commercial codes. The new laws provide unifying analytical criteria and set out the ultimate objective of market regulation: protect competition and increase consumer welfare.

Although Italy has operated under the umbrella of Articles 85 and 86 of the Treaty of Rome since 1957[5], and thus has had to conform to European Community (EC) decisions on restrictive agreements and abuses of dominant position, the country has delayed, sometimes for decades, in applying EC directives and recommendations aimed at liberalising the industries operating under state monopoly concession[6]. To understand the origins of Italy's attitude towards competition policy and industrial policy programmes in general, one must look at the provisions in the Constitution and the Civil Code, which, until the adoption of the antitrust law of 1990, were the national legislative standard.

Article 41 of the Italian Constitution establishes a broad mandate according to which "private economic activity is free" but cannot be undertaken in contrast with social utility or cause harm to the security, liberty and dignity of humanity. The Constitution then leaves to the legislature the task of establishing controls and programmes aimed at influencing private and public economic activity to attain social goals; it thus lacks any reference to monopolies and restriction of competition. As will be shown in the following paragraphs, this concept of planning and co-ordination took Italy down a path diametrically opposite the one suggested by antitrust philosophy. It is here that the EC finally caught up and forced a re-evaluation of the concept of "economic liberty"; imposed the new interpretation, which championed the concept of markets and their protection; and conceptualised state intervention as setting rules to protect competition rather than interfering with the market[7].

The period from the late 1920s to the early 1940s saw the state take control of the private economy in the dual effort to avert crises like that of 1929 and to impose more direct control over the development of the economy. This occurred through the extensive granting of exclusive monopolies, the nationalisation of industries, the institution of administrative controls over the right to participate in certain economic activities and the creation of administered prices for whole series of products[8]. The existing regime also applied its authoritarian philosophy by enacting laws which created and disciplined mandatory consortiums — including professional associations[9].

Towards the end of this period the Italian legislature implemented other laws, the main objective of which was not the protection of "competition" or consumer welfare, but rather the restriction of firms' behaviour. In the case of monopolies, the law specified that a *legal* monopolist could not refuse to deal with a potential client in an indiscriminate manner[10], but this law did not apply to monopolists — or dominant firms — that had gained their position through their own efforts, and thus ignored the wider issue of "dominant firm" behaviour in favour of guaranteeing consumer access to essential goods and services[11]. In the case of cartels, once again, the legislature limited the government's antitrust role by expressly exempting cartels which were limited to a particular activity, had a short duration (five years) and were circumscribed to specific geographic areas[12].

The lack of an antitrust culture in Italy must be seen in the perspective of the active debate witnessed both in parliament and in academia as early as the 1950s[13]. The proposed ministerial directive for the regulation of cartels in 1950[14] and the legislative proposal for the protection of competition in 1955[15] represent valid efforts to impede restrictive collusive behaviour and protect consumers from anticompetitive practices.

During the 1960s, industrial policy was implemented through three basic programmes. The first was aimed at directing strategic investments by the public sector (universal housing, adequate national health care system) and the private sectors in a territorially balanced way (north/south); the second tried to strengthen and reorganise public enterprises in an effort to create a growing source of revenue; and the third was an effort to inform the private sector of the objectives of industrial policy. These instruments of industrial policy, however, were intermixed with direct subsidies and incentives that — in the name of development, employment and aid to specific sectors of the economy — became the heart of industrial policy. Indeed, industrial policy shifted away from specific objectives, orienting itself to subsidising and to making subsidies conditional on other factors[16]. The crises of the 1970s — labour disputes, the bloating of public expenditures in response to social demands and the oil crisis — all contributed to rendering useless the programmes started in the previous decade and led the Italian legislature to buttress industrial policy with the neglected tool of antitrust legislation.

Historically speaking, the governments of all three countries considered here have condoned and even encouraged the creation of industrial blocs. In Venezuela and Mexico this occurred through the application of import-substitution development policies whereby the government protected national industries by creating import barriers and heavily regulating competition at home. The theory was that in developing countries characterised by market imperfections and structural deficiencies, state intervention became crucial in filling the gap between private and social rates of return. In particular, the state needed to encourage expenditure in the production of non-traditional goods since domestic private rates of return underestimated the advantages of investment in industry[17]. By instituting these incentives, the governments reinforced business's perspective that there was nothing wrong with the cartelisation or monopolisation of certain industries. The concept of what was "rational" for firms to do and what was "efficient" in general welfare terms became confused as criteria other than the maximisation of competition were used. Indeed, the Latin American experience points to a situation where import-substitution development policies encouraged the formation of oligopolistic[18] and monopolistic market structures while at the same time the existing antitrust laws became complements to price control policies and were used to "protect" consumers from price rises[19].

Origins of the law in the three countries

The catalyst which pushed the Italian government to adopt this new law is multidimensional but can be traced primarily to the desire to participate in the creation of an integrated European market[20]. The adoption of "traditional" antitrust legislation was thus a response to a regionalisation trend. This explanation seems decisive in the cases of Italy and Mexico, but has a different relevance for Venezuela. In Mexico's case, the economic bloc into which entry was sought was the North American Free Trade Agreement (NAFTA); as in the Italian case, acceptance to this club is conditional on the standardization of the rules by which the game is played. As such, Mexico's latest version of the Antitrust Law — which brings it at least to par with the legislations of its NAFTA companions — is consistent with this goal of "integration". Indeed, this new law is to evaluated as an integral augmentation to Mexico's numerous trade barrier reforms, exchange rate realignments, and industrial programmes aimed at easing entry by foreign competitors and increasing allocative efficiency[21]. For Mexico and Venezuela, the broader economic reforms were also pushed by the need to reduce dependence on oil revenue as the sole source of foreign currency and of buying power.

Another impetus for the adoption of these new laws came from the fall of the Eastern bloc, which left, by default, the market model as the only viable alternative[22]. Italy took a definitive turn towards a "market" approach to managing the economy and away from a "public" strategy. In contrast to the historical divisions over the objectives of competition policy and on the means of achieving those objectives, this view is currently shared by political parties along the entire spectrum. This turn was translated into increased privatisation[23] as a means of streamlining bloated and inefficient government operations, rejection of tariff and non-tariff trade barriers as tools for economic growth[24], price liberalisation[25] and the establishment of competition rules to eliminate monopolistic practices which misallocated resources, caused inefficiencies and decreased consumer welfare.

The Latin American countries also opted to turn away from public-sector involvement and turned towards a market-oriented, open-trade development policy, but they did so for slightly different reasons. In Venezuela, while there was pressure from the outside to implement a series of market-oriented reforms, there was also an internal populist movement that saw the antitrust law as a means of fighting the power of the "big companies" — and thus pushed for its adoption[26]. The main creative push, however, came from the technocrats (many of whom were trained abroad) nominated to key governmental positions in the 1989-90 period by newly elected President Pérez. These "outsiders" to politics helped establish and maintain the intellectual climate which served as a breeding ground for many of the liberalising reforms — including the antitrust law. Also contributing to this rethinking were the failure of the import-substitution industrialisation plans and the effects of a mounting fiscal burden in the context of the distortions induced in national markets by price controls[27].

Between the suspension of economic rights[28] in 1962 and the adoption of the competition law in 1992, the Venezuelan government exerted direct control over the economy through executive decrees (in fixing prices) and judicial regulations (legitimisation of cartels). In July 1991 the right to economic liberty was reinstated, thus restoring the power of the legislature to regulate the market and protect the right of the individual to participate in whatever branch of the economy he chose. The direct consequence of this change was the abrogation of the decrees restricting economic liberty and the adoption of antidumping, consumer protection and competition laws, among others.

The modern competition law of Mexico is based on Article 28 of the 1917 Constitution. This article prohibits monopolies and monopolistic practices which, through the excessive concentration of control over "necessary consumer goods", can be detrimental to the public or to a particular social class. This characterisation of monopolistic practices led to wholesale price regulation of a series of goods that the executive deemed "necessary", ranging from medical supplies to cement[29]. The first competition law in Mexico, dating from 1934, provided enforcement parameters too difficult to apply and introduced antitrust concepts which tended to "protect" competitors rather than competition[30]. In 1950, the Law on Economic Powers of the Federal Executive formally established the power of the executive to set maximum prices for a series of goods[31] (of an authorised size); to intervene in situations characterised by insufficient production by rationing, affecting distribution and imposing "priorities"; to eliminate "useless" middlemen who only add to the final cost of the good; and in extreme cases to oblige firms to produce "necessary consumer goods" and to provide compensation when this caused an economic loss to the producer. The new competition law of 1993 abrogated the laws of 1934 and 1950, and served to reinstate property rights, which had been limited under the strictly regulated regime.

Comparison of the Italian, Venezuelan, and Mexican laws

The analysis here utilises the Italian law and experience as a benchmark against which to evaluate the Venezuelan and Mexican laws and the direction that enforcement may take in those countries. The classic antitrust policy tools are: merger policy, control of dominant firm behaviour and restrictive agreements, and an advocacy programme aimed at preventing the adoption and persistence of anticompetitive laws and regulations. The ability of the state to influence the strategic behaviour of economic interests through antitrust laws depends in large part on the political objectives of the legislature and on the interpretations adopted by the chief enforcer: the legislature can facilitate the work of the enforcer by providing him or her with incisive investigatory powers and well-defined evaluation criteria, and by creating an autonomous administrative structure; the degree of ambiguity and discretion built into the law can make it subject to opportunistic interpretation by the enforcer and thus reduce its effectiveness in the long run.

General considerations

The three bodies of legislation are primarily patterned after the EC competition law, in that they set up autonomous administrative agencies responsible for protecting competition through the control of abusive behaviour by dominant firms, the prevention of distortions created by collusive agreements, and the prohibition of mergers that create a dominant firm able to restrict competition. The Venezuelan and Mexican laws differ from the Italian law in that they include *per se* provisions for handling restrictive collusive agreements and certain abusive behaviours by dominant firms[32]. Another important distinction is that the Italian law establishes joint responsibility, thus creating the possibility of heterogeneous application of the law, while in the Latin American cases enforcement powers are centred in only one agency.

Administrative structure and selection of chief enforcer

The three laws protect the autonomy of the respective antitrust agencies by granting them administrative and decisional independence. The difference lies in how the chief enforcers and presidents are selected and in the provisions set up for their removal. Of the three, the Venezuelan law provides the widest discretionary powers for removing the superintendent[33]. This could give rise to two kinds of problems. First, it may encourage the so-called spoils system, whereby the entrance of a new chief enforcer has a domino effect on the other positions in the structure and thus creates a discontinuity in the functioning of the administration. Second, the awareness that exogenous factors can cause the removal of the chief enforcer can adversely condition his or her behaviour. The Venezuelan law has a built-in safeguard: while the chief enforcer can be removed, the selection criteria guarantee that the replacement will meet the same standards met by the outgoing chief enforcer. All three laws prohibit their chief enforcers from holding any outside non-academic employment, and in Italy even academic employment is forbidden.

Shared enforcement responsibility

As mentioned above, the Italian law is the only one of the three that stipulates joint responsibility for enforcement. The Italian Antitrust Authority shares responsibility with two other entities: the Bank of Italy for firms active in the credit industry, and the Media Authority for firms in the radio, television and print industries. In both cases the agencies also have regulatory and oversight responsibilities. This configuration is the compromise solution which arose, in large part, as a result of efforts by long-standing institutions to prevent any erosion in the magnitude or scope of their power; it is not a model that should be followed.

One peculiar aspect of the Italian law is that it grants the executive branch exceptional powers of intervention in merger cases dealing with the privatisation of state-owned enterprises or in mergers between Italian firms and firms from countries which do not have similar antitrust laws. The first of these provisions, however, is tempered in that the executive can only issue broad guidelines that are not case-specific and that in any event must conform to specific principles.

Procedural transparency and right to defence

Perhaps the most important characteristics of the various antitrust laws, in terms of how administrative reform can strengthen the creation of democratic institutions, are the degree of procedural transparency and the extent to which the right to defence is protected. Procedural transparency increases the effectiveness and efficiency of administrative action and reduces the possibility of strategic behaviour by the state by imposing on the appropriate office or division the unequivocal responsibility for dealing with a particular matter within a predetermined and objectively set period of time[34]. Similarly, guaranteeing the right to be heard at the various steps of the administrative proceeding and the right of immediate access to the counterpart's depositions decreases the possibility that the administration or the state may infringe on the individual's rights.

Areas of intervention

Collusive behaviour

The article in the Italian law dealing with agreements does not distinguish *a priori* between vertical and horizontal agreements; rather, it focusses on the magnitude and duration of the effects that an agreement can have on competition[35]. The standard of evaluation used is the rule of reason: the authority must show that the objective or effect of an agreement is the consistent restriction of competition[36]. The approach taken by the Mexican legislature to control this type of anticompetitive behaviour is more direct in that it specifically mentions a list of horizontal agreements as *per se* violations; the Venezuelan law includes all agreements and leaves to the Exemption Regulation the task of excluding vertical agreements. Both approaches minimise the costs borne by the antitrust agencies, which need not expend scarce resources to prove the anticompetitive effects of such practices but merely demonstrate that the practice occurred; in addition, this straightforward formulation provides clear criteria for private sector firms to follow. This is perhaps the biggest and most crucial difference between the Italian and the two Latin American laws.

As for the possibility of exempting restrictive agreements, the Italian example creates a paradox which, if taken to its extreme interpretation, can lead to a distorted application of the law. More specifically, the fact that an agreement can be considered restrictive and subsequently exempted can, under the guidance of particularly interventionist or power-hungry enforcers, lead to abusive application of this two-step procedure (the subjection of as many agreements as possible to administrative control). In this regard the three laws differ in their philosophy. At one end of the spectrum stands the Venezuelan law, which prohibits all restrictive agreements and permits a subsequent exemption for those that entail efficiency considerations and increases in consumer welfare; Italy follows a rule-of-reason approach for evaluating, on a case-by-case basis, the merits of granting an exemption; and Mexico stands at the opposite end, as its law does not provide for the possibility of granting exemptions to restrictive horizontal agreements.

Merger policy

For merger policy, the three laws take slightly different approaches in determining notification and evaluation criteria and in specifying intervention powers. The Venezuelan law has a *per se* prohibition against mergers that create dominant positions or restrict competition; it thus applies a mix of absolute and relative standards[37]. The Italian law prohibits mergers that create a dominant position such as to restrict competition. Finally, the Mexican law prevents mergers whose purpose or effect is to diminish or harm competition[38]. All three sanction only those dominant positions which are attained through mergers, which means that the antitrust enforcer cannot restrain a monopolist who through his own efforts has attained dominance in a market, but can only react to eventual abuses.

Dominance

The Italian law leaves the concept of dominance undefined, thus giving the antitrust enforcer the responsibility of determining on a case-by-case basis the characteristics and existence of dominance and the possible restriction of competition. In contrast, the Mexican and Venezuelan laws spell out the criteria that must be met to identify whether an economic agent has substantial market power and whether competition is harmed. With regard to definitions, the Italian law is patterned after EC law and thus makes reference to a growing body of jurisprudence to determine whether dominance exists. In practice this has translated into determining whether the firm under consideration has the power to act independently of its competitors.

Restrictions on legal monopolists

All three laws provide for dealing with legal monopolists. In the case of Italy and Mexico exemptions are granted for all economic activities strictly connected to the monopoly concession, while all other related activities fall under the scrutiny of the law. The Venezuelan law handles the legal monopolists in a slightly different manner: unless the law granting the monopoly concession specifies operating conditions that condone particular kinds of anticompetitive behaviour, the monopolist must act in conformity with the competition law.

Furthermore, the Italian law allows economic entities to produce goods and services for their own use, even if those goods and services fall under a monopoly concession granted to another entity. This right and the tendency to prohibit the extension of a dominant position — acquired as a result of a monopoly concession — to contiguous markets that do not fall under the strict definition of the concession are the main interventionist tools of the authority. A case in point is the cellular telephone market, which according to the authority's interpretation falls outside the basic concession granted to the *Società Italiana per l'Esercizio delle Telecomunicazioni p.a.* (S.I.P.), and thus must operate under competition rules.

Advocacy programme

Both Italy and Mexico have specific articles in their laws giving antitrust authorities the power to issue non-binding advisory opinions on proposed and existing legislation that is deemed to introduce competitive distortions. The Venezuelan law has no such provision, but nothing prevents or has prevented the Antitrust Authority from making its opinion known[39]. Although the omission of this provision from the law has done little to restrict the authority's activities in this area, it may increase the potential for delegitimisation and for institutional inactivity.

Enforcement, investigatory powers and sanctions

The effectiveness of an antitrust authority depends in large part on its ability to ascertain the existence of anticompetitive behaviour and on the powers at its disposal to impose remedies. In all three of the countries under consideration, violation of the antitrust law qualifies as a civil offence and not as a criminal one[40].

The Italian authority has the power to initiate investigations, subpoena documents and conduct on-site inspections; to investigate statutory situations which create distortions in the market and to conduct informative inquiries in economic sectors where competition may be harmed (in the latter case it enjoys lesser inquisitory powers than when it is conducting an investigation); and to stop mergers, prohibit or exempt cartels and restrict abusive behaviour by dominant firms. It also has the power to initiate investigations *ex officio* under all three of the prosecution articles — collusive agreements, abusive dominant behaviour and mergers. In all three cases there are provisions for imposing fines, when violations of the law are encountered or firms provide false information, as well as defined time restrictions that take effect at each step of the investigation. The Mexican and Venezuelan laws provide their respective enforcers with similar investigative and acquisitory powers.

Where sanctions are imposed for violations of the articles relating to abuses of dominant position and restrictive collusive behaviour, the Italian and Venezuelan systems impose fines as a percentage of the annual income of the violator. For non-compliance, failure to co-operate or false declarations, the Italian and Venezuelan laws establish fixed fines[41]. Mexican legislation sets all fines similarly and as a multiple of the minimum wage, except for very serious violations, in which case fines of up to 10 per cent of annual sales or 10 per cent of assets (depending on which is greater) are levied.

In theory, the objective of administrative fines should be to punish and prevent recurrence of illegal behaviour without provoking the exit of an economic operator from the market. If maximum fines are established, firms might well find it profitable to continue violating the law. In effect, the fine then becomes a mere "tax" paid on illegally earned profits. If minimum fines are set, paying the penalty could send firms into bankruptcy, which in turn could lead to a loss in consumer welfare and harm competition by reducing the number of operators in the market. Thus, in theory the best policy is one that, taking into consideration aggravating (persistence of violation, amount earned as a result of illegal behaviour, size of market share, leading role in violation) and mitigating factors (co-operation, possibility of failure, follower role in violation), imposes a fine that is clearly not inferior to the gain earned by the violator but does not cause exit from the market[42].

The Italian law instituting the Guarantor of Competition and Markets

The Italian parliament took a deliberate step towards strengthening competitive market conditions when it adopted its antitrust law in 1990[43]. This law — a direct extension of Article 41 of the Constitution, which protects and guarantees the right to economic activities — also served to bring the Italian legal system in tune with EC antitrust standards[44].

Administrative autonomy

In brief, the Italian antitrust law established an independent government agency headed by a president and four commissioners who are charged with enforcing the law as it pertains to two broad areas: on one hand, the control of mergers (Articles 5 and 6), abuses of dominant position (Article 3), and restrictive collusive agreements (Articles 2 and 4); on the other, the fact-finding investigations and advocacy programmes (Articles 12 and 20-21 respectively).

The members of the authority hold non-renewable seven-year appointments and are nominated via a joint recommendation of the presidents of the House and Senate. The law specifically grants to the authority the power to request and obtain the co-operation of other public entities in its undertakings. In cases involving the insurance and the print advertising sectors, the law requires the authority to ask the regulatory agencies for an advisory opinion before reaching a decision.

For its financing the authority depends on the budget of the Ministry of Industry, Commerce and Crafts, as approved by the Ministry of the Treasury and the General Accounting Office. This dependence does not translate into *de facto* control of the day-to-day operations of the authority, but there are two provisions which grant the minister of industry the power to disapprove a merger and to issue broad guidelines for the approval of mergers to monopoly. In the latter case, the minister can determine, *a priori*, a set of general principles on the basis of which the Antitrust Authority can then approve a merger to monopoly if (1) it is deemed to be in the general economic interest of the nation and integral to the European integration process (a so-called national champion), and (2) it is shown that the merger will not create competitive distortions other than those justified by the general interest. Conversely, the minister can stop a merger if he or she determines that one of the merging parties originates from a country that does not have a competition law similar to the Italian one.

Shared responsibilities

The authority shares responsibility for enforcing the antitrust law with two other entities: the Bank of Italy for firms in the credit industry, and the Media Authority[45] for firms in the radio, television and print industries[46]. In both cases the other agencies also have regulatory and oversight responsibilities.

It is important to analyse the possible conflicts of interest that can arise from the integration of regulatory powers with the power to enforce the competition law, since the two mandates can be contradictory. Indeed, owing to a specific provision in the regulation law or to control of the regulator by special interest groups, the regulator is more likely to be interested in maximising stability in the industry, conformity to technical standards, the provision of a "basic" service and possibly the protection of individual economic entities; the enforcer of antitrust law, by contrast, is interested in protecting the process of competition and consumer welfare. Thus the agencies that share in the enforcement of the antitrust law may choose (and have on occasion chosen) to apply the law utilising different criteria.

In a recent case[47], the Media Authority chose to grant an exemption to a horizontal restrictive agreement proposed by the major print advertising companies. The objective of this agreement was to ensure that subscribers refrained from entering into "advance payment" contracts with publishers. The supporters of the agreement stipulated that these clauses were hurting the advertising agencies because they imposed too high an operating cost given the declining trend in the industry. In particular, it was stated that the clauses discriminated against small advertising agencies by excluding them from whole sections of the market. Thus, the agreement would allow for a greater number of firms to survive and operate profitably. While the Media Authority concurred with the advisory opinion of the Antitrust Authority that the agreement restricted competition and did not result in efficiencies or economic benefits to consumers, it nonetheless appealed to the constitutionally established right to "informational plurality", saying that the agreement would contribute to this objective and thus should be allowed.

Scope and depth of powers

The authority has the power to initiate investigations, subpoena documents, and conduct on-site inspections into alleged restrictive collusive behaviour. It also has the power to investigate statutory situations which create distortions in the market and to conduct informative inquiries in economic sectors where competition may be harmed (in the latter case, it enjoys lesser acquisitory powers than when it is conducting an investigation).

The law has one interesting aspect which conditions the behaviour of both the Antitrust Authority and firms: for mergers of companies meeting certain income levels, notification of the authority is compulsory; for agreements between firms, however, the notification step is voluntary.

In terms of its enforcement powers, the Antitrust Authority may stop mergers, prohibit or exempt cartels and restrict abusive behaviour by dominant firms. In all three cases there are provisions for handing out fines when violations of the law are encountered or where firms provide false information.

The authority has the power to initiate investigations *ex officio* under all three of the prosecution articles — collusive agreements, abusive dominant behaviour and mergers. In all three cases there are well-defined time restrictions that take effect at each step of the investigation.

Enforcement policy under Antitrust Law No. 287/1990

The enforcement policy of the authority has been primarily one of reactive control. The authority has had to balance the need to create internal administrative and analytical procedures to handle its case load with the need to react to a series of short turn-around deadlines. All of this has been complicated by the need to establish solid legal precedents in a field that until now has been explored only at the EC level. In so far as it has been able, the authority has also initiated in-house investigations into distortionary practices.

Mergers

Since its inception the Antitrust Authority has devoted the majority of its resources to screening mergers; it has examined over 1 200 notifications in almost three years[48], stopping only a very few. The Italian law prohibits only those mergers that create or strengthen a firm's dominant position in such a way as to eliminate or substantially reduce competition. Thus, the evaluation of a merger proceeds in two steps: determining whether the merger creates a dominant firm, and evaluating the consequences of such a merger.

The Italian law provides three definitions of a merger[49]: the merger of two or more firms, creation of a joint venture and acquisition of control of a firm. For the first category, contrary to EC law, the Italian law does not limit its definition of mergers to operations involving previously independent firms. Thus, group reorganisations fall under the scrutiny of the antitrust enforcer even though the external economic effects of such operations are negligible, at best[50]. The second class of mergers refers to the creation of an autonomous economic entity whose objective is not the co-ordination of its own behaviour with that of the founding firms[51]. The third type of merger is a catch-all which encompasses all mergers accomplished through means other than a direct merger and the constitution of a joint venture. The decisive factor in meeting this definition becomes the acquisition of a "determinant influence" on a firm by another.

Abuses of dominant position

The Italian experience points to the existence of three basic types of cases that fall under this category: abuses by firms that have gained their dominance in one market through leverage on a legal monopoly in a contiguous market[52]; abuses by firms that, through some governmental or legislative disposition, have gained an anticompetitive advantage over their competitors[53]; and abuses by firms that have reached a dominant position due to market considerations[54]. The antitrust enforcer treated all cases by issuing rulings that prohibit specific abusive practices and has not imposed "structural" solutions. The notion of abusive practice is primarily "welfare"-oriented in that the practice must reduce the benefits to consumers or restrict competition. The one clause that finds a difficult application is that which refers to unjust prices, as it imposes on the antitrust enforcer the difficult task of calculating the marginal cost faced by the firm.

Collusive behaviour

The Italian law does not distinguish *a priori* between horizontal and vertical agreements, but focusses on the magnitude and duration of the effects that an agreement can have on competition[55]. The standard of evaluation utilised is the rule of reason: the authority must show that the objective or effect of an agreement is the **consistent** restriction of competition[56]. The sectors of the economy investigated by the authority have varied from the food products industry to the transportation sector. The gamut of agreements examined includes agreements between firms or trade associations, consortium articles of association, merger-related clauses (such as non-competition agreements) and regulations of trade associations[57]. As of the summer of 1993, no exemption from the law has been granted, although numerous requests have been made[58].

Sector analyses

A series of sector analyses has been conducted in industries where the authority has determined the potential existence of distortion in the way competition operates. Often the findings of these analyses have been used to initiate investigations into restrictive collusive practices and abusive behaviour by dominant firms.

Legislative proposals

The Italian Antitrust Authority has a programme for monitoring the parliamentary legislative agenda, which is designed to avoid the introduction of laws or regulations that can create distortions in the competitive process[59]. The authority also tries to anticipate EC intervention directed at enforcing the articles of the Treaty of Rome and the EC directives aimed at liberalising particular sectors[60].

The Venezuelan law instituting the Superintendency for the Promotion and Protection of Free Competition

The primary objectives of the Venezuelan law are the promotion and protection of competition and the protection of efficiencies which benefit producers and consumers. The law also aims at prohibiting monopolistic and oligopolistic practices which can limit competition. It thus seeks to maximise competition while, where there are efficiency considerations, allowing certain restrictive practices. The law defines the relevant concepts to be used as benchmarks in determining whether certain practices occur[61].

It has an umbrella prohibition (Article 5) against all practices or agreements which restrict competition and eight articles which list the "specific" prohibitions (Articles 6-13). As interpreted by the Venezuelan Antitrust Authority in its first decision[62] the general provision is a "residual" clause which is in place to catch all of the practices deemed anticompetitive, but for which no specific prohibition is postulated. Thus, to prove a violation of Article 5 the authority needs to show that competition is restricted, while for violations of Articles 6-13 it need only show that the practice occurred. In the case of abuses of dominant position the Venezuelan law provides for a mix of *per se* and rule-of-reason provisions (see Table 1).

The Venezuelan Antitrust Authority has also issued an exemptions regulation which lists the practices and agreements that are allowed in so far as they do not restrict competition. These non-distorting practices are actually interpreted as falling outside the scope of the law; indeed, it is assumed that the true intention of the legislature was to grant exemptions to agreements that restrict competition but entail efficiencies and benefits for consumers. Thus the regulation is to be seen against the backdrop of Articles 10 and 12 (agreements) and Article 13 (dominant firm behaviour), as it provides for the possibility of restrictive vertical agreements that do not violate the definition of effective competition (Article 16), and also limits the prohibitions against dominant firms by allowing price discrimination that is justified on the basis of normal business practices[63].

The Venezuelan law prohibits mergers that result in the restriction of competition or the formation of a dominant position. The articles relating to mergers have not yet taken effect, as the Antitrust Authority has not issued the relevant merger guidelines. Once it does, the authority will be faced with the tricky problem of enforcing the law without overly restricting economic activity. This problem may arise since the small size of the Venezuelan economy implies that most of the mergers falling under the jurisdiction of the law will also be in violation of it[64].

As we have seen, the Venezuelan Antitrust Authority plays an active advocacy role in the promotion and adoption of competitive laws by submitting comments to the parliament and the council of ministers[65]. In addition, it has a seat and a voice on the inter-ministerial councils empowered with overseeing the activities of the legal monopolists.

Of minor importance to the enforcement aspect of the law, but nonetheless of major importance in revealing the true intent of the legislature, is the conflict-of-interest provision (Article 28), which sets strict standards of conduct for employees and thus minimises the possibility of individual and institutional capture.

Table 1. **Comparison of Italian, Venezuelan and Mexican Antitrust Laws**

		MEXICO	**VENEZUELA**	**ITALY**
General provisions				
Date of adoption of the law and related regulations		23 June 1993 Not yet approved	13 January 1992 23 February 1993 (exemption reg.)	10 September 1990 10 October 1991 (procedural reg.)
Nature of agency & degree of independence		- autonomous administrative body of the Ministry of Commerce and Industrial Development - independent decision making - appeals are heard by the commission itself, and eventually by the courts	- functionally autonomous body administratively tied to the Ministry of Development - decisions are challenged only at the Supreme Courts	- independent administration subject to court review & limited executive intervention
Joint enforcement responsibility with other governmental agencies		No	No	Yes (Bank of Italy & Media Authority)
Direct civil enforcement		Yes	All cases must be initially filed with the Antitrust Agency, which then can prosecute, remand to private court, or close down	Yes
Conflict of interest rules		employees cannot hold any other job except for academic positions	- employees or their relatives cannot work for an investigated firm, or related firm for the period of 1 year following the investigation	- employees cannot hold any other employment
Enforcement areas				
Enforce-ment policy	*Per se* (absolute ban on certain behaviours regardless of results)	- horizontal activities: price fixing, restricting output, splitting up of markets, and bid rigging	horizontal or vertical activities: price fixing, restricting output, splitting up of markets, tying contracts abuse of dominant position: price discrimination, tying contracts, and refusal to deal	No *per se* provisions

228

Table 1. (end)

		MEXICO	VENEZUELA	ITALY
		Enforcement areas		
	Rule of reason (anticompeti-tive value judgement is required to decide on legality)	See cell below	- resale price maintenance	<u>vertical or horizontal agreements:</u> resale price maintenance, restricting output, splitting up the market, price discrimination, and tying contracts
	Dominance (behaviour prohibited specifically to "dominant" firms)	- exclusive distribution contracts - resale price maintenance - tying contracts - refusal to deal - coercive retaliatory behaviour - any act which impedes competition	- restricting output - price discrimination	- unjust pricing - price discrimination - restricting output - tying contracts
Advocacy powers		- offer opinion on restructuring official programmes detrimental to competition - issue non-binding comments on existing and proposed laws - participate in the signing of international agreements regulating competition	- the law does not have an article giving the power to undertake interventions, nor does it prevent the authority from doing it	- propose non-binding comments on existing and proposed legislation
Merger policy		prohibit mergers which create "uncontestable" monopoly situations	prohibit mergers which create dominant firms or restrict competition	prohibit or impose changes in mergers to avoid creation or strengthening of dominant position such as to restrict competition
Restrictions on legal monopolies		legal monopolies are not subject to the competition law	- legal monopolies are subject to the competition law <u>unless</u> the concession itself specifies an exemption	- the right to production for own consumption is guaranteed - legal monopolist is exempt for competition law <u>only</u> for those activities which are <u>strictly</u> connected to the concession

The Mexican law instituting the Federal Competition Commission

The primary objective of the Mexican antitrust law is protection of the competitive process through the prevention and elimination of monopolies, anticompetitive practices and other restraints on the efficient operation of markets[66]. The Mexican law incorporates many provisions which facilitate enforcement by providing clear-cut definitions of the concepts of dominance, relevant market and competition, and by providing the tools necessary for minimising enforcement costs.

The law includes two articles which distinguish between absolute monopolistic practices[67] and relative monopolistic practices[68]. In the first case the law has a series of *per se* provisions which render restrictive horizontal agreements illegal. Abuses of dominant position and vertical restrictive agreements fall under the second category, which requires the authority to prove that the practices have the objective or effect of "unfair" elimination of other agents from the market, the creation of entry barriers or discrimination. To a certain extent this approach deviates from the Italian and Venezuelan methodologies in that it is not a "consumer" welfare approach, being concerned more with the protection of "competitors"[69].

The law deals strictly with absolute practices because cartels which restrict output, fix prices or split geographic markets are highly unlikely to entail efficiency benefits to consumers, while they surely have a negative impact on welfare.

Conclusion

In theory, given perfect — or almost perfect — national markets characterised by the absence of trade barriers, the role of antitrust legislation as a tool for disciplining markets is reduced as the removal of entry barriers disciplines the "contestable" markets to competitive outcomes[70]. However, a series of factors linked to developing countries in particular, and to countries undergoing economic liberalisations in general, can increase the effectiveness of this policy tool. More specifically, in countries where oligopolistic market structures have been maintained by import-substitution development policies, any subsequent trade liberalisation and reduced government subsidies may not be sufficient to impose competitive conditions, as it takes time to set up distribution networks and business relationships. The reasoning that trade liberalisation coupled with antitrust policy should have the desired outcome of creating competitive markets is subject to a caveat: these practices may continue even in the presence of an antitrust law, as special interest groups can lobby the state to grant them legitimacy through monopoly concessions or other forms of "protected" status. The antitrust authority therefore becomes helpless unless it can act as an effective constraint on the legislative process[71]. In so far as the state can adopt a pre-commitment strategy designed to reduce the incentives for strategic behaviour (by making an effort to distance contract enforcement, property rights, and bankruptcy proceedings from political decisions), it can foster investor confidence and increase the likelihood that new competitors will enter domestic markets.

An antitrust law that creates transparent proceedings for evaluating anticompetitive behaviour by both the private and public sectors can do a great deal to strengthen the development of democratic institutions. Indeed, by limiting the interventionist role of the state, the legislature can ensure that the freedom to pursue an economic activity is constrained only in those cases where market anomalies create distortions in competition and fail to protect consumer welfare. Thus, the government does not have the power to favour particular political or economic groups arbitrarily, but must apply the same rules to everybody. In this light, the advocacy programme becomes crucial in ensuring that the state does not circumvent the framework created by the competition law in an effort to behave opportunistically.

Notes and References

1. For a discussion of the interrelation between democracy and capitalism, and the role of property rights and competition policy, see Martin L. Weitzman (1993), "Capitalism and Democracy: A Summing Up of the Arguments", in S. Bowles, H. Gintis and B. Gustafsson, eds (1993), *Markets and Democracy: Participation, Accountability and Efficiency*, Cambridge University Press, Cambridge.

2. Italy enacted its law in October 1990, Venezuela in January 1992, and Mexico in June 1993.

3. Albert Fishlow (1990), "The Latin American State", *Journal of Economic Perspectives*, Vol. 4, No. 3 (Summer), pp. 61-74.

4. This is particularly true for countries with relatively smaller industrial sectors where the attainment of minimum economies of scale may imply a high domestic concentration.

5. The principles contained in Articles 85 and 86 have been introduced into Italian jurisprudence by ordinary judges, who, in the absence of a national antitrust law, used them to give a new interpretation to Article 2598 of the civil code in cases of "unfair competition".

6. Italian Antitrust Authority (1993), *Annual Report to the Prime Minister*, p. 8.

7. Giuliano Amato (1992), "Il Mercato nella costituzione", *Quaderni Costituzionali*, a. XII, no. 1 (April), p. 16.

8. Vincenzo Donativi (1993), "Introduzione Storica", in Aldo Fringnani, Roberto Pardolesi, Antonio Patroni Griffi, and Luigi Carlo Ubertazzi, eds, *Diritto Antitrust Italiano* (Bologna: Zanichelli), pp. 52-53.

9. Donativi (1993), p. 53.

10. *Codice Civile*, Titolo X, Capo I, Sezione I, Art. 2597.

11. Donativi (1993), p. 59.

12. *Codice Civile*, Titolo X, Capo I, Sezione I, Art. 2596.

13. For a discussion of the debates on the role of the state in regulating monopolies and anticompetitive practices during the early 1950s, see Leopoldo Piccardi, Tullio Ascarelli, Ugo La Malfa, and Ernesto Rossi (1955), *La Lotta Contro i Monopoli* (Bari: Laterza).

14. Dispositions for the monitoring of consortiums presented to the House of Representatives on 13 July 1950 by the Hon. Togni, Minister of Industry and Commerce.

15. "Norms for the Protection of Competition and the Market", legislative proposal presented 16 March 1955 by Representatives Malagodi and Bozzi.

16. Amato (1992), p. 14.

17. Fishlow (1990), pp. 62-63. This underestimation was caused by ignoring the savings from costly imports, the benefits from externalities related to technological development and increases in labour skills, and the benefits from concerted production activities.

18. See Moisès Naím (1992), "The Launching of Radical Policy Changes: The Venezuelan Experience, 1989-1991", in Joseph Tulchin, ed., *Venezuela: Democracy and Political and Economic Change* (Boulder: Lynne Reiner), p. 78; Ignacio DeLeon (forthcoming), *The Venezuelan Law on Competition*, p. 3.

19. Malcom B. Coate, Rene Bustamante, and Armando Rodriguez (1992), "Antitrust in Latin America: Regulating Government and Business", *University of Miami International Law Review*, Vol. 24, No. 1 (Fall), pp. 37-85.

20. Italian Antitrust Authority (1993), p. 7.

21. Nora Lustig (1992), "Mexico's Integration Strategy with North America", in Colin I. Bradford, Jr., ed., *Strategic Options for Latin America in the 1990s* (Paris: OECD Development Centre and IDB), pp. 155-179.

22. For a discussion of the "marketisation" of Eastern European countries and the role of competition policy see Langenfeld and Blitzer (1992), "Is Competition Policy the Last Thing Central and Eastern Europe Need?", *American University Journal of International Law and Policy*, Vol. 6:325, p. 35.

23. The Amato government introduced a law decree on 11 July 1992 which started Italy on the path of privatisation (Law Decree No. 333/92, *Misure Urgenti per il Risanamento della Finanza Pubblica*).

24. See adhesion to EC directives liberalising the insurance sectors, the shipping sector, and others.

25. Liberalisation of cement, salt, milk, bread, gasoline and others.

26. The original Venezuelan antitrust law reflected this opinion and established restrictive rules governing acquisitions by firms above a certain size. This was partially circumvented by the adoption of the new regulation, which softened the merger intervention powers. The regulation also widened the legal window of opportunity for granting exemptions from the prohibition on restrictive agreements.

27. Naím (1992), p. 119.

28. The exercise of individual economic rights was protected by Article 96 of the 1961 Constitution; suspension of these rights, which lasted for 30 years, was approved under an exceptional constitutional regime and characterised as temporary, transitory and exceptional (DeLeon, forthcoming, p. 2).

29. *Reglamento sobre Artìculos de Consumo Necesario* of 1941, as published in the *Official Gazette* of 23 December 1941 (and subsequent amendments).

30. See Article 1 of the *Ley Organica del Articulo 28 Constitucional en Materia de Monopolios*, published in the *Official Gazette* of 31 August 1934.

31. Producers or distributors of goods falling under this category were prohibited from marketing these same goods under different guises (size of container, new varieties, new style of container) unless previously authorised.

32. See Table 1 for a breakdown of the detail of the three laws.

33. The three criteria are criminal conviction, violation of any of the six original selection criteria during the term of office, and dereliction of duty and proven ineptitude.

34. The trend towards increased transparency in administrative proceedings was further strengthened by the adoption of Law 241/90 on administrative proceedings and the right of access.

35. Of the fifteen collusive agreement cases closed in 1992, four concerned vertical relationships (Italian Antitrust Authority, 1993).

36. In this respect the Italian law differs from EC law, having introduced the parameter of consistency which is absent in the latter. In this particular case the Italian law actually refers to the "game of competition", a concept which is then left undefined.

37. As the Venezuelan merger guidelines had not been issued at the time of writing, the analysis here is restricted to the examination of the broad provisions in the law itself.

38. Whether the Mexican or Venezuelan law will require notification of within-group mergers (i.e. mergers between non-independent firms) remains to be seen. The law does not explicitly preclude from the definition of mergers those occurring between economic entities that are not independent, and the merger guidelines had not been issued at the time of writing.

39. Indeed, the Venezuelan Antitrust Agency sees this advocacy role as perhaps the most important objective of competition policy as applied in developing countries; unlike the United States, where antitrust was instituted as a curb against big business, in Venezuela it was the state itself that, through the granting of privileges to special interest groups and the creation of state monopolies, imposed a series of limitations to the economic freedom of the individual (speech by Ignacio DeLeon, General Legal Council of the Venezuelan Antitrust Authority, at UNCTAD conference on restrictive business practices, October 1993).

40. Contrary to US law, where the violators of some of the antitrust statutes can face jail terms in addition to fines.

41. In Italy's case these fines change on a yearly basis depending on the changes in the GNP index.

42. It could be argued that if a firm is at risk of failing even after behaving like a monopolist and extracting monopoly rents, it should not be in the market at all.

43 The Autorità garante della concorrenza e del mercato (Italian Antitrust Authority) was instituted by Law No. 287, 10 October 1990.

44. Treaty of Rome establishing the European Community, 25 March 1957, Article 85 (restrictive collusive agreements), Article 86 (abuse of dominant position); and EEC Regulation No. 4064, 21 December 1989 (mergers), in *Official Gazette* of the EC (*OGEC*), 1989, No. L. 395/1, ratified in *OGEC*, 1990, No. L. 73/34. The very first article of the Italian antitrust law ordains that the law is to be interpreted as an application of EC legal principles relating to abuses of dominant position and restrictive agreements. Furthermore it establishes broad parameters for deciding whether the case is to be examined by the national authority or the EC Commission. In theory, if a case has the potential of introducing distortions in the competitive process such as to restrict trade amongst the member nations then the case comes before the Commission; if this condition does not hold, the national authority has competence.

45. The Autorità garante per la radiodiffusione e l'editoria was instituted by Law No. 416, 5 August 1981.

46. The Media Authority has jurisdiction over firms enrolled in the National Print Register (Article 11, Law No. 416, 5 August 1981) and the National Broadcast Register (Article 12, Law No. 223, 6 August 1990).

47. Decision of 14 July 1993 relative to case 3886/RNS/AAGG.

48. This number is weighted down by the prevalence of *intragruppo* — or in-house — mergers, which account for almost 60 per cent of the merger notifications.

49. A merger notification is required when the joint income of the interested parties exceeds 560 billion lira (approximately $300 million) or when the income of the acquired firm is greater than 56 billion lira (approximately $30 million). These values are incremented each year in accordance with the GDP deflator.

50. The justification for using such a definition points to the peculiarities of the Italian economic system, in which firms with state participation are active. These firms, though dependent on the same group, and thus subject to joint control, enjoy a marked degree of decision-making autonomy.

51. These concentrative joint ventures are to be seen in contrast to co-operative joint ventures, which fall under the "agreements" article of the law whose objective is the co-ordination of the economic behaviour of the firms involved.

52. Resolution No. 1028 of 24 March 1993 relative to the monopolist telephone company's extending its dominance in the market for the resale of portable phones; and Resolution No. 1017 relative to the Rome Airport Authority's extending its dominance in airport activities not falling under the original concession.

53. See case against Tirrenia di Navigazione S.p.A., a shipping company that due to its state subsidies was operating, at a loss, in competition with other "private" shippers and abusing its dominant position (Resolution No. 453 of 10 April 1992).

54. Indicative of the role played by the Italian Antitrust Authority is the fact that no such cases had ended in a condemnation at the time of writing.

55. Of the fifteen collusive agreement cases closed in 1992, four concerned vertical relationships. Italian Antitrust Authority (1993).

56. The Italian law actually refers to the "game of competition", a concept which is then left undefined.

57. Italian Antitrust Authority (1993), p. 29.

58. The usual formula is for firms to request that the authority issue a decision as to whether the accord violates the law. If the accord is found to be in violation, the firms then usually request that the authority issue an exemption, since invariably — in the words of the firms — these accords have a positive effect on the way the good is offered to the consumers.

59. See Legislative Draft No. 1710 of the Senate relative to the restructuring of the port system, and Legislative Draft No. 1926 on the reorganisation of the cinema industry.

60. See EC Directives 88/301 and 90/388 on the liberalisation of telecommunication services and telecommunication terminals, on the basis of which the Italian Antitrust Authority found against the state telephone monopolist concerning its behaviour in the market for telephone credit cards (Resolution No. 412 of 3 March 1992).

61. The law provides two basic definitions which are key in interpreting the articles on restrictive practices and abuses of dominant position: dominance (Article 14), effective competition (Article 16), and competition (Article 3).

62. Resoluciòn No. SPPLC/0002-93; Premezclado y Prefabricados de Concreto S.A., Premezclado Tucon C.A., y Mezcladora Mixto-Listo Consolidada C.A.

63. Thus quantity and prompt-payment discounts, low-risk premiums and so on are allowed, whereas fidelity discounts are not.

64. DeLeon (forthcoming), p. 8.

65. The Venezuelan authority has also published a series of pamphlets aimed at educating the public on the role of antitrust in society, and on how to lodge complaints against alleged violators of the law.

66. Article 1 of the Federal Competition Law.

67. Article 9 of the law specifies the following as *per se* violations of the law: horizontal price fixing, restrictions on output, division of the market, and fixing of bids.

68. Article 10 of the law states that the following are relative monopolistic practices: exclusive distribution contracts, resale price maintenance, tying contracts, refusal to deal, coercive retaliatory behaviour, and — a final umbrella provision — any act which impedes competition.

69. In the articles relating to abuses of dominant position the Italian law always explains its restrictions by stating "...as it can hurt consumers" or "...detrimental to competition".

70. For a discussion of the impact of market structure on the pattern of international trade and the development of domestic industry see C.D. Jebuni, J. Love, and D.J.C. Forsyth (1988), "Market Structure and LDCs' Manufactured Export Performance", *World Development*, Vol. 16, No. 12, pp. 1511-1520.

71. Armando Rodriguez (1993), "Economic Liberalization and Rent Seeking Behavior: Assessing the Effectiveness of Antitrust Policies in the Developing Countries", Federal Trade Commission Working Paper, in progress.

Fourth Part

CONCLUDING REFLECTIONS

New State-Society Relations
in Latin America

Manuel Antonio Garretón

The new socio-historical context

Some major transformations have recently come about in Latin American societies, at different periods and to varying degrees.

The first of these has resulted in the prevalence of political and institutional models providing a framework for concerted action and conflict resolution, which have tended to replace the dictatorships, civil wars and revolutionary formulas of the preceding decades[1].

Second, inward-looking development has run its course. As activity has slowed down in the public sector as well as in the urban industrial sector, this development model has given way to adjustment and stabilization policies leading to new forms of integration into the world economy and ultimately consolidating the capitalist model[2].

Third, a relentless rise in poverty and marginalisation, and a growing precariousness in educational systems and job markets, have altered social structures and stratification systems. All of this has given rise to a new configuration of social actors and challenged traditional forms of collective action[3].

Finally, the model of modernity has been redefined to contain a critical view of the Western or North American type of modernisation that has dominated in Latin American society, particularly amongst the power elite[4].

The future of Latin American countries, therefore, lies in their ability to meet at least four challenges, or to initiate four processes.

The first is that of building political democracies. The problem today is not so much the transition from authoritarian or formal military regimes to democracy, as to avoid authoritarian regressions, to complete unfinished transformations while overcoming inherited authoritarian enclaves, and to extend democratic institutions to all the different social spheres. The point is to consolidate political democracies, and above all, to make these democracies effective so as to neutralise the *de facto* power structures which could easily replace the formal political regime[5].

The second challenge could be called that of "social democratisation": incorporating that segment of society which has hitherto been excluded, which in certain countries amounts to as much as 60 per cent of the total population[6]. The terms of the problem are different today: the so-called marginal sector has ceased to be a grouping of defiant actors; it is now made up of people who are simply unwanted, who are no longer needed by society and those "within" — not even to be exploited.

The third challenge has to do with defining the development model. The inward-looking development model is out, but market economy or open economy, as merely principles or instruments, cannot in themselves define a development model. Even the definition of capitalism, which is no more than a model of accumulation, cannot account for the complexity of a model of development and integration into the world economy. The discussions surrounding the Asian experiences show just how much the various Latin American countries are still at the stage of breaking with the former model, whether they are in the adjustment or post-adjustment phase[7].

The fourth challenge can be regarded as the synthesis of the others, but it has its own dynamic. It consists in defining the type of modernisation that Latin American countries will adopt. As Octavio Paz has often pointed out, Western rationality or the North American mass-culture model is not adapted to the culturally mixed or hybrid nature of modernity in these countries. Modernity can no longer be defined in terms of historical models of modernisation or of any single aspect of modernisation, whether its most scientific aspect, its most expressive aspect, or simply the historical memory of a national identity. Each society combines these three aspects differently and develops its own modernity[8].

The challenges and changes that have taken place over the past decades — or are just taking shape for the future — have considerable implications for collective action and the role of the state.

The problem of social change can no longer be resolved with a project aiming to transform the whole of society by acting on a single one of its structures or dimensions. Rather, the current trend is to differentiate the various social spheres and to generate projects, each of which affects a single social dimension. In other words, certain challenges in progress can not be understood in terms of sequences, consequences, or mechanical effects. This also means that each of these processes has its own internal dynamic, which implies that they should be undertaken simultaneously and that the state has a different role in each. A single model of state intervention or action would therefore be inconceivable, even in each specific society[9].

The concept of reform does not quite apply to the changes just mentioned. Having been radically redefined since the 1960s, the concept is now indicative of the economic climate of the 1980s and 1990s. In the 1960s, "structural reform" referred either to the changes in relations between socio-productive structures such as agriculture or industry, or to institutional changes, specifically to the changes in the property or dominance relations defined as power structures. All of this was charged with a mobilising and revolutionary force, and the military regimes of the last decades were considered precisely to be reactions against these structural reforms.

None of this remains today in the current meaning of structural reform and reform of the state, terms usually used in close connection with economic reform of the "adjustment" type. These terms carry an exclusively economic connotation and refer to the so-called new market-economy model, usually accompanied by an ideology professing an opposition to both the state and the redistribution of wealth: the exact opposite of what structural reform meant in the 1960s. We must therefore get away from an ideological view of structural reform which defines a model of society where the market, and measures such as privatisation, are considered not just as instruments but as the "correct" parameters of society[10].

Political, economic and cultural changes, as well as changes in the organisation of society, are directed at the transformation of the constitutive or socio-political matrix of a society. By socio-political matrix, we are referring to the relations, mediated by the political regime, that link the state, the political-representation system and the socio-economic base of social actors. It seems clear that what might be called the "classic matrix" of these elements — a matrix characteristic of a certain kind of state, development model and political culture — has been profoundly disassembled. We are witnessing the possible emergence of a new socio-political matrix that neither traditional conservative political paradigms nor known revolutionary utopias can explain. Different countries might well follow different paths in this matter. Some will undergo a long decomposition process with no new matrix coming forth. Others will try to reconstitute the classic matrix. In others, it is very likely that the basic feature of a new matrix will be its openness, that is, the growing autonomy of its components and the subsequent tension amongst them, despite the survival of features characteristic of the decomposing classic matrix[11].

The state and the socio-political matrix

We are far cry from a Manichean definition, according to which the state is exclusively an agent of domination, which should either be taken over or destroyed. We must also dismiss another simplistic view of the state as a neutral set of agencies and institutions with which we can dispense or which are limited to a purely instrumental dimension. The state has symbolic, institutional, and instrumental dimensions; it can be an actor or an autonomous agent. In addition, depending on what social sphere it is dealing with, its functions can be coercive, integrative, redistributive, or regulatory. This complexity and versatility of the state derives from the fact that it is many things simultaneously: a moment of unity for a historical society called a nation, a development agent, the crystallisation of dominance relations and the set of public institutions holding the functions we have mentioned previously. The state cannot be restricted to any of these dimensions or functions, even if in certain historical situations it can appear to be particularly identified with one or another particular aspect of its manifold significances.

The state's multidimensional nature is only part of its complexity, because in fact it is never isolated or posited in a social void. The state is always part of a set of

241

relations, and it cannot be historically defined without this context. Hence the idea of a socio-political matrix as the relation linking **the state, a representation system** (or political-party structure — the moment of the sum of constituents' overall claims and political demands) and **the socio-economic base,** made up of social actors having their own cultural orientations, which is the interface with the civil society. The relation, or institutional mediation, linking the three components of the socio-political matrix is what we call the **political regime**, which decides how a society is to be governed, what sort of relations are established between the state and the people (citizenship), and how social conflicts and demands are dealt with. Democracy, strictly speaking, is a political regime characterised by a number of specific principles and mechanisms: popular sovereignty, a constitutional state that guarantees public rights and freedom, and in general human rights, universal suffrage for the election of governing representatives, alternation in governance and ideological pluralism in politics (a pluralism of which political parties are the main, but not the sole expression).

No analysis of the state and of state reform can avoid referring both to its different dimensions and to its existence as a component of the socio-political matrix.

Thus, the basic question is whether, beyond the changes in political regimes (as exemplified by transitions from authoritarian to democratic regimes), beyond the changes in economic models (as exemplified by adjustment leading to an open-market economy), we are in the presence of a new type of society, that is, a new socio-political matrix[12]. In some Latin American countries that have experienced regime transitions, the old matrix fell apart in such a way as to wipe out the three elements that made it up. In other countries, populist and *caudillo*-style forms of government have made a comeback, trying this time around to apply neoliberal development models entailing the sort of tensions inherent to any unnatural combination. It is undeniable, however, that in addition and in contradiction to these trends, other trends are pointing to the growing autonomy and strength of the state, the political-party system and the social base, and to tensions between these complementary elements. All of this is redefining classic politics and cultural orientations. This central hypothesis defines not only an emerging trend but also a normative orientation.

Latin American societies have favoured a socio-political matrix where elements linking the state, the representation system and the social actors have been, depending on the case, in a relationship of **fusion, imbrication, subordination or elimination**.

In some countries, for instance, fusion of these elements has occurred around the figure of the populist leader. In others, fusion has taken place through the identification of the state and a political party, or on the basis of the articulation between social organisation and the political-party leadership. In other countries, the party system has been the basis for the fusion of all social divisions, or corporatist groups have taken over the whole of collective action, leaving no room for an independent political life. Such a matrix has used the qualifier "national-popular" (*Nacional Popular*), has been known to take many forms (populist, militarist, etc.) and has been able to survive a variety of political regimes. In this matrix, the state has played a referential role for all collective action — development, social mobility and mobilisation, redistribution of wealth, and the integration of the grassroots sector — but it has had little autonomy with regard to society and is the target of all sorts of pressures and demands. This interpenetrating of society and state has given politics a central role, but except in a few remarkable cases, the politics has been more of the mobilising than of the representative type, and the institutions of representation have been the weakest aspect of the matrix. The principle of the state, though present throughout the whole of society, has not included institutional autonomy or a capacity for effective state action[13].

It was in opposition to this matrix and type of state that the military regimes of the 1960s and 1970s were built. Subsequent transition or redemocratisation has coincided with the void left by the disappearance of the former matrix, which was dismembered by authoritarian regimes and not successfully replaced[14]. This void has generally been filled by a variety of substitutes that counteract the potential reinforcement of precisely these three elements (state, regime and political actors, and social actors and civil society) by eliminating one of them, by subordinating them, or by deifying one of them.

Two extreme poles seem to be striving to take the place of this vanishing matrix. The first is the extreme modernising pole consisting of rationalism and instrumental reason; collective action is replaced by technocratic reason, thus neutralising politics, and market logic seems to overrule any other dimension of society. The principal manifestation of this pole is its neoliberal version, where the state is considered only as an instrument with a dubious past. This is why its aim is to reduce state power through, for example, the privatisations that epitomise this type of state reform. Nonetheless, all changes based on this conception have been forced to rely on very strong state intervention, sometimes with an increase in its coercive capacity.

The other pole attempts to negate politics on the basis of a certain irrationalism, replacing political action with the universalising principle of **expressive-symbolic** logic. In this case, collective action loses its political nature and becomes moral or religious action.

Between these two extremes, populist, clientelist or partisan nostalgias are re-emerging, this time with no invitation to grand ideological projects or to highly integrative mobilisations. Such nostalgias now appear as fragmentary forms presenting corollaries such as anomie, apathy and atomism, and in some cases felonious components, such as narcotics trafficking and corruption.

All the same, these visions can be countered by suggesting that out of the ashes of the old matrix of political action a new matrix and a new political culture are emerging, which could be defined by the reinforcement of each of the three components: the state, the regime and its political actors, and the civil society or social actors. In addition, we can contend that the future of democratic regimes depends on the consolidation of this new matrix, on this three-sided reinforcement and on the establishment of a relationship among the three components that is no longer one of fusion or imbrication, but one of mutual **tension** and complementarity.

State and society; autonomy and complementarity

First of all, the empirical inaccuracy of anti-state assertions must be recognised. Such assertions are formulated from two contradictory angles, one declaring the free market to be a universal panacea and the other viewing the people as in opposition to the state. They stand in contradiction to trends showing that public opinion, while rejecting a bureaucratic and inefficient type of state, strongly supports the state's role as redistributing agent, principle of national unity, and defence against the current weakness of social actors. Such ideas also stand in contradiction to the historical fact that no recent national development has taken place without the state's having played a strong role as development agent in relation with the other social agents. The issue at hand is not to have the state play a lesser role, but rather to reform the state: to modernise it, decentralise it and reorganise it in such a way as to make it participative.

If we consider the state within the framework of a new socio-political matrix, the principle of "stateness" is not to be eliminated; rather, it is to be built upon and strengthened. This idea concurs with that of Guillermo O'Donnell on the need to extend and give more depth to the "rule of law", which is absent in a number of spheres of society[15]. However, this reinforcement of the principle of state autonomy and of the role of the state as an agent of national unity and development, requiring elimination of its most bureaucratic tendencies, must be accompanied by a simultaneous reinforcement of the levels of participation and of representation of society.

There are at least two aspects to this. One has to do with decentralisation and the strengthening of local and regional authorities; this involves not just the problem of administration, management and grassroots actors' participation, but also the collection and allocation of taxes.

The other aspect touches on the topic of parties and the political class. The inefficacy of parties — or, depending on the case, their undue interference in society, their penchant for destroying or absorbing other parties, or their exaggerated focus on or complete indifference to ideology — must give way to a **strong party system** characterised by a propensity for inclusion, for internal democracy, for negotiation and concerted action, capable of forming large coalitions and of establishing channels with society to make sure new issues, social conflicts and differences are expressed — in short, capable of being really representative. The possibility of forming **majority coalitions** in turn implies institutional changes in the system of government. This challenges the existing, exorbitantly strong presidential system in Latin American countries and suggests the need to introduce certain elements of a parliamentary system, not only from the point of view of accountability (as Stephan Haggard and Robert Kaufman argue[16]), but also from that of the constitution of majorities and party reinforcement.

Reinforcement of the principles of "stateness" and representativity means a transformation in politics and requires in turn that civil society — that is, social actors who are autonomous with regard to the state and the party system — increase in strength and density. This brings up the importance of supporting the enterprising actor to offset the reinforced state. The growth, diversification and strengthening of social actors implies an increase in participation levels, which should not be limited to a symbolic dimension but should also be directed at the effective solution of problems. This brings us back to the issue of the decentralisation of state power.

A rather complex reality confronts us today, in that we seem to be witnessing a general weakening of collective action and social movements. As a consequence, even to speak of social actors and the civil society may seem nostalgic or excessively idealistic[17].

The classic socio-political matrix featured a type of collective action focussed on the state and on political objectives, as well as a type of social movement that was founded on principles of developmentalism, modernisation, nationalism, populism and social integration. The epitome of such action was the workers' movement, to which other movements deferred, at least in ideological terms. The military regimes and various authoritarian regimes, as well as the economic crisis of the past decades, ultimately shattered this form of action. During that period of authoritarianism, these nationalistic, populist movements were pushed into the background by what could be called the democratic movement, which subordinated every other struggle to the acquisition of democratic institutions, previously regarded as "bourgeois".

Now that the classic matrix has broken down and democratic transitions have been completed, the unifying principle of social action has disappeared. In fact, all principles seem to have diversified, sometimes even into mutual contradiction, and are now expressed through totally different actors; most important, the forefront has come to be occupied by so-called public opinion, which makes itself known through surveys and with which a relation is established through mass media, rather than through mobilising and representational organisations.

The constitution of social actors faces an even more serious problem than that of the diversification of the principles of action and struggle and the lack of unifying principles and issues. It is the matter of social exclusion mentioned above. All social categories are currently experiencing the fracture between those "on the inside" and those excluded, as well as the breach between the different models of modernity held by those on the inside. The first rift defines not a conflict but an exclusion. The second defines a conflict wherein the subordinate actors are very weak and at a high risk of exclusion at any moment. In these situations, there are no actors organised on a regular basis; what we find is sporadic mobilisation and fragmented, defensive action.

The problem now is to rethink the configuration of actors. It must be acknowledged that no social and political actor is capable of producing the field of tensions and articulating the various principles of action that emerge in the processes of modernisation and social democratisation. This brings to light a paradox in the role of the state. We must not expect the state to be a unifying agent for the life of society and the diversity of its actors, but we definitely need state intervention for the constitution of spaces and institutions within which actors can come forth who are autonomous with regard to the state, without being marginal. If the state and — in some cases — the political parties do not attend to this task, the paucity of actors and the representation crisis are likely to last indefinitely.

In order to avoid matrices where collective action is dominated by the state, political parties or corporatist interest groups, then the three levels — state, parties, and socio-economic base and social actors — must be strengthened simultaneously.

A socio-political matrix with the above-mentioned features, however, is not yet a reality. Rather, as we have previously mentioned, our reflections show that we are currently observing a variety of phenomena: breakdowns, the persistence of former elements, attempts to re-establish the classic matrix and attempts to set up a new one. These complex processes are taking three directions. The first leads to breakdown with no further prospect of change. The second is a regression to the classic matrix. The third consists in building a new matrix wherein the components are both autonomous and mutually complementary. The resulting combinations vary according to the country, and it is too soon to foretell their outcome. Nonetheless, the institutional framework will clearly be democratic. It is more difficult to say how effective it will be or to what degree it will be replaced by *de facto* power structures.

Conclusions: the principles of state reform

An attempt has been made in this essay to analyse the state from a broader perspective by placing it in the context of its relations with society, particularly the system of representation and the base for the constitution of social actors — or civil society. State reform or transformation must take these relations into account and avoid the instrumental or administrative illusion which responds to the exclusive demand of effectiveness without acknowledging the complexity inherent to the state's insertion within society. It would be a mistake, however, to overlook its instrumental dimension, which could be seen as the "inner" dimension of the state. Ultimately, speaking of state reform or transformation also leads to specific strategies affecting a set of institutions and organisations which, in turn, are to take on the more general problems of social transformation we have mentioned above.

So let us conclude by enunciating several principles that follow from what we have said thus far and that should be applied when undertaking state reforms aimed at building a new socio-political matrix characterised by the reinforcement, autonomy and complementarity of its components[18].

First, state reform cannot be limited to a dogmatic matter of size or breadth: consideration must be given to the principles and functions that make the size of the state a dependent variable. It is necessary to steer away from a tradition that solved problems by adding new departments and agencies to the state without altering them, as well as from the neoliberal contention that the magic solution to all problems lies in reducing the state apparatus. This might mean that in certain areas, such as justice or targeted redistribution, beyond the necessary reforms of the existing structures, consideration will have to be given to an increase in human, institutional, administrative and bureaucratic resources, that is, to an increase in the size of the state apparatus. Conversely, thought should be given to the reduction of this apparatus in certain of the state's economic functions and above all in some of its military functions. Generally speaking, where size is concerned, functions relating to redistribution of wealth and integration should follow an opposite pattern to that of coercive functions.

Second, in order to reinforce the principle of state or "stateness" without falling into the trap of state domination, a clear distinction should be made between that which constitutes state policy and that which constitutes government policy. The first is mainly to be founded on consensus, while the second follows the majority principle. New problems such as those relating to human rights, to the environment and especially to exclusion and poverty, should come under a national state policy.

Third, it is indispensable to differentiate the areas where state reform consists in carrying out an in-depth transformation affecting norms and personnel — as in the field of justice — from the fields where reform is mainly aimed at modernisation, a lighter bureaucracy, decentralisation and retraining of civil servants. In addition, it appears that there are some new issues that the state will sometimes have to address in an executive capacity, and sometimes only in a regulatory capacity. This will require either new structures (environment, innovation), or new norms (communication, information technology), or even a restructuring of existing agencies with new responsibilities (culture, education) related more to regulation, orientation and assessment than to management.

Finally, the terms of the problem of access to the state for both individuals and society have changed. Insofar as the state's services are concerned, the issue is no longer — even for the most marginalised sectors — one of mere access to the services or how widely they extend; rather, it is one of their quality. This means that quality has become a question of equity and that we can no longer separate these two aspects. This observation applies not only to housing and health, but also — and especially — to education and justice.

As far as state decisions are concerned, while upholding the principles of state autonomy and of "stateness", it is important to promote the institutional participation of individuals and society at both the central and decentralised levels, either by introducing principles of direct democracy for certain matters, or by reforming the state structure in such a way as to allow the presence of non-corporatist groups on national commissions or councils in various fields of state endeavour.

Notes and References

1. Among the many publications on this subject, see C. Barba, J.L. Barros and J. Hurtado, eds, *Transiciones a la democracia en Europa y América*, FLACSO, Universidad de Guadalajara, Angel Porras, México, 1991, 2 vols.

2. CEPAL, *Equidad y transformación productiva: un enfoque integrado*, UN-CEPAL, Santiago, 1992.

3. CEPAL, *Transformación ocupacional y crisis social en América latina*, Santiago, 1989; A. Touraine, *La parole et le sang*, Editions Odile Jacob, Paris, 1988.

4. N. García-Canclini, *Culturas híbridas: estrategias para entrar y salir de la modernidad*, Grijalbo, México, 1989.

5. M.A. Garretón, "Transformaciones sociopolíticas en América latina", in M.A. Garretón, *Los partidos y la transformación política en América latina*, FLACSO, Santiago, 1993; G. O'Donnell, "Delegative Democracy", mimeo, University of Notre Dame, 1991; M. Cavarozzi, "Más allá de la transición", *Revista Estudios Políticos*, No. 74 (1991), Segunda Epoca.

6. F. Weffort, *A America errada*, CEDEC, São Paulo, 1990.

7. See, for example, H. de Soto and S. Schmiheiny, eds, *Las nuevas reglas del juego: hacia un desarrollo sostenible en América latina*, Oveja negra, Bogotá, 1991.

8. O. Paz, "La búsqueda del présente", *Vuelta*, Año 15, México (January 1991); A. Touraine, *Critique de la modernité*, Fayard, Paris, 1992.

9. F. Calderón and M. Dos Santos, "Hacia un nuevo orden estatal en América latina: veinte tesis socio-políticas y un corolario de cierre", *Revista Paraguaya de Sociología*, No. 77 (1990).

10. M.A. Garretón, "La dimensión política de los procesos de transformación en Chile", Documento de trabajo, FLACSO, Santiago, 1993.

11. These notions of the state and its insertion into a socio-political matrix are developed in M.A. Garretón and M. Espinosa, "¿Reforma del estado o cambio en la matriz socio-política?", *Perfiles Latinoamericanos*, México, Año 1, No. 1 (December 1992).

12. G. O'Donnell, "On the State, Various Crises and Problematic Democratization", mimeo, Kellogg Institute, University of Notre Dame, March 1992; M. Cavarozzi, "La política: clave del largo plazo latinoamericano", mimeo, FLACSO, México, 1992.

13. A. Touraine, *La parole et le sang, op. cit.*

14. On contemporary authoritarianism in Latin America, see D. Collier, *The New Authoritarianism in Latin America*, Princeton University Press, Princeton, 1979; on the

democratisation process, see G. O'Donnell, P. Schmitter and L. Whitehead, eds, *Transiciones desde un gobierno autoritario*, Ed. Paidós, Buenos Aires, 1988, 4 vols.

15. See the chapter by O'Donnell in this volume.

16. See Haggard and Kaufmann's contribution to this volume.

17. M.A. Garretón, "Social Movements and the Politics of Democratization", paper presented at the Nordic Conference on Social Movements in the Third World, Department of Sociology, University of Lund, 18-21 August 1993; A. Touraine, *La parole et le sang, op. cit.*

18. M.A. Garretón and M. Espinosa, *op. cit.*, examine the case of Chile in the light of these principles.

Some Reflections on Redefining
the Role of the State

Guillermo O'Donnell

As Colin Bradford says in his Introduction to this volume, "The economic debate in the 1980s was extremely narrow, focusing on structural adjustment, trade policy and exchange rate reform as if they constituted the entire economic agenda. Economic issues overwhelmed all other policy priorities in the 1980s." Bradford goes on to say that nowadays there exist "new imperatives for social equity, growth and environmental sustainability, as well as for political and state reform". This volume, like the conference in which it originated, is a good expression of these concerns.

The assault on the state

Why the neglect that Bradford observes? The conventional — mainstream — answer is "If the house is on fire...". In other words, inflation (in some cases hyperinflation), severe external sector imbalances, and other related plagues were so intense that what was done — taming inflation, restoring some basic macroeconomic balances, and trimming as fast as possible an overblown state — was all that could be done. Some side effects were considered unavoidable, such as increasing poverty and neglect of environmental problems. Furthermore, these and other regrettable consequences were already being generated by the preceding economic crisis, and the perpetuation of the crisis would probably have further worsened them.

This argument is invalid, especially because it claims an exclusive and one-dimensional rationality as appropriate for a social world that is immensely more complex. The hard truth is that those who disagreed were unable to come up with a credible alternative program for extinguishing the fire that, indeed, was devastating the house[1]. Furthermore, purely normative lamentations were not deemed, for good reasons, to carry much weight. What some of the dissidents did was to argue that other policies could have been applied simultaneously with the harsh policies of economic stabilization; the fire was not so violent that other parts of the house could not be saved, parts that not only would be very important for resuming growth and aiming at minimally decent levels of social equity but that also are important *per se*.

The extent to which the state was destroyed was enormous, and unnecessary, particularly in the light of the adverse conditions which preceded the economic crisis, and was accentuated by the economic policies discussed here. It can be attributed as much to "objective" conditions as to two closely related policy factors: economic policies that were too simplistically addressed to short-term economic goals, and the intensely anti-statist ideologies that so dominated the 1980s[2]. Two dimensions need to be considered.

The first is the destruction of the state as an apparatus, as a set of public organizations which should be actively useful for the attainment of various (and changing) societal goals. The reduction of fiscal deficits was in fact achieved by drastic drops in public investments (including those that mainstream economics would recommend), and by no less drastic losses in the real salaries of public employees[3]. The fall of public investment was probably temporarily unavoidable, but the policies of the state toward its employees seemed tailor-made for justifying the worst apprehensions of anti-statist ideologies. First, the state and its employees were demonized: they were the source of all evils, and were seen as the only actors engaged in rent seeking[4]. Second, the programs aimed at getting rid of the "excess personnel" which indeed existed, combined with the extremely low salaries, dismal working conditions and sharp drop in social status that followed those programs, induced many — if not most — of the better qualified and motivated individuals to leave public employment. Consequently, many less qualified personnel who were already surplus to requirements remain in public service, and some old problems — including poor motivation, inefficacy and corruption — have worsened. If career prospects are almost nil and salaries too low for even a minimal standard of living, these consequences are hardly surprising. Even corporations in the United States are suffering from the negative consequences of hasty and indiscriminate attempts to reduce their personnel[5]. As several chapters in this volume argue, there are many tasks which a transformed and vastly improved state apparatus should undertake, even from the narrow point of view of consolidating the economic reforms. More sensible, forward-looking and, indeed, less aggressive policies toward public employees were possible and were not prohibitively expensive. Such policies would have left the state in much better shape for the tasks ahead.

The second dimension of the destruction of the state requires a brief excursus. The state is not only a set of bureaucracies. It is also a legal order. Normally, this legal order textures social relations along the territory covered by an entity internationally recognized as a nation-state. This texturing is effective when most social agents, even though they may lack detailed knowledge of the law, abide by it, expect others to do so, and know that, in case of conflict, they may have access to fair adjudication by one segment of the state apparatus, the judiciary. Civil and political rights (democracy) as well as contract and property rights (capitalism) may be written on paper, but they are effective only when and where the above expectations are actually met[6]. As Alain Touraine observes in his chapter of the present volume, the last two decades have increased (or, as in the case of Argentina, have generated) the profound dualism of Latin American countries. This, of course, is directly related to the drama of social destitution and exclusion. There are huge areas on the territorial periphery of these countries, and many parts of the cities which are supposed to be the dynamic centers of both democracy and capitalism, to which the effectiveness of the state-as-law does not extend.

These "brown areas"[7] are ruled in ways that have very little to do with the constitution and the laws; without the *public* dimension of the state entailed by the effectiveness of the law none of the conditions for democracy and for a *market* economy can exist. Both democracy and markets presuppose for their adequate functioning the effectiveness of the law; otherwise individuals may vote and exchange, but these acts are embedded in a context that leads to all sorts of predatory behavior. This behavior expresses naked (i.e. not legally and institutionally mediated) power relations which, among other things, tend to reinforce existing inequalities. The recent attack on the state apparatus has had serious consequences in this respect. The data show that in state-level agencies located in these regions, the lowering of salaries and working conditions (and surely the demoralization) suffered by employees went even further than in the national agencies. The programs of "decentralization" which transferred responsibilities but not resources to peripheral regions (thus helping to show, domestically and internationally, reductions in the national budget deficit) were part of the reason for this devastation. If we consider that these regions (both those on the geographical periphery and those in the big cities) contain a large part of the population, we are forced to conclude that the rule of law has a tenuous hold over the territory of many Latin American (and, indeed, post-communist) countries.

Only recently have efforts begun in the uphill task of upgrading the judiciary. This task is complicated by the low salaries, the poor training, the politicization of appointments, and the poor working conditions that prevail almost everywhere in Latin America. A further complication is that in the brown areas more than the judiciary is required if the law is to become effective. Owing to the naked power relations that prevail there, honest and competent judges are scarce, and too often no other powers are willing to enforce or comply with their decisions. In particular, the corruption of the police, its manipulation by informal (if not criminal) powers, and its recurrent violence against the disadvantaged is another crucial challenge to be met.

A less indiscriminate and aggressive policy toward the state apparatus and a less obssesive concern with showing rapid reductions in the fiscal deficit would not have solved long-standing socio-structural problems, but it could have cushioned some of social and economic deterioration that occurred with particular intensity in the peripheries of Latin American countries. This is particularly important if one considers that in the brown areas civil society and the formal economy are weak, the legal guarantees for the proper functioning of markets are intermittent, and the boundaries between the informal and illegal economies are often blurred[8]. In other words, in these areas a reasonably agile and efficacious state is badly needed. This is fundamental, quite obviously, to the eventual expansion and consolidation of these democracies, but it is no less crucial for a reasonably working market economy.

Some consequences of social exclusion

Surely the last remark is less than obvious. It may be argued that it is hopeless to expect such an economy to work without the social exclusion of what in Latin America amounts to approximately 50 per cent of the population. At least insofar as democracy is no less of a value than a growing economy, this exclusion sounds politically unfeasible — not because the poorer, more excluded segments of the population will spontaneously revolt (this is seldom the case), but because such a degree of dualism and social exclusion cannot but impregnate the whole national political process. In particular, building strong, effectively working institutions becomes extremely difficult. Congress, the judiciary, agencies that implement, say, tax, social and education policies with reasonable efficacy across the whole territory, not only in privileged segments — these "political" institutions are indispensable not only for democratic consolidation, but also for a reasonably adequate functioning of markets and hence for sustainable economic growth. (Italy, a long-established democracy and a rather prosperous economy, shows the dire consequences of deeply entrenched dualism, even at levels of unequality and poverty that are far lower than those of Latin America.)

The problems of dualism and exclusion will take a long time to resolve, but they must be brought to the fore, for two reasons. First, too often policies are made at the national center, taking into consideration only the center and its connections with the international arena. This tendency has been reinforced by the high degree of political isolation in which the economic reforms have been undertaken. Second, as already noted, it is very hard to imagine that, in peripheral areas, the state would not have a very active role to play: strengthening the judiciary; improving the workings of state legislatures and executives; reforming the police, so it can become a helpful part of and not an egregious antagonist to the rule of law; and making sure that education and other social policies are implemented without huge discontinuities across the territory. One may not logically expect the existence (and eventual reinforcement) of sharp intra-national dualism to be a dominant consideration for macroeconomic policies such as those of the 1980s, but the territorial and social dimensions entailed by this dualism should not be ignored when dealing with both the consolidation of democracy and the medium- and long-run prospects of economic growth.

As Bradford argues, the task ahead is no less than reshaping the state in ways more adapted to facilitating economic growth and to ameliorating inequities. To this must be added two interrelated aspects: ensuring the overall effectiveness of the rule of law, and taking seriously into account the territorial and social dimension of all these issues. Nonetheless, a serious risk looms on the horizon: trying to do too much too soon.

To begin with, no one knows how to reform the state, even in highly developed countries (witness the troubles of the Clinton administration in this respect, to say nothing of Italy). What can be done, then? The obvious answer is "be selective and modest", but the selection of priorities is always the result of a complex political process.

Different approaches

The essays in this volume are clearly "centrist". They do not include the views of the "orthodox", i.e. those who would adamantly refuse any reactivation of the role of the state, and who would probably consider that attempting to redress inequalities by means which are not exclusively market-based will only worsen the situation of those supposedly favored[9]. Neither do they include the views of "radicals", i.e. those who condemn *in toto* the economic policies of the 1980s and advocate their sharp reversal.

Within this center, three overlapping positions have emerged:

1) *Economic maximizers*: Yes, the state must be reformed and take a broader role than in the past years, but this should be limited to the institutional and policy areas which are indispensable for advancing the economic reforms already under way (e.g. increase regulatory capabilities, increase state capabilities for export promotion and international negotiations, and the like). Other goals may be worthwhile but, for the time being at least, trying to achieve them would spread scarce resources too thin, and jeopardize what has been already achieved[10].

2) *Eclectic maximizers*: A more active and broader role of the state is necessary not only for advancing economic reforms but also for tackling some of the more urgent problems related to poverty. Better sanitation, education and the like (and, in some more political arguments, such as the ones presented by Stephan Haggard and Robert Kaufman in this volume, a stable party system) are necessary conditions for the advancement of economic reforms. According to the more political arguments, these achievements would also help to consolidate democracy. Notice that here the postulated causal connections are more nebulous than in the first argument.

3) *Fuzzy optimizers*: Goals such as the ones postulated by the maximizers are undoubtedly valuable in economic terms, but there are others (such as alleviation of poverty, the redress of environmental degradation[11], and, on another plane, the consolidation of democracy) that are valuable *per se*, regardless of their presumed instrumentality in maximizing the achievement of the economic goals. Here the causal connections are even more nebulous than in the previous category. Indeed, they almost evaporate since, at least at this level of generality, one can not do much more than express the hope that in the medium or long run these two sorts of goals will converge without too much conflict. Furthermore, in contrast with both kinds of maximizers, if fuzzy optimizers stop here they are left with no criteria for deciding the difficult trade-offs that will be unavoidably faced along the way. Fortunately, some seminal efforts have been recently made that show a clear awareness of the need to analyze those trade-offs, and the (ethical and political, not only "technical") conflicts they are likely to pose or to activate[12]. This is the way to proceed, even if one may want to introduce the further complication that fuzzy optimizers may be prone (if not logically mandated) to be democratic maximizers, i.e. to believe that the paramount consideration should be, first, the preservation of existing democracies and, second, their institutional consolidation and social expansion (a task that, in itself, might also pose difficult trade-offs between, for example, expansion and consolidation).

Democratic political processes

At this point we must introduce the political process. In situations of deep and protracted socio-economic crisis, particularly if it has included episodes of hyperinflation, it is possible for a governing group and its international supporters to set narrow but highly salient goals to which most of society acquiesces. This has happened in several contemporary cases, not only in Latin America. Whether those efforts fail or succeed, however, it is impossible to stick to those limited goals for too long. They unavoidably lead to other issues, and rather soon civil society begins to reassert itself. The policy agenda widens, and typically heats up debates that span the full spectrum from orthodox to radicals. By that time, whether we like or not, we are back to competitive politics. This type of competition exists, at times vigorously, under authoritarian regimes, except that under the more cohesive and repressive of these regimes the voices of most of civil society are muted and outcomes of the conflicts tend to be more decisive (to be on the losing side can mean far more than losing a governmental job...). Here, however, we are interested in democracies, something whose preservation, consolidation and expansion is, at least for some of us, valuable *per se*. There are good reasons, exhaustively analyzed in the literature, why high economic development and democracy tend to go hand in hand[13].

After much research, however, there is no decisive empirical evidence to prove that authoritarian or democratic regimes are more apt (or, for that matter, if political regimes make any difference at all) for one of the challenges that Latin America faces: finding paths that will lead it to higher levels of economic development[14]. This indecisiveness of the historical evidence and the less than exemplary functioning of many new democracies may mean that, as has happened in the past, those who want to maximize existing economic achievements will coalesce with other forces that for their own, probably more primordial reasons, prefer to terminate democracy. This is not a foregone conclusion, of course; one hopeful signal that we have finally left the 1980s and fully entered into the 1990s is that the ranks of politically influential orthodox and economic maximizers (including the most important international financial organisations) have been thinning in favor of eclectic maximizers.

The democratic political process *is* confused, but not necessarily confusing. This process is nothing if it does not include several coalitions trying to place at the top of the national agenda the issues that are salient for them, and their proposed solutions. Shaping the national agenda of attention (i.e. engaging in the continual struggle to determine public priorities) is a crucial aspect of what political power is about. There is nothing nicely geometric in this process. What is and what is not an issue (and the criteria which should be applied in deciding this question) is the perpetually challenged result of the interaction of fields of forces that cut across civil society, the economy, and the state apparatus. Public agendas reflect the balances and imbalances of those forces (including ideologies). Consequently, the resulting priorities are never fully consensual or consistent. The political process (particularly but not only the democratic political process) at best optimizes only fuzzily. This means that, although at a price in terms of logical rigor and precision of postulated causal connections, a plea for fuzzy optimization may be a plea for — democratically congenial — realism[15].

Exceptional circumstances (such as a protracted crisis accompanied by extremely high inflation or hyperinflation) may allow, and necessitate, that "somebody" located at the apex of the state dictate a narrow agenda, and that most of the population temporarily acquiesce to that *diktat*, but this case is exceptional and temporary, and should be recognized as such. Policy-makers and advisors may long for the freedom, the political insulation, and the daring commitment to recognizably positive goals with which they acted under those circumstances. It is sheer cognitive and political *hubris*, however, to think that beyond this evanescent period they will be able to define priorities for the whole country and that civil society will accept or acquiesce to that definition.

The attempt to impose a set of presumably consistent priorities from above not only is impossible but would, especially under democratic conditions, be self-defeating: there is no way in which the diverse demands springing from civil society, and indeed from the state apparatus, could be suppressed. What results from those demands is anything but consistent. This is good, if at times bewildering: it expresses the diversity of interests and identities without which civil society is submerged in the nightmare of totalitarianism. Willing democracy entails not the resigned acceptance of this diversity but valuing it for the avenues of social innovation and discovery that it uniquely offers. This is one reason why, beyond easily uttered generic statements, a democratic commitment is not always an easy one, particularly in democracies that have a weak institutional structure and, consequently, a very uncertain and fluctuating public agenda[16].

Reforming the state (prudently)

If this is the case, one must ask again: what can sociologists, political scientists and public administration experts do? The search for a theory that would tell us how to reform the state would be futile: with whom, for whom, and for what the state is to be reformed are and will always be inherently debatable questions. These analysts can, however, make some contributions which, from this perspective, are not minor. First, they can derive, from experience and from some middle-range theories, prudential rules about how, under given contextual circumstances (which should be researched and specified), some state agencies may enhance their efficacy in the attainment of certain goals (assuming that those goals are acceptable). Second, they can try to influence actors incorporated in the policy process with their views about what priorities such actors should strive to inscribe on the public agenda (although they should know that normally their goals will have been diluted during the process that, in the best of cases, leads to such inscription). Alternatively, and very importantly from the perspective of expanding democracy, one may try to help excluded actors enter into the policy process, for example by helping them to arrive at more self-conscious and mobilizing definitions of their own interests. For both cognitive and ethical reasons, the advice to be given on how to reform parts of the state must be very self-conscious of its prudential limits, of the kind of goals which those reforms are supposed to help achieve, and of the set of actors that, in a properly democratic context, would be supposed to have a fair hearing in relation to those reforms. The real-life conditions of experts' contracts — particularly the pretence that experts' advice is "apolitical" — are not very propitious for achieving this ideal, but this should not be an overwhelming impediment.

In this context, the contributions to this volume by Teresa Albánez and J. Samuel Valenzuela are especially important. Albánez raises the question of how much and for how long Latin American democracies can withstand so much misery. Valenzuela analyzes the conditions under which labor movements can be strengthened and, against much current conventional wisdom, cogently argues that such an outcome would be favorable for both democracy and economic growth. In other words, by more or less explosive or institutionalized processes, the public agenda will become even more complicated in the near future than it is today, in terms of both the issues to be dealt with and the actors to be taken into account. To be sure, this statement presupposes the continuation of democracy; but authoritarian alternatives, except during extremely repressive periods, would be no more able than democracies to evade the complication of their agenda, and their institutional conditions for dealing with it would be worse.

It is important to recognize that, as any observer of well-established democracies can testify, democratic politics is messy, all the more so in countries where most problems are more demanding and where there are few institutions that filter and aggregate the issues that claim priority. The complexity is further compounded by the fact that states must be able not only to make good decisions but also, and no less importantly, to implement them. Weak states, democratic or not, can excel at making decisions (at least they make a lot of them), but they are very bad at implementing those decisions. Most policies flounder because of a combination of administrative incapabilities and the resistance of affected interests. In contrast, strong states (almost all of which are democratic today) make fewer decisions but are much better at implementing them. The negotiations, compromises and changing sets of relevant actors typical of the democratic process are no less weighty (and no less inimical to clear-cut, consistent policies and priorities) during policy implementation than during policy formulation.

It is in this kind of world that prudent efforts must be made to enhance selectively but persistently the devastated state that the 1990s has inherited.

Notes and References

1. A recent argument in this sense is made by Stephan Haggard and Robert Kaufman, *The Political Economy of Democratic Transitions* (forthcoming). The authors note that their argument does not extend much beyond initial policies aimed at taming inflation and diminishing huge fiscal and balance-of-payments deficits. A number of issues remain contentious, within and outside mainstream economics: for example, the degree, timing, and sequencing of financial and trade liberalization and of privatization, and the advisability of income and industrial policies.

2. Guillermo O'Donnell, "Delegative Democracy", *Journal of Democracy* (forthcoming) [first published in *Novos Estudos*, CEBRAP, No. 31 (October 1991), pp. 25-40]; and "On the State, Democratization and Some Conceptual Problems: A Latin American View with Glances at Some Postcommunist Countries", *World Development*, 21, No. 8 (1993), pp. 1355-1369.

3. In Argentina, Brazil and Peru, the real salaries of middle- and lower-level national public employees were at least 50 per cent lower in 1990 than in 1980.

4. Paul Streeten argues against the view that only state agents are rent seekers, in "Markets and States: Against Minimalism", *World Development*, 21, No. 8 (1993), pp. 1281-1298.

5. *Business Week* ("How Goliaths can act as Davids", 8 September 1993, pp. 192-201) reports a study by Kim S. Cameron of the Business School of the University of Michigan. This study concludes that in three-quarters of 150 "restructuring" US corporations (including IBM, General Motors and Eastman Kodak) there have been serious performance losses due to this kind of indiscriminate policy.

6. For thoughtful arguments on this and related points by an author who is hardly suspect, see Vito Tanzi, "Fiscal Policy, Growth, and the Design of Stabilization Programs", in Mario Blejer and Ki-Young Chu, eds, *Fiscal Policy, Stabilization, and Growth in Developing Countries* (Washington, D.C.: International Monetary Fund, 1989), pp. 13-32. For broader perspectives, see Colin I. Bradford, Jr., Introduction to this volume; Streeten, *op. cit.*; Manuel Antonio Garretón and Malva Espinoza, "Reforma del estado o cambio en la matriz socio-política?", *Estudios Sociales* (Chile), No. 74 (1992), pp. 9-35; and Pablo Gerchunoff and Juan Carlos Torre, "What Role for the State in Latin America?", in Simón Teitel, ed., *Towards a New Development Strategy for Latin America: Pathways from Hirschman's Thought* (Washington, D.C.: Inter-American Development Bank, 1992), pp. 259-278.

7. O'Donnell, "On the State...", *op. cit.*

8. Current work on post-communist countries has been usefully conceptualizing the various "economies" that are emerging or surviving in addition to the one related to formal employment in the capitalist economy. See Richard Rose, "Toward a Civil Economy", *Journal of Democracy*, 2, No. 3 (April 1992), pp. 14-26; and Endre Sik, "From the Second to the Informal Economy", *Journal of Public Policy*, 12, No. 2 (1992), pp. 153-175.

9. This is close to Albert Hirschman's "perversity thesis": the argument that "...any purposive action to improve some feature of the political, social, or economic order only serves to exacerbate the condition one wishes to remedy" [*The Rhetoric of Reaction* (Cambridge: Belknap Press of Harvard University Press, 1991), p. 7].

10. This seems to be Hirschman's "jeopardy thesis": the argument that "...the cost of the proposed change or reform is too high since it endangers some previous, precious accomplishment" (*op. cit.*, p. 7).

11. Those who place environmental issues as one of their top priorities are condemned to be fuzzy optimizers; it is not clear how, except perhaps in the — very fuzzy — long run, they can plausibly argue that solving environmental problems will help maximize the advancement of current economic reforms. Consistently with this point of view, in this volume Margaret Keck argues for linking environmental issues with an invigorated democratic process.

12. This is clearly the case of this volume and most of its contributions. For a more detailed statement in this direction, see Colin I. Bradford, Jr. 1994, "Toward an Integrated Policy Framework", *in* B. Fischer, A van Gleich and W. Grabendorf (eds.), Latin America's Competitive Position in the Enlarged European Market, Nomos Verlag, Baden Baden and Bradford's Introduction to Bradford, Colin I. Jr. *The New Paradigm of Systemic Competitiveness: Towards More Integrated Policies in Latin America*, forthcoming, OECD Development Centre, Paris. See also Luiz Carlos Bresser Pereira, José María Maravall and Adam Przeworski, *Economic Reforms in New Democracies: A Social-Democratic Approach* (New York: Cambridge University Press, 1993).

   The great challenge is to pursue these efforts, at the level of analytical formulation and of a detailed tracing of the interactions among various, not only economic, policy areas.

13. For a careful assessment of this correlation, see Larry Diamond, "Economic Development and Democracy Reconsidered", *American Behavioral Scientist*, 35, Nos. 4-5 (March-June 1992), pp. 450-499.

14. See Adam Przeworski and Fernando Limongi, "Political Regimes and Economic Growth", *Journal of Economic Perspectives*, 7, No. 3 (Summer 1993), pp. 51-69 for a good discussion of this largely undecided issue.

15. This view does not imply that social and political actors are not rational. Rather, it is their contextually situated rationality which leads to this kind of outcome.

16. The author has argued this point elsewhere. In addition to "Delegative Democracy" and "On the State...", *op. cit.*, the reader may want to check Guillermo O'Donnell, "Transitions, Continuities and Paradoxes", in Scott Mainwaring, Guillermo O'Donnell, and J. Samuel Valenzuela, eds, *Issues in Democratic Consolidation: The New South American Democracies in Comparative Perspective* (Notre Dame: University of Notre Dame Press, 1992), pp. 17-56.

Some Conclusions from the Conference Discussion

Colin I. Bradford, Jr.

The conference that led to this book was perhaps unusual in that members of at least three different professional groups — economists, political scientists and government officials — participated in the discussion. These professional domains are not always conversant with one another's preoccupations and perspectives, and experts from each field are only in infrequent communication with one another.

The conference benefited from the interaction which resulted from bringing different experiences to bear on a problem which is not bounded by the limits of a single discipline or professional lens. Despite these differences in professional perspectives, agreement on some basic points emerged.

There are many **new factors** in the current context which make redefining the role of the state a priority. These include the increasing urgency of social needs; the rising importance of human development for international competitiveness and economic growth; the over-extension of the state; changes in development strategy; and shifts in civil society and industrial organisation. The degree of disintegration, disarticulation and decomposition of the state in the last decade under the pressure of adjustment and the fiscal problem has made the reform of the state more difficult but also more pressing. This admittedly profound crisis of the state has nonetheless opened the possibility of building up new capacities from the remains of recently destroyed state capacity.

These pressures lead to a redefinition of the **role of the state**. The strength and vitality of civil society and the innovativeness and initiative of the "civil economy" provide the bases for a redefinition of the role of the state away from a large "mobilising" state perceived as responsible for national well-being to one which is interactive with society and the private sector. The new role of the state is embodied in associative, facilitative and supportive behaviours that enhance strengths in society rather than merely providing benefits.

The Latin American state of the 1990s relies on the initiatives and assets of society. This redefinition is neither the old concept of state-led development with strong public sector participation in directly productive activites and heavy intervention in markets, nor the more recent idea of the minimalist state which relies on market forces alone to address social and economic problems. Rather, the new definition suggests a strategic role for the state in establishing the framework for economic direction, for the interaction between the public and private sectors; and a catalytic role in assembling disparate economic agents, instruments and factors around national objectives.

The **capacity of the state** to play this new supportive, rather than provisioning, role depends on a leaner, more flexible, and more intelligent bureaucracy and civil service. The agenda for the reform of the state includes administrative and civil service reform, as well as increased education, training and remuneration for government officials. Although narrow, this definition of the reform agenda is nevertheless critical. It goes beyond reducing government expenditure and the privatisation of state enterprises, to streamlining the bureaucracy, improving the civil service and creating a new culture of public service which will encourage more innovative ways of relating the state to civil society.

The creation of **new modalities of interaction** between society and state has become vital to fulfilling the new role of the state. This is a challenge for innovation in both domains. New forms of association are emerging in Latin America; the Brazilian National Forum — a pluralist organisation of business, labour, university, religious and political leaders, whose aim is to generate a consensus on future directions for the nation — has been an extremely successful example.

Labour unions with the right balance between factory-level loyalty, branch-level activity and nation-wide perspectives can facilitate rather than resist the changes needed for increasing competitiveness and upgrading skills. The capacity of the state to interact with these organisations of civil society and the capacity of political parties to represent broad social interests in building coalitions and support for reform become extremely important.

The new pressures on the state to play a key role in social development make far-reaching **tax reform** imperative to generate the revenues necessary for a sound fiscal basis. Fiscal reform is central in overcoming the financial crisis inherited from the past and in enabling the state to play a positive role in the future. Broad-based income tax reforms are more effective than piecemeal tax policies, from the point of view of both revenue raising and economic incentives.

The tax system is nevertheless a major instrument for defining income distribution outcomes and hence expressing social values. It is also an important instrument of environmental policy. In the struggle for influence within variegated political systems in Latin America, tax reform becomes a crucial instrument for achieving multiple objectives among and between diverse groups. Policy choices are intrinsically political and inevitably involve conflicts between significant social groups.

Another dimension of the challenges of the present conjuncture is **the rise of horizontal issues** in policy making in Latin America. Social development, technological innovation and environmental issues are good examples of increasingly important policy goals which cannot be addressed effectively by any single instrument, and which require, instead, a cross-cutting policy approach. The old hierarchical, centralised, bureaucratic state apparatus is ill-equipped to deal with these policy co-ordination problems. The limited number of civil servants able to deal with the new issues in their broader context clearly constrains the capacity of the state in Latin America to move forward on the new agenda and to assume its newly defined role, especially when reform requires confrontation with established groups on a broad front.

The redefinition of the role of the state towards a broad integrative and interactive role is intimately related to the social fabric of each country. The **rule of law and the role of the judiciary** become crucial elements in shaping and maintaining the social order as well as providing essential support for private sector transactions and development. Therefore, new programmes to support judicial and legal reform, on which the Inter-American Development Bank has already embarked, are important innovations in this field.

Decentralisation of governmental functions seems to be an important component of redefining the role of the state from mobilising to associating functions. Widespread experience with structural adjustment suggests, however, that centralisation has increased rather than decreased in recent years, making the current effort to reverse the trend still more difficult. In addition, state-federal relations are extraordinarily complex in many countries where further decentralisation may run contrary to the need for fiscal discipline. Also, political influences on public resource allocation are likely to be more prevalent in decentralised systems.

A **national project** is essential to moving society towards a new future. However difficult it may be to develop an integrated policy approach to social, economic and political development on a practical basis, it is nonetheless critical for national leaders to provide society with visions of the future which are holistic in nature and on which societies can make choices through democratic procedures. The National Forum experience in Brazil seems to be one means of generating an integrated vision of modernisation around which opinions can crystallise to form the basis for more specific choices and actions. Without a national project, individual reform proposals seem to society to represent a desirable menu without a distinguishable direction, and there is no basis for differentiating between the meaning of individual measures.

Countries define different projects according to their individual cultural and historical contexts. Democracy provides societies with the means of making decisions, once alternative futures are articulated and represented.

Politicians and analysts, political scientists and economists all have **different languages and perspectives on the major issues** facing Latin America today. The economic reform agenda of the 1980s is giving way to a second phase of broader economic, social and political reforms in the 1990s. The naïve assumption that social reforms will necessarily help make economic reforms sustainable and in turn will strengthen democracy needs to be viewed with scepticism. Rather, the more complicated reforms of the 1990s require facing the inherent tensions, contradictions and conflicts inherent in different reform "logics".

Social policy reform may consume more political and economic resources than it generates, especially in the short run. Tough-minded decisions need to be made to advance the new reform agenda in situations in which the capacity of all actors is limited, political processes are less than perfectly representative and economic resources are restricted.

Conflict is an inevitable part of the reform process, especially as political participation increases. To understand the interaction of these different dimensions and to avoid sterile dialogues within the confines of circumscribed discourses, communication across disciplines and professions will be especially important in advancing the broader agenda facing Latin America in the 1990s.

Programme

Monday 8th November, 1993

Chairperson	Jean Bonvin, President, OECD Development Centre
Welcoming Remarks	Jean Bonvin, President, OECD Development Centre Nancy Birdsall, Executive Vice-President, Inter-American Development Bank
Overview Papers	*Redefining the Role of the State: Political Processes, State Capacity and the New Agenda in Latin America* Colin Bradford, OECD Development Centre
	The IDB and Modernisation of the State Luciano Tomassini, Corporación de Investigaciones para el Desarrollo, Santiago
Overview Comments	Manuel Antonio Garretón, FLACSO, Santiago Guillermo O'Donnell, University of Notre Dame, Indiana

Discussion

EUROPEAN AND LATIN AMERICAN POLITICAL PERSPECTIVES ON THE ROLE OF THE STATE

	The State and Society in the Reform Era Alain Touraine, École des hautes études en sciences sociales, Paris
Discussion	Jesus Silva Herzog, Former Minister of Finance, Mexico; Mexican Ambassador to Spain Gabriel Valdés, President of the Senate of Chile

CONSOLIDATING DEMOCRACY

	The Role of Political Institutions and Political Process Stephan Haggard, University of California, San Diego and Robert Kaufman, Rutgers University, New Brunswick

Administrative Reform and State Capacity
Luciano Cafagna, Autorità garante
della concorrenza e del mercato, Rome

THE NEW PARADIGM AND INTEREST GROUP RELATIONS WITH THE STATE

Business and the State
João Paulo dos Reis Velloso, Instituto Nacional
de Altos Estudos, Rio de Janeiro

Labour and the State
Samuel Valenzuela, University of Notre Dame,
Indiana

Tuesday 9th November, 1993

Chairperson   Nancy Birdsall, Executive Vice-President,
                                   Inter-American Development Bank

THE NEW AGENDA, STATE CAPACITY AND POLITICAL PROCESS

Policy Reform and the Reform of the State
Ricardo Hausmann, Former Minister
of Co-ordination and Planning, Venezuela

*Toward a Social Agenda and Social Services
Reform*
Teresa Albánez, Minister for the Family, Venezuela

*Toward the Integration of Environmental
Sustainability into Politics, Policy
and Administration*
Margaret Keck, Yale University, New Haven

*Toward Tax Reform as an Instrument for Achieving
Growth, Social Development and Sustainability*
Guillermo Perry, Fedesarrollo, Bogotá

POLITICS, ECONOMIC POLICY REFORM AND THE ROLE OF THE STATE IN LATIN
AMERICA AND EAST ASIA

Albert Fishlow, University of California at Berkeley
Nancy Birdsall, Executive Vice-President,
Inter-American Development Bank

SUMMARY AND CONCLUSIONS: A NEW SYNTHESIS FOR LATIN AMERICA
DEMOCRACY, REFORM AND THE STATE

Guillermo O'Donnell, University of Notre Dame,
Indiana
Manuel Antonio Garretón, FLACSO, Santiago

Participants

Co-Chairpersons

Ms Nancy BIRDSALL

Executive Vice-President
Inter-American Development Bank

Mr Jean BONVIN

President
OECD Development Centre

Authors

Ms Teresa ALBÁNEZ BARNOLA

Ministra
Ministerio de la Familia
Venezuela

Mr Colin BRADFORD

Head of Research Programme
OECD Development Centre
France

Mr Luciano CAFAGNA

Componente
Autoritá garante della concorrenza
e del mercato
Italy

Mr Albert FISHLOW

Department of Economics
University of California, Berkeley
United States

Mr Manuel Antonio GARRETÓN

Facultad Latinoamericana de Ciencias
Sociales (FLACSO)
Chile

Mr Ricardo HAUSMANN

Instituto de Estudios Superiores
de Administración (IESA)
Venezuela

Mr Robert R. KAUFMAN

Department of Political Science
Rutgers University
United States

Ms Margaret KECK

Department of Political Science
Yale University
United States

Mr Guillermo O'DONNELL

Academic Director
The Helen Kellogg Institute for Latin
American Studies
United States

Mr Guillermo PERRY RUBIO	Fundación para la Educación Superior y el Desarrollo (Fedesarrollo) Colombia
Mr João Paulo dos REIS VELLOSO	Presidente Instituto Nacional de Altos Estudos (INAE) Brazil
Mr Luciano TOMASSINI	Corporación de Investigaciones para el Desarrollo (CINDE) Chile
M. Alain TOURAINE	Directeur Centre d'analyse et d'intervention sociologiques École des hautes études en sciences sociales France
Mr J. Samuel VALENZUELA	The Helen Kellogg Institute for Latin American Studies United States

Participants

Mr Oscar ALTIMIR	Director Economic Development Division UN Economic Commission for Latin America and the Caribbean Chile
Mr Claude AUROI	Executive Secretary EADI Switzerland
M. Georges COUFFIGNAL	Directeur Institut des hautes études de l'Amérique latine (IHEAL) France
M. Maurício DIAS DAVID	Économiste, chercheur associé au Centre de recherches sur le Brésil contemporain (EHESS) et à l'Université Paris-XIII France
Mr Hugo FERNANDEZ FAINGOLD	Former Minister of Labour Uruguay
Mme Fabienne GAME	Futuribles International France
Mr Wolf GRABENDORFF	Director Institute for European-Latin American Relations (IRELA) Spain

Mr Helio JAGUARIBE

Decano
Instituto de Estudios Politicos
e Sociais (IEPES)
Brazil

Mr Julio LABASTIDA MARTIN DEL CAMPO

Secretario General
Facultad Latinoamericana de Ciencias
Sociales (FLACSO)
Costa Rica

Mr Alexander R. LOVE

Chairman
Development Assistance Committee
OECD
France

Ms Nora LUSTIG

Senior Fellow
The Brookings Institution
Foreign Policy Studies Program
United States

Mr Klaus MEYER

Botschafter a.D.
University of Leipzig
Germany

M. Bruno REVESZ

Directeur de recherche du CIPCA (Pérou)
France

M. Giuseppe SACCO

Institut d'études politiques de Paris
France

Mr Jesus SILVA HERZOG

Embajador de México en España
Spain

Mr Georg SORENSEN

Department of Political Science
University of Aarhus
Denmark

Ms Barbara STALLINGS

UN Economic Commission
for Latin America and the Caribbean
Chile

Ms Rosemary THORP

The Latin American Centre
University of Oxford
United Kingdom

Mr Gabriel VALDÉS

Presidente del Senado
Chile

Diplomatic Representations in Paris

Argentina	Mr Horacio M. DOVAL, Economic and Commercial Affairs
Brazil	H.E. Mr Carlos Alberto LEITE BARBOSA, Ambassador Mr Paulo R. DE ALMEIDA, Counsellor
Chile	H.E. Mr José-Miguel BARROS, Ambassador Mr Eduardo GALVEZ, First Secretary
Mexico	H.E. Mr Ignacio MORALES LECHUGA, Ambassador Mr Héctor CAMACHO, Minister for OECD Affairs Mr Jorgé del VALLE, Counsellor for OECD Affairs
Peru	Mr Eduardo BERNALES, Economic Affairs
Venezuela	H.E. Mr Antonio José OLAVARRIA, Ambassador Ms Liliana SHILLING, Minister Counsellor Mr Luis Fernando PEREZ-SEGNINI, Second Secretary

National Delegations to the OECD

Belgium	Mr Lionel A.E. DE MEY, Minister Plenipotentiary, Bilateral Economic Relations with Latin America, Foreign Ministry, Brussels
Canada	Mr Rolando BAHAMONDE, Policy Programme and Evaluation Division (Asia Branch), Canadian International Development Agency (CIDA), Canada Mr Ian WRIGHT, Counsellor, Permanent Delegation
EC	Ms Françoise MOREAU, DG I, Brussels
Spain	H.E. Mr Claudio ARANZADI, Ambassador Mr Juan M. ROMERO DE TERREROS, Minister Counsellor Mr Jesús GONZALEZ REGIDOR, Counsellor

France	Ministère des Affaires étrangères
	Direction d'Amérique
	    M. Jean-Jacques SUBRENAT,
	    Directeur-adjoint
	    M. Alain FORT
	    Mme Marie-Claire GERARDIN
	    Mme Élisabeth LAFARGE
	    Mme Stéphanie SEYDOUX
	Direction des affaires économiques
	    M. Marcel ESCURE, Secrétaire
	    des affaires étrangères
	
	Ministère de l'Économie
	Direction du Trésor
	    M. Michel LAFFITTE, Chef du bureau
	    des biens d'équipement, services
	    et opérations en capital

Germany	Mr Thomas SCHURIG, Counsellor, Permanent Delegation
Greece	Mr Panos MAVROKEFALOS, Counsellor, Permanent Delegation
Netherlands	Mr Rudolf BEKINK, Deputy Permanent Representative
Norway	Mr Helge SELAND, Second Secretary, Permanent Delegation
Portugal	Mr Luis BARROS, Counsellor, Permanent Delegation
Switzerland	Mr Roger PASQUIER, Counsellor, Permanent Delegation
Sweden	Mr Fredrik SVEDÄNG, First Secretary, Permanent Delegation

OECD Secretariat

Mr Bernard WOOD — Director, Development Co-operation Directorate

Mr Richard CAREY — Deputy Director, Development Co-operation Directorate

Mr Maldwyn JONES — Private Office of the Secretary General

Ms Raundi HALVORSON-QUEVEDO — Development Co-operation Directorate, Financial Policies and Private Sector Division

Ms Elaine LALOUM — Directorate for Science, Technology and Industry, Sectoral Issues Division

OECD Development Centre

Mr Jean BONVIN — President

Mr Colin BRADFORD — Head of Research Programme

Mr Giulio FOSSI — Head, External Co-operation

Mr Christian MORRISSON — Head of Research Programme

Mr David TURNHAM — Head of Research Programme

Mr Charles OMAN — Principal Administrator

Mr David ROLAND-HOLST — Principal Administrator

Mr Hartmut SCHNEIDER — Principal Administrator

Ms Catherine DUPORT — Administrator

Mr Colm FOY — Administrator, Information and Publications Unit

Mr Henny HELMICH — Administrator, External Co-operation

Inter-American Development Bank

Ms Nancy BIRDSALL — Executive Vice-President

Ms Nohra REY DE MARULANDA — Manager, Economic and Social Development Department

Mr Jorge ELENA — Special Representative in Europe

Mr Jean-Michel HOUDE — Alternate Representative in Europe

Mr Ziga VODUŠEK — Senior Economist, European Office

Mr Rod CHAPMAN — Senior Press and Information Officer, European Office

MAIN SALES OUTLETS OF OECD PUBLICATIONS
PRINCIPAUX POINTS DE VENTE DES PUBLICATIONS DE L'OCDE

ARGENTINA – ARGENTINE
Carlos Hirsch S.R.L.
Galería Güemes, Florida 165, 4° Piso
1333 Buenos Aires   Tel. (1) 331.1787 y 331.2391
Telefax: (1) 331.1787

AUSTRALIA – AUSTRALIE
D.A. Information Services
648 Whitehorse Road, P.O.B 163
Mitcham, Victoria 3132   Tel. (03) 873.4411
Telefax: (03) 873.5679

AUSTRIA – AUTRICHE
Gerold & Co.
Graben 31
Wien I   Tel. (0222) 533.50.14

BELGIUM – BELGIQUE
Jean De Lannoy
Avenue du Roi 202
B-1060 Bruxelles   Tel. (02) 538.51.69/538.08.41
Telefax: (02) 538.08.41

CANADA
Renouf Publishing Company Ltd.
1294 Algoma Road
Ottawa, ON K1B 3W8   Tel. (613) 741.4333
Telefax: (613) 741.5439
Stores:
61 Sparks Street
Ottawa, ON K1P 5R1   Tel. (613) 238.8985
211 Yonge Street
Toronto, ON M5B 1M4   Tel. (416) 363.3171
Telefax: (416)363.59.63

Les Éditions La Liberté Inc.
3020 Chemin Sainte-Foy
Sainte-Foy, PQ G1X 3V6   Tel. (418) 658.3763
Telefax: (418) 658.3763

Federal Publications Inc.
165 University Avenue, Suite 701
Toronto, ON M5H 3B8   Tel. (416) 860.1611
Telefax: (416) 860.1608

Les Publications Fédérales
1185 Université
Montréal, QC H3B 3A7   Tel. (514) 954.1633
Telefax : (514) 954.1635

CHINA – CHINE
China National Publications Import
Export Corporation (CNPIEC)
16 Gongti E. Road, Chaoyang District
P.O. Box 88 or 50
Beijing 100704 PR   Tel. (01) 506.6688
Telefax: (01) 506.3101

DENMARK – DANEMARK
Munksgaard Book and Subscription Service
35, Nørre Søgade, P.O. Box 2148
DK-1016 København K   Tel. (33) 12.85.70
Telefax: (33) 12.93.87

FINLAND – FINLANDE
Akateeminen Kirjakauppa
Keskuskatu 1, P.O. Box 128
00100 Helsinki

Subscription Services/Agence d'abonnements :
P.O. Box 23
00371 Helsinki   Tel. (358 0) 12141
Telefax: (358 0) 121.4450

FRANCE
OECD/OCDE
Mail Orders/Commandes par correspondance:
2, rue André-Pascal
75775 Paris Cedex 16   Tel. (33-1) 45.24.82.00
Telefax: (33-1) 45.24.81.76 or (33-1) 45.24.85.00
Telex: 640048 OCDE

OECD Bookshop/Librairie de l'OCDE :
33, rue Octave-Feuillet
75016 Paris   Tel. (33-1) 45.24.81.67
                                 (33-1) 45.24.81.81
Documentation Française
29, quai Voltaire
75007 Paris   Tel. 40.15.70.00
Gibert Jeune (Droit-Économie)
6, place Saint-Michel
75006 Paris   Tel. 43.25.91.19
Librairie du Commerce International
10, avenue d'Iéna
75016 Paris   Tel. 40.73.34.60
Librairie Dunod
Université Paris-Dauphine
Place du Maréchal de Lattre de Tassigny
75016 Paris   Tel. (1) 44.05.40.13
Librairie Lavoisier
11, rue Lavoisier
75008 Paris   Tel. 42.65.39.95
Librairie L.G.D.J. - Montchrestien
20, rue Soufflot
75005 Paris   Tel. 46.33.89.85
Librairie des Sciences Politiques
30, rue Saint-Guillaume
75007 Paris   Tel. 45.48.36.02
P.U.F.
49, boulevard Saint-Michel
75005 Paris   Tel. 43.25.83.40
Librairie de l'Université
12a, rue Nazareth
13100 Aix-en-Provence   Tel. (16) 42.26.18.08
Documentation Française
165, rue Garibaldi
69003 Lyon   Tel. (16) 78.63.32.23
Librairie Decitre
29, place Bellecour
69002 Lyon   Tel. (16) 72.40.54.54

GERMANY – ALLEMAGNE
OECD Publications and Information Centre
August-Bebel-Allee 6
D-53175 Bonn 2   Tel. (0228) 959.120
Telefax: (0228) 959.12.17

GREECE – GRÈCE
Librairie Kauffmann
Mavrokordatou 9
106 78 Athens   Tel. (01) 32.55.321
Telefax: (01) 36.33.967

HONG-KONG
Swindon Book Co. Ltd.
13–15 Lock Road
Kowloon, Hong Kong   Tel. 366.80.31
Telefax: 739.49.75

HUNGARY – HONGRIE
Euro Info Service
POB 1271
1464 Budapest   Tel. (1) 111.62.16
Telefax : (1) 111.60.61

ICELAND – ISLANDE
Mál Mog Menning
Laugavegi 18, Pósthólf 392
121 Reykjavik   Tel. 162.35.23

INDIA – INDE
Oxford Book and Stationery Co.
Scindia House
New Delhi 110001   Tel.(11) 331.5896/5308
Telefax: (11) 332.5993
17 Park Street
Calcutta 700016   Tel. 240832

INDONESIA – INDONÉSIE
Pdii-Lipi
P.O. Box 269/JKSMG/88
Jakarta 12790   Tel. 583467
Telex: 62 875

IRELAND – IRLANDE
TDC Publishers – Library Suppliers
12 North Frederick Street
Dublin 1   Tel. (01) 874.48.35
Telefax: (01) 874.84.16

ISRAEL
Electronic Publications only
Publications électroniques seulement
Sophist Systems Ltd.
71 Allenby Street
Tel-Aviv 65134   Tel. 3-29.00.21
Telefax: 3-29.92.39

ITALY – ITALIE
Libreria Commissionaria Sansoni
Via Duca di Calabria 1/1
50125 Firenze   Tel. (055) 64.54.15
Telefax: (055) 64.12.57
Via Bartolini 29
20155 Milano   Tel. (02) 36.50.83
Editrice e Libreria Herder
Piazza Montecitorio 120
00186 Roma   Tel. 679.46.28
Telefax: 678.47.51
Libreria Hoepli
Via Hoepli 5
20121 Milano   Tel. (02) 86.54.46
Telefax: (02) 805.28.86
Libreria Scientifica
Dott. Lucio de Biasio 'Aeiou'
Via Coronelli, 6
20146 Milano   Tel. (02) 48.95.45.52
Telefax: (02) 48.95.45.48

JAPAN – JAPON
OECD Publications and Information Centre
Landic Akasaka Building
2-3-4 Akasaka, Minato-ku
Tokyo 107   Tel. (81.3) 3586.2016
Telefax: (81.3) 3584.7929

KOREA – CORÉE
Kyobo Book Centre Co. Ltd.
P.O. Box 1658, Kwang Hwa Moon
Seoul   Tel. 730.78.91
Telefax: 735.00.30

MALAYSIA – MALAISIE
Co-operative Bookshop Ltd.
University of Malaya
P.O. Box 1127, Jalan Pantai Baru
59700 Kuala Lumpur
Malaysia   Tel. 756.5000/756.5425
Telefax: 757.3661

MEXICO – MEXIQUE
Revistas y Periodicos Internacionales S.A. de C.V.
Florencia 57 - 1004
Mexico, D.F. 06600   Tel. 207.81.00
Telefax : 208.39.79

NETHERLANDS – PAYS-BAS
SDU Uitgeverij Plantijnstraat
Externe Fondsen
Postbus 20014
2500 EA's-Gravenhage   Tel. (070) 37.89.880
Voor bestellingen: Telefax: (070) 34.75.778

**NEW ZEALAND
NOUVELLE-ZÉLANDE**
Legislation Services
P.O. Box 12418
Thorndon, Wellington   Tel. (04) 496.5652
                              Telefax: (04) 496.5698

NORWAY – NORVÈGE
Narvesen Info Center – NIC
Bertrand Narvesens vei 2
P.O. Box 6125 Etterstad
0602 Oslo 6   Tel. (022) 57.33.00
                              Telefax: (022) 68.19.01

PAKISTAN
Mirza Book Agency
65 Shahrah Quaid-E-Azam
Lahore 54000   Tel. (42) 353.601
                              Telefax: (42) 231.730

PHILIPPINE – PHILIPPINES
International Book Center
5th Floor, Filipinas Life Bldg.
Ayala Avenue
Metro Manila   Tel. 81.96.76
                              Telex 23312 RHP PH

PORTUGAL
Livraria Portugal
Rua do Carmo 70-74
Apart. 2681
1200 Lisboa   Tel.: (01) 347.49.82/5
                              Telefax: (01) 347.02.64

SINGAPORE – SINGAPOUR
Gower Asia Pacific Pte Ltd.
Golden Wheel Building
41, Kallang Pudding Road, No. 04-03
Singapore 1334   Tel. 741.5166
                              Telefax: 742.9356

SPAIN – ESPAGNE
Mundi-Prensa Libros S.A.
Castelló 37, Apartado 1223
Madrid 28001   Tel. (91) 431.33.99
                              Telefax: (91) 575.39.98

Libreria Internacional AEDOS
Consejo de Ciento 391
08009 – Barcelona   Tel. (93) 488.30.09
                              Telefax: (93) 487.76.59

Llibreria de la Generalitat
Palau Moja
Rambla dels Estudis, 118
08002 – Barcelona
                   (Subscripcions) Tel. (93) 318.80.12
                   (Publicacions) Tel. (93) 302.67.23
                              Telefax: (93) 412.18.54

SRI LANKA
Centre for Policy Research
c/o Colombo Agencies Ltd.
No. 300-304, Galle Road
Colombo 3   Tel. (1) 574240, 573551-2
                   Telefax: (1) 575394, 510711

SWEDEN – SUÈDE
Fritzes Information Center
Box 16356
Regeringsgatan 12
106 47 Stockholm   Tel. (08) 690.90.90
                              Telefax: (08) 20.50.21

Subscription Agency/Agence d'abonnements :
Wennergren-Williams Info AB
P.O. Box 1305
171 25 Solna   Tel. (08) 705.97.50
                              Téléfax : (08) 27.00.71

SWITZERLAND – SUISSE
Maditec S.A. (Books and Periodicals - Livres
et périodiques)
Chemin des Palettes 4
Case postale 266
1020 Renens   Tel. (021) 635.08.65
                              Telefax: (021) 635.07.80

Librairie Payot S.A.
4, place Pépinet
CP 3212
1002 Lausanne   Tel. (021) 341.33.48
                              Telefax: (021) 341.33.45

Librairie Unilivres
6, rue de Candolle
1205 Genève   Tel. (022) 320.26.23
                              Telefax: (022) 329.73.18

Subscription Agency/Agence d'abonnements :
Dynapresse Marketing S.A.
38 avenue Vibert
1227 Carouge   Tel.: (022) 308.07.89
                              Telefax : (022) 308.07.99

See also – Voir aussi :
OECD Publications and Information Centre
August-Bebel-Allee 6
D-53175 Bonn 2 (Germany)   Tel. (0228) 959.120
                              Telefax: (0228) 959.12.17

TAIWAN – FORMOSE
Good Faith Worldwide Int'l. Co. Ltd.
9th Floor, No. 118, Sec. 2
Chung Hsiao E. Road
Taipei   Tel. (02) 391.7396/391.7397
                              Telefax: (02) 394.9176

THAILAND – THAÏLANDE
Suksit Siam Co. Ltd.
113, 115 Fuang Nakhon Rd.
Opp. Wat Rajbopith
Bangkok 10200   Tel. (662) 225.9531/2
                              Telefax: (662) 222.5188

TURKEY – TURQUIE
Kültür Yayinlari Is-Türk Ltd. Sti.
Atatürk Bulvari No. 191/Kat 13
Kavaklidere/Ankara   Tel. 428.11.40 Ext. 2458
Dolmabahce Cad. No. 29
Besiktas/Istanbul   Tel. 260.71.88
                              Telex: 43482B

UNITED KINGDOM – ROYAUME-UNI
HMSO
Gen. enquiries   Tel. (071) 873 0011
Postal orders only:
P.O. Box 276, London SW8 5DT
Personal Callers HMSO Bookshop
49 High Holborn, London WC1V 6HB
                              Telefax: (071) 873 8200
Branches at: Belfast, Birmingham, Bristol, Edin-
burgh, Manchester

UNITED STATES – ÉTATS-UNIS
OECD Publications and Information Centre
2001 L Street N.W., Suite 700
Washington, D.C. 20036-4910 Tel. (202) 785.6323
                              Telefax: (202) 785.0350

VENEZUELA
Libreria del Este
Avda F. Miranda 52, Aptdo. 60337
Edificio Galipán
Caracas 106   Tel. 951.1705/951.2307/951.1297
                        Telegram: Libreste Caracas

Subscription to OECD periodicals may also be
placed through main subscription agencies.

Les abonnements aux publications périodiques de
l'OCDE peuvent être souscrits auprès des
principales agences d'abonnement.

Orders and inquiries from countries where Distributors have not yet been appointed should be sent to:
OECD Publications Service, 2 rue André-Pascal,
75775 Paris Cedex 16, France.

Les commandes provenant de pays où l'OCDE n'a
pas encore désigné de distributeur devraient être
adressées à : OCDE, Service des Publications,
2, rue André-Pascal, 75775 Paris Cedex 16, France.

                                        2-1994

OECD PUBLICATIONS, 2 rue André-Pascal, 75775 PARIS CEDEX 16
PRINTED IN FRANCE
(41 94 04 1) ISBN 92-64-14089-1 - No. 46993 1994